D0088977

Justice Corrupted

JUSTICE CORRUPTED

How the Left Weaponized Our Legal System

TED CRUZ

Regnery Publishing
WASHINGTON, D.C.

Regnery® is a registered trademark and its colophon is a trademark of Salem
Communications Holding Corporation

Cataloging-in-Publication data on file with the Library of Congress

ISBN: 978-1-68451-361-1
eISBN 978-1-68451-369-7
Library of Congress Control Number: 2022941052

Published in the United States by
Regnery Publishing
A Division of Salem Media Group
Washington, D.C.
www.Regnery.com

Manufactured in the United States of America

10 9 8 7 6 5 4 3 2

Books are available in quantity for promotional or premium use.
For information on discounts and terms, please visit our website:
www.Regnery.com.

This book is dedicated to Hon. Edwin Meese, the seventy-fifth attorney general of the United States and the chairman of my national leadership team when I first ran for the Senate.

It is also dedicated to Charles J. Cooper, who served as General Meese's right hand, who clerked for Chief Justice William Rehnquist, who is one of the most talented constitutional litigators alive, who was my first boss, and who taught me how to be a lawyer.

CONTENTS

PREFACE

I t was every father's nightmare. Your fourteen-year-old daughter, your little girl, being sexually assaulted at school. In the girls' bathroom. By a boy wearing a skirt.

Horrific. But in any sane environment, the consequences would have been swift. The boy would have been prosecuted, convicted, and imprisoned. The criminal justice system would have worked, if not as a deterrent, then at least as a punishment.

But Loudoun County, Virginia, was no longer a sane environment. Here, a group of left-wing ideologues had taken over the local public school system, turning their town into the kind of woke experiment that was being replicated in radical school districts across the United States. When the school board got word of this horrible assault, they covered it up, refusing to prosecute the boy. Instead, they transferred him to another school, where, to the surprise of nobody rational, he assaulted yet another young girl.

Why did the system fail? We know why. Because the crime was inconvenient for the prevailing political narrative. That narrative—the one that says gender doesn't exist, and that children can switch between male and female at will—was more important to these zealots than the physical safety of the children in the care of Loudoun County Public Schools. Boys dressed as girls never—*never!*—commit sexual assaults. And they certainly don't commit them in the girls' bathroom, a place that the new leftist elite insisted should be available to anyone who "identified" as a girl. It didn't matter if the person in question had just begun identifying as a girl yesterday, or even if he still had a beard and male reproductive organs.

The father of the first girl assaulted, a plumber named Scott Smith, was devastated and outraged. You would be, too, if the same thing happened to your daughter or the daughter of someone you love. Shortly after the incident, Smith went to his daughter's school to try to make sure justice was served. When he got there, he found out that the school's principal had no intention of taking disciplinary action against the boy or even of calling the police. This, understandably, outraged Smith even further.

By the end of that day, the police were finally called to the school. But not to arrest the boy who had sexually violated Smith's daughter. Rather, the police were called *on Scott Smith himself.* The school's principal called the police, according to an excellent investigative report on the incident published in the *Daily Wire*, because he was "making a scene" about his daughter's assault.[1]

As the weeks went on, anger about various policies in Loudoun County grew. Aside from rumors about the sexual assault of Smith's daughter, parents had recently learned that much of what their children were being taught in school was absolute nonsense. During the pandemic, when Loudoun County kids were forced to learn remotely, many of their parents had peered over their shoulders to see lessons on white guilt, systemic racism, and gender studies on the screens of their iPads and laptops. During a few contentious school board meetings, many of these parents had made their concerns known, leading to several high-profile arguments in public. The next meeting, Smith learned, would be held on June 22.

During the meeting, the school board was in full defense mode. The board members knew that parents were concerned about the school's open-door bathroom policy and the potential for sexual assaults that came with it. They also knew that these fears had been realized just a few weeks earlier, when Smith's daughter had been assaulted. But as the concerned parents came to the microphone (more than 250 had signed up to speak that day), the members of the school board lied about the incident time and time again.

When Beth Barts, a school board member who had clashed with Loudoun County parents in the past, had the chance to address these serious concerns, she dismissed them, almost mocking anyone who would be concerned about such things.

"Our students do not need to be protected," she said. "They are not in danger."

Turning to another member of the school board, she asked whether assaults occurred in bathrooms and locker rooms.

"To my knowledge," interjected Scott Ziegler, the superintendent of Loudoun County Public Schools, "we don't have any record of assaults occurring in our restrooms."

This was a lie, as Ziegler knew and had admitted in an email to the board members on the day of Smith's daughter's assault.[2] Perhaps that is why he quoted *Time* magazine for the rest of his answer. The magazine had printed a report the previous year claiming that "the data was simply not playing out that transgender students were more likely to assault cisgender students in restrooms." Ziegler then went on to say that "the predator transgender student or person simply does not exist."

Of course, Ziegler knew full well that at least one "predatory transgender student" did, in fact, exist, and that the school board was protecting him (or her, or them, or xim, or xer). Scott Smith, who sat in the audience that evening with his wife, Jess, knew it too.

For the next hour or so, parents from both sides of the cultural divide took to the microphone and made speeches. Some parents demanded to know exactly how many of these assaults had occurred; others screamed wildly that anyone who raised such concerns was a bigot, a sexist, and a racist, too.

All the while, Scott Smith sat quietly, knowing that if the school board had its way, the story of what had happened to his daughter would soon be buried to serve a dishonest woke narrative. At some point during the commotion, a woman came up to him and said hello. She wore a rainbow t-shirt. Smith's wife said she recognized her, and even believed they were friends. When this woman, who would later turn out to be a fierce left-wing ideologue, asked why the Smiths had come to the meeting, they told her what had happened to their daughter: the assault, the cover-up, and all the details in between.

The woman grew upset, even angry. Through gritted teeth, she said, "That's not what happened."

This, apparently, was the breaking point for Scott Smith, and understandably so. For weeks, he'd been hearing that what had happened to his daughter was not only not a big deal, but that it hadn't actually occurred at all. For a moment, Smith raised his voice and grew agitated. The woman looked at his t-shirt, which advertised his plumbing business, and declared that she was going to "ruin the business on social media."

Smith argued back at her, although not for long.

Before he knew what was happening, Smith felt his arm being jerked by a police officer who'd been watching the exchange from the far side of the room. Alarmed, Smith yanked his hand away, and the officer came at him with his full weight. Soon, they were wrestling on the ground, and the whole thing was being filmed by cameras. Images of Smith, his pants half down and his t-shirt up pulled up over his stomach, would soon go out to millions of people on news networks all over the world. It was just one more in a line of horrible indignities that he had been forced to endure.

While her husband was being tackled and thrown to the ground, Jess Smith yelled out, "My child was raped at school, and this is what happens!"

Sadly, almost no one could hear her amid the clamor that ensued after her husband was assaulted. Instead, they watched as her husband, who had come to the school board meeting simply to listen to the people who were covering up his daughter's sexual assault, was again treated like a criminal by the police force of Loudoun County. All the while, the boy who had raped their daughter was walking free, preparing to assault another young girl at his new school.

In the following days, the image of Smith being tackled by police became emblematic of a war that had raged for a long time—a war between parents who demanded to know exactly what was going on at their children's schools and arrogant school officials, nearly all of whom had been indoctrinated by woke ideology, who attempted to hide it from them. Across the country, elected Democrats on school boards were facing thousands of enraged parents on a host of issues: sexual assaults on campus, woke bathroom policies, Critical Race Theory, and more. These parents were angry, and rightfully so.

In a democratic system, when people are angry, elected officials are supposed to listen. These elected officials don't always have to agree on the substance—that's why we have elections—but the First Amendment to our Constitution explicitly protects the right of the people to "petition their government for the redress of grievances."

But democracy is messy. Listening to your constituents can be hard, and if they're angry, it can be unpleasant. For the Democrats on school boards across the country, there was a simpler solution. Rather than listening, they could simply use law enforcement to intimidate parents who disagreed with them into silence. In cases that involved parents like Scott Smith who refused to be intimidated, they could shut them down by force.

But there was only so much they could do at the local level.

So, shortly after the incident in Loudoun County, the National School Boards Association (NSBA) enlisted the Biden White House as their enforcers. They talked with political operatives at the White House who shared their warped view of the world, and with input from those operatives they drafted a letter to President Biden.

In the letter, the NSBA said that public schools and education leaders in the United States were "under an immediate threat."[3] They claimed that there was "a growing number of threats of violence and acts of intimidation occurring across the nation," and said "immediate assistance" was "required to protect our students, school board members, and educators who are susceptible to acts of violence affecting interstate commerce because of threats to their districts, families, and personal safety." The line about interstate commerce was added so that the Department of Justice would have justification to take action at the federal level, because the Constitution gives the federal government the power to regulate interstate commerce.

Later in the letter, the NSBA wrote, "as these acts of malice, violence, and threats against public school officials have increased, the classification of these heinous actions could be the *equivalent to a form of domestic terrorism* and hate crimes."[4] In the list of these "acts of malice, violence, and threats against public school officials," they included numerous incidents of parents getting fed up at school board meetings, many of which included nothing more than raised voices or peaceful demonstrations. The NSBA suggested that the Biden Justice Department use the Patriot Act, a controversial Bush-era law meant for the pursuit and punishment of terrorists, to go after these parents.

Early in the list, of course, was the case of Scott Smith, the man who had come to a school board meeting in peace only to be tackled by police at the behest of the school board itself. In the eyes of the Biden administration and their political allies, this father should now be classified as a domestic terrorist.

The NSBA letter was sent to the Biden Justice Department on September 29, 2021. Now, normally, the Biden Justice Department is glacially slow and often defiantly unresponsive. In 2021 alone, I sent seventeen letters to the Justice Department in an attempt to hold them to account. As one of the more senior members of the Senate Judiciary Committee, I have the responsibility—as does the full committee—to conduct oversight of the DOJ. I've sent multiple letters demanding answers on a variety of issues. On June 7, 2021, I sent a letter demanding to know why so few people who participated in violent riots during the summer of 2020 were prosecuted or punished for their crimes; a few days later, I joined a letter written by Senator Chuck Grassley that sought information about how sensitive taxpayer records were leaked to the media by the Internal Revenue Service. Also last year, I sent letters demanding information or action on the protection of rights of conscience for pro-life doctors, the need to prosecute Dr. Anthony Fauci's multiple lies under oath to Congress, the public disclosure of John Durham's report on the FBI's Crossfire Hurricane investigation, and many other important issues.

As Republicans are currently in the minority in the Senate, I do not currently have the ability to issue a subpoena or coercive measure to compel answers from the DOJ. All I can do is ask nicely. For virtually all of these oversight letters, the DOJ delays weeks or months; then, finally, the response is little more than a form letter. They routinely dodge and deflect; the DOJ responses say, in effect, "Thanks for your letter. So sorry, but we're not going to answer your questions."

Their defiance is not purely partisan. DOJ often ignores Senate Democrats as well. Senator Sheldon Whitehouse, for instance, one of the most liberal Democrats on the Judiciary Committee, has railed against the Biden DOJ for its lack of response to questions from Congress.

"There is something going on over there," he said, "that looks an awful lot like a formal policy not to answer our questions.... We are going to have to come to a proper resolution of this so that the oversight capacity of all of us as senators is not completely blunted by blockades in the executive branch."[5]

To be sure, the Department of Justice has been slow under Republican presidents, too. It's not uncommon to have a pile of unanswered letters from concerned senators sitting on a desk somewhere, especially when those letters have come from the opposing party. But the Biden Department of Justice has been substantially worse, elevating non-responsiveness to an art form. Their refusal to answer people who are tasked with overseeing them reflects their arrogance and unbridled hubris. They believe they are accountable to no one—not to members of Congress, and certainly not to the American people.

But when partisan politics demands it, the Biden Department of Justice can be lightning fast. Ergo, on October 4, 2021, just *six days* after they received the letter from the National School Boards Association, Attorney General Merrick Garland issued a formal memo addressed to the FBI and the criminal division of the Department of Justice. In it, Attorney General Garland said he was taking the incidents described in the memo seriously, and that the Justice Department would "use its authority and resources to discourage these threats, identify them when they occur, and prosecute them when appropriate." He also directed the FBI to convene meetings with local leaders to "facilitate discussion of strategies for addressing threats against school administrators, board members, teachers, and staff" to open "dedicated lines of communication for threat reporting, assessment, and response."

Shortly thereafter, Garland testified before the Judiciary Committee, and I took the opportunity to demand answers. Just a few weeks earlier, the boy who had sexually assaulted Scott Smith's daughter in a public-school bathroom had been found guilty of a *second* count of sexual assault. According to local reports, he had lured another innocent girl into an empty classroom, where he proceeded to "hold her against her will and inappropriately touch her."[6] After he was convicted, the court ordered that he register as a sex offender for the rest of his life.

Yet Merrick Garland and the Biden Department of Justice still had the memo up on their website that labeled Scott Smith, the father of this sick boy's first victim, as the problem, and potentially a domestic terrorist. They had not moved to edit or retract this memo or to send another one clarifying the false and offensive sentiments contained therein. The community of Loudoun County had taken notice. On October 26, for instance, hundreds of students participated in a walkout, many of them chanting "Loudoun County protects rapists."

A few days before the Senate hearing was set to take place, Attorney General Garland had participated in an oversight hearing in the House of Representatives. Under questioning from representatives who were similarly outraged about the incident in Loudoun County and the Biden DOJ's response to it, Garland had said that he "could not imagine any circumstance…where [parents of schoolchildren] would be labeled as domestic terrorists."

Somehow, Garland had managed to get away with this non-answer in front of the House committee. I did not intend to let him do the same thing. Under the terms of his memo, the Biden Department of Justice was attempting to treat concerned parents as criminals, and he was the one directly responsible. Garland had explicitly referred to innocent parents such as Scott Smith as "potential threats." Given that even a cursory glance at the facts of the case would have revealed this to be untrue, Garland was either misinformed about the case or lying about it. I didn't know which was worse, but I intended to find out.

I decided not to begin my line of questioning with the usual pleasantries. I had done so at Attorney General Garland's confirmation hearing, during which he agreed with me that it would be "totally inappropriate for the Department [of Justice] to target any individual because of their politics."[7] Now that he had gone directly against his own admonition, I figured it was best to get down to business.

I began by asking Garland how many incidents of violence were cited in the letter written to President Biden by the National School Boards Association—a letter which, according to his testimony under oath in front of the House committee, had been the entire basis for his decision to write a memo directing the FBI to investigate and target parents as if they were domestic terrorists.

He said he didn't know, so I told him that the answer was twenty. When I asked how many were actually "violent," as he had claimed in his letter—meaning someone had engaged in actual physical violence, beyond saying angry words or making gestures that were displeasing to Democrats—he fumbled again for an answer. I asked whether he or anyone on his staff did *any* independent research into the inflammatory claims in the school board association's letter—a letter for which the NSBA had subsequently issued a lengthy apology, admitting there was "no justification for some of the language included." Garland stammered again, and it became clear that neither he nor anyone on his staff had done any research at all.

As I pointed out during my questioning, Attorney General Garland began his career as a law clerk to Justice William Brennan. He'd also had many law clerks during his two-decade career as a judge. If he had come into the office of a Supreme Court justice during his time as a clerk claiming that there was a "disturbing pattern of violence," and then cited nothing but a shoddy memo written by a partisan advocacy group as evidence, he'd have been fired on the spot (and the United States of America may have been better for it). This, as I pointed out, was yet another case of the Justice Department going after the Biden administration's political enemies in a way that was sinister, wrong, and, as if the rest weren't bad enough, downright sloppy.

In the end, Garland admitted that when Scott Smith expressed his displeasure with the way he'd been treated by the school board in Loudoun County, his outburst was protected by the First Amendment. Of course, the attorney general is supposed to study the facts of the case *before* sending the FBI out to investigate parents like Smith. But this was not law enforcement; instead, Garland and the Biden DOJ were using the machinery of the Justice Department to attack their political enemies.

When there are credible threats of actual violence, law enforcement can (and should) act. It doesn't matter what party the person making the threats is affiliated with. But when there is peaceful speech—even loud, passionate, and angry speech—law enforcement has no authority to silence American citizens.

Merrick Garland knows that. He explicitly agreed with that during both his confirmation hearing and my questioning over Loudoun County.

But for both Garland and Joe Biden, politics was more important. It still is. The Biden White House wanted to satisfy its Democrat stakeholders, and so the DOJ moved with alacrity in responding to the ridiculous (and false) letter written by the National School Boards Association. The DOJ was more than happy to enlist the FBI to frighten, intimidate, and silence parents who had the temerity to disagree with their elected school boards.

The travesty in Loudoun County, and the Biden DOJ's complicity in the cover-up, had major political consequences. Parents across Virginia were outraged. In recent years, Virginia has become a reliably blue state. In the 2020 election, Joe Biden won it by 10 percent of the vote; four years earlier, Hillary Clinton won it by 5 percent. But when the far-left Biden regime began meddling in the affairs of parents, that changed.

The Democrat running for governor in Virginia was Terry McAuliffe, an unabashed partisan who was more than happy to go along with his party's platform of outright contempt for parents. During a debate on September 29, 2021, he said, "I don't think parents should be telling schools what they should teach," setting off a firestorm of controversy among families in Virginia. Even the *Washington Post* admitted that the line was probably the "last hurrah" for the candidate.[8] Then, in the closing days of the campaign, McAuliffe appeared alongside Randi Weingarten, the arrogant and sanctimonious leader of one of our nation's largest teachers' unions. Over the past year, Weingarten had done enormous damage to students all over the nation, leading the charge for extended school closings long after they were remotely justifiable.

But moms and dads in Virginia, quite understandably, did not like being called domestic terrorists. They didn't appreciate the Biden DOJ sending the G-men to go after soccer moms and concerned fathers. On election night, to the shock of political pundits everywhere, voters in Virginia elected Glenn Youngkin, a Republican, as governor.

I endorsed Youngkin early. He's a friend, and the man I believed was most capable of leading Virginia out of the crisis it had found itself in thanks to a decade of liberal leadership. During the campaign, I spent two days barnstorming the state of Virginia with Glenn to help him win the race. That Republicans could win in blue Virginia, as well as in school board races across the country, augurs well for the likely electoral results in 2022.

Scott Smith, meanwhile, had traveled a Kafkaesque journey. From having his daughter brutally assaulted to seeing the school board deny it ever happened, to having major figures in the corporate press call him a liar and being forcefully thrown to the ground and arrested, to having the attorney general of the United States send the FBI after him as a domestic terrorist, nothing about the last year had been easy for him.

Fortunately, his name has since been cleared thanks to several hard-working investigative reporters who were willing to look into his story, find the truth, and publish it, particularly Luke Rosiak at the *Daily Wire*. Thanks to the work of these real journalists, Scott Smith's story is known. Of course, the corporate media was utterly AWOL. The *Washington Post*, whose motto is "Democracy dies in darkness," couldn't be bothered to cover the story. Gone are the days of Woodward and Bernstein aggressively tracking down and reporting on government corruption and abuse of power. Today, apparently, the *Post* has turned its erstwhile motto into a perverse mission statement. It took small conservative outlets to do the real work of journalism required to expose the truth.

But that doesn't change the fact that this courageous father was targeted by the Department of Justice and singled out as a potential domestic terrorist threat by his government—all for the crime of showing up at a public meeting and attempting to defend his wronged child.

And it all happened because under President Biden, the justice system—and justice itself—has been corrupted.

That's not the way it's supposed to work.

THE WAY IT'S SUPPOSED TO WORK

Justice is blind. She wields a sword and holds a set of scales. The sword represents the terrible punishment government can inflict, up to and including taking a human being's life. The scale stands for fairness, a careful measuring of the facts and the evidence in any given case.

But neither one of these potent symbols matters as much as the blindfold over Lady Justice's eyes. Her eyes work fine, of course, but she *chooses* not to see. Race, gender, wealth, privilege—Justice should see none of them.

The same goes for party and ideology. The Department of Justice should not be Republican or Democrat. It should be utterly apolitical, and the attorney general should enforce the law fairly and justly regardless of party affiliation.

Justice without the blindfold is a vengeful angel wielding power as a weapon to intimidate and oppress, not the guardian on whom we all rely in our hours of need. Lord Acton famously observed, "Power tends to corrupt, and absolute power corrupts absolutely." Our nation's founding fathers understood this principle, and for that reason the

Constitution was designed, as Jefferson put it, as chains to bind the mischief of government.

When America came into being, the notion of blind justice was a radical concept. Indeed, for much of human history, government had been a means of exercising unchecked power. The vast majority of people who have lived on planet Earth have lived under monarchial rule. From ancient civilizations to medieval times to well into the nineteenth century, kings and queens and czars and emperors have ruled mankind.

English philosopher Thomas Hobbes posited that government power—the "Leviathan," as he dubbed it—was necessary because without it, the world would descend into chaos. The state of nature without some kind of government, in his words, is "nasty, brutish, and short." Marauding outlaws (think Mad Max in the Thunderdome) make for a miserable existence, and so instead monarchy provided order and stability.

Religion was frequently enlisted in support of monarchy. From Samuel anointing first Saul and then David with oil to Aztec rulers imbued with their own divinity and popes crowning kings across the centuries, the most common justification for a ruler's power was that God gave him that authority. Sovereignty came from God to the monarch directly.

Later, when the notion of "rights" emerged, they began as beneficences from the king to the people. They were given like crumbs from his table to the subjects being ruled. But just as rights were given by grace, they could be taken away by whim.

The framers of our Constitution upended all of that. Revolutionaries in the literal and figurative sense, they carried guns and bayonets, but they also carried even more potent weapons: new ideas that still form the bedrock of our nation.

Our framers' moral and philosophical revolution turned on two radical concepts. First, that rights come from God rather than from a monarch. And second, that sovereignty in turn comes from the people.

Madison, Jefferson, Franklin, and Adams all studied the work of English philosopher John Locke, who had argued powerfully for the "natural rights" of man, specifically the rights to life, liberty, and property. Every human being, Locke argued, had those rights because we are created in the image of God.

Hence, Jefferson penned those foundational words in the Declaration of Independence: "We hold these truths to be self-evident: that all men are created equal, and that they are endowed by their Creator with certain unalienable rights, that among those are life, liberty, and the pursuit of happiness."

America was founded on the idea that our rights come from our Creator, not from government.

And with that insight, the framers inverted the notion of sovereignty. Rather than flowing from God to king to people, sovereignty instead flows from God to the people and only then to the government. From the beginning, our founders understood that the true function of our government was to safeguard the rights of citizens. To that end, thirteen years after the Declaration of Independence, Congress passed the Judiciary Act of 1789, which set up the federal court system of the United States.

For the most part, our justice system was based on English Common Law, deriving its principles from documents such as the Magna Carta, the first major document to declare that there was effectively no difference between kings and their subjects, at least in the eyes of God. That, in turn, is reflected in the bedrock principle of American law that "no man is above the law." For nearly a hundred years, these principles governed much of life in the United States. When justice is served properly, it protects the rights of all.

Tragically, for the first century of our nation's history, many Americans' rights were not protected. Women had only limited rights under law, and most African Americans were subjected to the horrific evil of slavery. In the eyes of the law, as reflected in the Supreme Court's infamous *Dred Scott* decision, African Americans were deemed not to be people, but merely property. After America paid the price of unspeakable bloodshed, the Civil War, President Lincoln's Emancipation Proclamation, and the Thirteenth, Fourteenth, and Fifteenth Amendments finally ended the abomination of slavery.

In the aftermath of the Civil War, our justice system faced an important test. Throughout the South, where hundreds of thousands of slaves had just been set free, roving bands of racist lunatics calling themselves the Ku Klux Klan made it their mission to keep African Americans oppressed, powerless, and out of public office. They did so through the use of horrible violence, often dragging African Americans out of their homes and hanging them from nearby trees. This horrific practice, known as "lynching," soon became so common throughout the nation that newspapers didn't bother reporting on every instance.

To respond to this grave threat, President Ulysses S. Grant—the man who had won the war for the Union and risen to the presidency shortly afterward—signed legislation forming the United States Justice Department, directing it to prosecute all members of the Ku Klux Klan to the fullest extent of the law. This, he reasoned, would set an example for anyone else who was thinking about donning robes and harassing innocent people of color. Over the next few months, Attorney General Amos T. Akerman and his army of lawyers at the Department of Justice crushed the Klan. Grant, like Lincoln before him, was a Republican. And the Klansmen were, almost without exception, Democrats.

In that time, according to a biography of President Grant, "federal grand juries, many interracial, brought 3,384 indictments against the KKK, resulting in 1,143 convictions. This conviction rate was even better than it sounded. The federal court system was burdened with cases and many federal judges, appointed before Grant, didn't sympathize with the anti-Klan crusade."[1] But in the end, the law prevailed. By 1872, the Klan was a shadow of its former self, a display to all Americans of the massive power that the United States government could have when it acts in the interest of fairness, justice, and the people.

In 1933, President Franklin Delano Roosevelt greatly expanded the responsibilities of the Justice Department, charging it with functions of "prosecuting in the courts of the United States claims and demands by, and [offenses] against, the Government of the United States, and of defending claims and demands against the Government, and of supervising the work of United States attorneys, marshals, and clerks in connection therewith, now exercised by any agency or officer."[2]

For almost a century, the Department of Justice mostly discharged its duties without fear or favor, bringing lawsuits against people who had violated the law. Although the president was formally in charge of the entire executive branch—of which the Department of Justice, as well as our nation's intelligence agencies, are a part—it was generally accepted that the Department of Justice, like the Supreme Court, was not supposed to dabble in partisan politics. Throughout history, there have been exceptions, several of which we will deal with in the pages to come. When President Richard Nixon was beginning to feel the heat from lawmakers asking questions about his crimes during the Watergate scandal, for instance, he attempted to use the full weight of the executive branch to crush his enemies. Indeed, Nixon expressly directed his attorney general to commit multiple serious crimes before firing him in what became known as the Saturday Night Massacre.

This kind of corruption was also commonplace during the administration of President John F. Kennedy, who defied historical precedent when he selected his own brother Robert as his attorney general. Together, the Kennedy brothers waged war on their enemies from the White House and DOJ in a manner that was quite uncommon in the American system of government, another topic we'll cover in this book.

But no president flouted the norms of judicial independence quite so brazenly as Barack Obama, who politicized and weaponized the Justice Department in a way that was directly contrary to over a century of tradition. In 2013, Attorney General Eric Holder described his role this way: "I'm still enjoying what I'm doing. There's still work to be done. *I'm still the president's wingman,* so I'm there with my boy."[3] Before Holder was nominated to be Obama's attorney general, he had built a reputation for being a relatively nonpartisan prosecutor—someone with integrity who could carry out the duties of his office honestly. Unfortunately, his tenure as attorney general did enormous damage to that reputation.

This partisan tradition, unfortunately, has been revived by President Joe Biden, a man who has no problem with calling concerned parents domestic terrorists, or with attacking voting laws to try to prevent the voters from electing Republicans all over the country.

In order to understand these impulses toward enemy-hunting and partisan witch hunts, it's important to review the history of presidents who have abused our justice system—the ones who attempted, and in some cases succeeded, in corrupting justice to suit their partisan goals.

We begin with Richard Milhous Nixon.

CHAPTER ONE

ENEMIES

Before the Storm

On the morning of his daughter Tricia's wedding, with four hundred guests about to arrive at the White House, Richard Nixon sat in the Oval Office with his chief of staff, H. R. Haldeman.

One of the most famous "hatchet men" in American politics, Haldeman had been with Nixon since the early 1960s. He'd stuck with Nixon through two failed campaigns—one for president in 1960, then another for governor of California in 1962. In that time, Haldeman had become well acquainted with the darker side of Nixon's personality. Around the building, he was known semi-affectionately as the president's "son of a bitch." When there was a job that Nixon didn't have the stomach to do himself—firing someone, for instance, or giving them direct orders that stretched the bounds of legality, and therefore shouldn't come straight from the president of the United States—Haldeman was more than happy to step in.

By the end of his tenure as chief of staff, this tendency would land Haldeman, as well as dozens of other men in Nixon's orbit, in prison.

But on that morning, June 12, 1971, the two men chatted idly, waiting for the storm clouds to pass. A light rain, which had been falling since before sunrise, had already delayed the outdoor wedding ceremony by about two hours. Despite several pleas from her father to move the whole event indoors to the East Room, Tricia Nixon had insisted on pushing the start time back until the sun came out. So, they waited—all four hundred friends and family members, many of whom had flown in from all over the country to see the president's daughter get married in the Rose Garden. That evening, many of them would sleep in the White House, filling the dozen or so guest bedrooms of the building for the first time since Nixon had won the presidency in 1968.

But Nixon's mind was not on the impending nuptials. Nor was it on the dozens of foreign and domestic disputes that were, at that very moment, threatening to sink his presidency.

He was thinking, as always, about his enemies.

For years, Nixon had been making lists of people who had wronged him. He wrote their names on yellow legal pads, scribbling constantly throughout the day like a madman, then letting those pads pile up around his home and office like old, dirty laundry. By the time he became president, the lists had grown so long that Haldeman, one of Nixon's designated enforcers in the White House, had to assign a full team of junior staffers just to keep track of them. During their first few years on the job, these aides would send memos back and forth with questions about the various lists and what they meant. They wondered, for instance, whether the people whose names Nixon had written on something called "The Freeze List" were more or less hated than those on the lists simply marked "enemies."

They rarely got clear answers.

"I'm sure he must have forgotten some of the people who did him wrong," Haldeman would later recall. "Because there were so many of them and he couldn't possibly remember all of them. He did have a remarkable ability, though, to keep most of them pretty well-catalogued."[1]

The real list, in other words, was in the president's head, usually somewhere near the top. Given a few minutes of silence, Nixon would often fill the time with lengthy, hateful diatribes about those who had wronged him. The audience mattered little to him; nor did the occasion.

On the morning of his daughter's wedding, for instance—a day for light and happy thoughts, if there ever was one—Nixon sat fuming. He ranted, according to an account of the morning by Nixon biographer John Farrell, about

> a hardy list that included: the "long-haired, dirty looking" protestors; the eastern establishment; feminists; teachers' union; Jews ("Goddamn, they are a vicious bunch"); African Americans ("We don't do well with Blacks...We don't want to do so damn well with Blacks"); the "softies" of the Ivy League; the "ass kissers and butter uppers" in the bureaucracy; and the "lousy, dirty...cowardly bastards" in the press.

After a few more minutes of idle chatter, which covered more and more groups of the president's enemies, the clouds began to lift. Sun shone in through the large windows in the Oval.

The two men exited the room and took their places for the ceremony.

For the rest of the evening, the event went off without a hitch. The assembled crowd, which included former presidents and many members of Congress, had a wonderful time. Even Richard Nixon, who had never been one to cut loose, danced and drank champagne. Toward the end of the evening, he pulled Lady Bird Johnson, the wife of his predecessor, Lyndon Johnson, out of the crowd and spun her around in circles on the dance floor.

The event was reported in the next day's newspapers as a roaring success, with the *New York Times* describing Tricia Nixon as "ethereal" and "beautiful."[2]

To a man who had always complained about rough treatment in the press, this should have been a rare bright spot.

But Nixon didn't seem to notice the article.

Instead, in typical fashion, he spent much of the next morning, a Sunday, in a foul mood. He asked about the press coverage and the guest list—he was angry that several high-profile people hadn't come—then moved on to the outlets that hadn't covered the wedding positively. In particular, he singled out the *Washington Post*, the paper that would ultimately bring about his downfall.

"They're never to be in the White House again," he said, speaking to his press secretary. "Never!"[3]

It was a few minutes after noon when Nixon finally slipped into the Oval Office to call General Alexander Haig, his deputy national security advisor, for an update on the state of the world outside the White House grounds. Toward the end of the call, Nixon learned that on the front page of that morning's *New York Times*, right beside the write-up of his daughter's wedding, was an article that would change the course of the Nixon presidency.

"The goddamn *New York Times*," General Haig said, "[ran] an exposé of the most highly classified documents of the war. It was a devastating security breach of the greatest magnitude of anything I've ever seen."[4]

This series of articles, among the most storied in American journalism, was based on a lengthy study of the Vietnam War that Defense Secretary Robert McNamara had ordered in the late '60s. Over the years, the series in the *Times* would reveal that the previous four administrations had not only bungled the war in Vietnam, but had also told bald-faced lies to the American people about how it was going. The leak would come to be known as the "Pentagon Papers."

Soon, it would be revealed that the source of the leak was Daniel Ellsberg, a former military analyst who was outraged that the American people had been repeatedly lied to about the progress of the war in Vietnam. Ellsberg had come into the Johnson administration straight from Harvard University, witnessing the government decision-making process firsthand. He had spent months photocopying the papers so that he could leak them to the press.

On Monday, June 14, 1971, the day after the first excerpt of the Pentagon Papers ran on the front page of the *New York Times*, Nixon called a meeting with Attorney General John Mitchell and John Ehrlichman, his domestic policy advisor. Both men were extremely loyal to the president. Mitchell, who had been a partner at Nixon's law firm before the presidency, would go on to play a major role in many of the "dirty tricks" for which the Nixon administration became infamous. So would John Ehrlichman.

President Nixon ordered Mitchell to stop the Pentagon Papers from being published.

For the next twelve hours or so, the Nixon administration exhausted all legal options to try to stop more excerpts of the report from coming out. But nothing worked. When the Supreme Court decided that the Nixon Justice Department did not, as a matter of law, have the right to stop the *Times* from publishing, it seemed that the battle was lost. The Nixon administration had played the game fair and square, attempting to stop the leaks by using the machinery of our justice system.

That effort had failed.

So, they began discussing options that were...let's say, not so legal.

A few days after the administration's public defeat in the Pentagon Papers case, H. R. Haldeman went to Nixon and let him know that there might be more documents floating around the capital. These documents, according to rumors, were much newer than the ones that had come out during the Pentagon Papers scandal; they might contain negative information not only about Kennedy and Johnson, but about Richard Nixon, too.

Luckily, according to Haldeman, he knew exactly where these documents were: sitting in a safe in the headquarters of the Brookings Institution, which happened to sit in a brand-new complex called the Watergate, just under a mile from the White House.

Leaning back in his chair behind the Resolute Desk, President Nixon began barking at his chief of staff.

"Bob?" he said. "Now, you remember Huston's plan? I want it implemented on a thievery basis. Goddamn it, go in and get those files. Blow the safe and get it."

Black Bag Jobs

Throughout his life, Richard Nixon had been willing to attack his enemies—both real and perceived—with uncommon ferocity. But interestingly, he rarely did so in a straightforward manner, and almost never face-to-face.

Instead, he attacked from the sides, using insinuation to make his points. During his first congressional race, which took place in California in 1946, he slyly accused the incumbent congressman, Jerry Voorhis, of being a secret Communist, knowing all the while that the accusation was false.

As Nixon's career progressed, these roundabout provocations grew to encompass outright spying and other dirty tricks. During that first race against Voorhis, for instance, Nixon listed "set up spies...in V. camp" among his top priorities, writing, as always, on the yellow legal pads that would soon be packed to the margins with the names of his enemies. Years earlier, fresh out of Duke Law School with no job prospects on the horizon, he had even filled out an application to become a special agent at the FBI. But the Bureau, which saw enough promise in the young man to grant him an interview, denied his application, noting (rather amazingly, considering the trajectory his career would take) that Nixon seemed to "lack aggression."[5]

Although Nixon never saw these notes, it almost seems as if he spent the rest of his career attempting to prove the FBI's assessment wrong.

As a young congressman serving on the House Un-American Activities Committee, or HUAC, Nixon went after Communists with an almost evangelical zeal. In one of the most famous episodes of his career,

Congressman Nixon managed to prove that Alger Hiss, a former State Department official who had worked at the highest levels of the American government, had in fact been a spy for the Soviet Union the whole time. It was a case full of espionage and intrigue; the hearings, which were televised all day during the summer of 1948, captivated the American public and made Nixon a star.

It was an episode that would serve as the centerpiece of Nixon's memoir *Six Crises*, written in the early '60s and published to great acclaim. For the rest of his career, Nixon would find ways to bring up the Hiss case in conversation, recounting the lessons he'd learned from it. One of the main lessons, oddly enough, was that committing a crime was one thing, but covering it up was what really got you in trouble.

During his time in Congress, Nixon also made the acquaintance of J. Edgar Hoover, the director of the FBI. Later, it would be revealed that Hoover, knowing that Nixon had applied for the Bureau and been rejected, had initiated the relationship, betting that the young Nixon might someday make something of himself. The bet paid off in spades. In time, though, they struck up a genuine friendship, which was somewhat odd considering the two men were not, to say the least, known for their warmth or generosity.

By the time he met Nixon, Hoover had already developed a reputation for ruthlessness and paranoia that would only grow as his career went on. He made even Richard Nixon, the deeply insecure congressman who planted spies in the campaigns of his enemies, look like a normal, well-adjusted American citizen. During his tenure as the director of the FBI, a post he had held since the early twentieth century, Hoover had often used the Bureau as a blunt weapon against his political enemies.

Hoover had used the Bureau to spy on civil rights icon Dr. Martin Luther King, Jr., for instance, making public his extramarital affairs and writing him threatening letters, even going so far as to encourage Dr. King to commit suicide. Hoover had planted listening devices in the homes and offices of countless activists, writers, and politicians. In order to plant these devices, Hoover had ordered agents to break into various buildings. These operations were called "black bag jobs," named for the small black bags that agents carried during break-ins and bugging operations. They were not remotely legal, so they were kept secret. The black bags, which anyone who's ever seen a spy movie would recognize, contained all kinds of tools of the espionage trade: wiretaps, lock picks, hammers, headphones, coils of rope, and more.

By the time Nixon won the White House in 1968, he had come to consider J. Edgar Hoover his "closest personal friend in all of public life."[6] Even during his years of exile from Washington—Nixon had lost the presidential election of 1960 to John F. Kennedy, then the race for governor of California in 1962, seemingly ending his political career—Hoover had remained in touch. They often had meetings in Hoover's house and on his boat. Shortly after Nixon's victory in 1968, Hoover went to visit him at the Pierre Hotel in New York, where the transition team was based. According to John Ehrlichman, who was usually present during Nixon's meetings with Hoover, the FBI director was "florid and fat-faced," adding that he "looked unwell."[7]

But, as historian Tim Weiner writes in *Enemies: A History of the FBI*, "[Hoover's] powers of speech were undiminished." The director, according to Weiner's account, "pointedly reminded Nixon about the powers of surveillance that were at a president's command." He spoke about how, at the direction of every president since Franklin Delano Roosevelt, the FBI had carried out operations that included breaking and entering, warrantless wiretapping, and other "black bag jobs." He reminded the new president that the FBI was, in Weiner's words, "especially adept at hunting down leakers," and that "wiretapping was 'the most effective means' it had." This meeting, it seemed, was a kind of offer from the FBI director to the president—one that Richard Nixon, a man who had spent his career carrying out small versions of the operations that the FBI was describing, longing to finally have the FBI and the United States Justice Department at his disposal, was all too happy to accept.

During the first years of his administration, the relationship between Nixon and the FBI prospered. Together, they harassed figures from John

Lennon to Muhammad Ali, wiretapping the Black Panthers and other antiwar leaders. Under this partnership, according to Nixon biographer John Farrell, "the military-industrial combine prospered, the state flourished, and the tentacles of surveillance crept through society."[8]

But soon the relationship began to sour. Nixon, who was perhaps even more eager than previous presidents to go after his enemies for personal and political reasons, repeatedly asked the FBI to go further and further in its surveillance and harassment of antiwar protestors. But Hoover, after over four decades at the helm of the FBI, was a little more cautious. A few years earlier, in 1965, he had been forced to endure a painful airing-out of the FBI's dirty laundry during several Senate hearings on the matter, after which he swore off some of the more extreme "black bag jobs" he had been carrying out for decades. More than once, Nixon and his aides complained that the intelligence they were getting from the FBI was weak, sloppy, and shoddily written.

Outside the White House, the political situation was growing dire. In the late '60s and early '70s, hundreds of thousands of people had filled the streets in protest of the war in Vietnam. Some of these demonstrations became violent, and many of them ended in skirmishes between protestors and counter-protestors. In a memo to the president, then-speechwriter Pat Buchanan wrote that the administration was now "in a contest over the soul of the country," and that the White House needed to engage in "heated political warfare" as a response.[9]

Clearly, they believed something needed to be done—and quickly.

In the early summer of 1970, a young White House aide named Tom Huston rose to the occasion. Over a few days, Huston drafted a plan designed to spring the FBI, the Justice Department, and even the CIA—which was legally forbidden from engaging in covert activities on American soil—into action against anti-Nixon forces in the United States. Due to the extreme political situation of the time, Huston suggested, the FBI needed to revive its "black bag jobs" and other illegal clandestine activities, including the surveillance of mail. The plan is a fascinating document, especially to modern readers, not least because its author, who had once been described by a superior as "intense and cadaverous," repeatedly acknowledged in plain language that his recommendations were illegal.[10]

"Present procedures should be changed," he wrote, "to permit intensification of coverage of individuals and groups in the United States who pose a major threat to the internal security.... Covert coverage [of the U.S. mail] is illegal and there are serious risks involved. However, the advantages to be derived from its use outweigh the risks."[11]

The plan also recommended a technique that the author refers to (in an extreme feat of understatement, considering the circumstances), as "surreptitious entry." In a section under this heading, Huston calls for "selective use of this technique against other urgent and high priority internal security targets." Again, he admits that "use of this technique is clearly illegal: it amounts to burglary. It is also highly risky and could result in great embarrassment if exposed. However, it is also the most fruitful and can produce the type of intelligence which cannot be obtained in any other fashion. The FBI in Mr. Hoover's younger days used to conduct such operations with great success and with no exposure."

When Tom Huston presented this plan to the heads of our nation's intelligence community in J. Edgar Hoover's office, everyone but the director of the FBI agreed to sign off on it. Hoover, however, flew into a rage upon hearing what the young Nixon aide had to say. Over the next few days, he got together with John Mitchell, the attorney general, to make sure that the plan would never be implemented. Even though Richard Nixon himself approved the Huston plan—and, by all accounts, was thrilled with it—Mitchell revoked it, citing Director Hoover's unwillingness to get back into the dirty business of widespread warrantless wiretapping, spying, and breaking and entering.

Nixon had asked the FBI to act as his enforcers, effectively taking Hoover up on the offer that he had made during the transition just a few years earlier, and the FBI director had refused. In many ways, this was the beginning of the end of J. Edgar Hoover. Soon after the Huston plan debacle, Nixon began looking for replacements within the Bureau for him—which wasn't a big step, given that Hoover, then seventy-five, was well past the mandatory retirement age. The relationship between the two men, which had remained strong through the darkest periods of their lives, would never recover. Although the FBI would carry out several surveillance operations for the Nixon White House in the years to come, the intelligence was never quite as reliable as Nixon would have liked.

The Huston plan, as the journalist Garrett M. Graff writes in his recent one-volume history of Watergate, titled *Watergate: A New History*, ended up on the desk of John Dean, a young aide who had just been hired as the White House counsel. When Tom Huston left the White House, the newly hired Dean inherited some of his duties, including the dirty tricks he'd performed for Richard Nixon.

"Dean placed [the Huston plan] in a safe," Graff writes, "where it sat like a time bomb, evidence that the Nixon White House repeatedly—and dubiously—explored the limits of legal activities aimed at its political opponents. As Senator Richard Schweiker would say years later: 'Even though the Huston plan was dead, I believe it had nine lives.'"

All the President's Goons

As the fallout from the Pentagon Papers case continued, Richard Nixon grew increasingly desperate. The FBI, which had long served as a one-stop shop for the kind of dirty tricks he wanted to carry out, had rebuffed him in stunning fashion. Nixon believed, and not without reason, that with the Vietnam War still raging and the possibility of documents that detailed his failures sitting in a safe at the Brookings Institution, he would almost certainly lose the presidential election of 1972.

Having already given the order to "blow the safe" and recover the documents from the Brookings Institution—documents that, strangely, would turn out never to have existed—Nixon turned to a man named Chuck Colson, known around the White House as a tough loose cannon, willing to take on the dirty jobs that most political aides wouldn't do. A hard-driving lawyer who once boasted, according to his obituary in the *New York Times*, that he would "walk over his own grandmother" to get Nixon reelected in 1972, Colson had a tendency to whip his boss into a frenzy, playing to the darker side of his personality. Once, according to Nixon biographer John Farrell, when Attorney General John Mitchell was asked what Chuck Colson's constituency was, he replied, "The president's worst instincts."[12]

Within a few days, Colson got together with a few associates and came up with a plan which, even against the backdrop of the Watergate scandal, still seems too insane to be true. At some point in the next few days, Colson said, he would have one of his White House associates break into the Brookings Institution in the Watergate building and start a fire. Then, amid the panic and chaos that was sure to ensue, he would break into the office, crack the safe, and run away with the documents.

When John Dean, the new White House counsel, learned of this plan, he was rightly alarmed—so alarmed, in fact, that he flew out to California immediately, where President Nixon was staying at the six-acre ranch in San Clemente that he called the "Western White House." Standing on the deck, Dean reminded the president that, first of all, starting such a fire would be a felony. Secondly, he said, if anyone died in the blaze, Richard Nixon, the president of the United States, would legally be able to be charged with murder. At Dean's urging, Nixon abandoned that particular plan, telling Colson to wait around for another assignment.

It didn't take long for one to appear—or, rather, for several to appear. Given his paranoia, Nixon was never short on work for the crazy amateur spies who had come to populate the White House. Repeatedly, he made himself quite clear about the type of "tough guys" he needed to carry out the operations.

"I really need a son of a bitch like Huston," he said on August 1, "who will work his butt off and do it dishonorably....I'll direct him myself."[13]

He ended up with several. One of them was a retired CIA operative named Howard Hunt, a slight, unassuming man who worked for a PR agency and wrote spy novels on the side. Oddly enough, he seemed to have been present for some of the CIA's most embarrassing episodes, including the disastrous Bay of Pigs invasion that had taken place in Cuba under President Kennedy. But Colson, who had somehow managed to become Nixon's most trusted man when it came to dirty tricks, believed that Hunt was the man for the job. President Nixon agreed, and Hunt was hired.

For a few months, Hunt kicked around and did minor jobs for the president, failing at every turn. When he was tasked with trying to find dirt on John F. Kennedy in the government's secret files, for instance, he failed miserably. But that didn't stop him from forging documents ostensibly from the State Department and leaking them to *Life* magazine.

Around the same time, when President Nixon found out that J. Edgar Hoover had been intentionally slow-rolling the FBI's investigation into Daniel Ellsberg, he demanded that the job be brought in-house. Once again, law enforcement had refused his most aggressive requests, and he was going to take matters into his own hands.

"I need a man," he said, venting in the White House to Chuck Colson, John Ehrlichman, and H. R. Haldeman. "A commander. An officer in charge here at the White House that I can call when I wake up, as I did last night, at two o'clock in the morning and I can say I want to do this, this, and this...a guy, also who will have the initiative to go out and do a few of these things."[14]

Naturally, the job fell to men like Howard Hunt. But by this point, he was no longer alone. Over the course of a few months that summer, President Nixon and his aides had formed a group called the Special Investigations Unit, originally intended to hunt down leaks and stop them, especially when the intelligence community wasn't acting quickly enough. The two men in charge of this unit, David Young and Egil Krogh, would soon become major figures on the national stage, along with just about everyone else who came through the basement office of the Executive Office Building where the unit made their plans and carried out their operations.

The group's mandate was simple: attack the president's enemies; do it by any means necessary. They had almost unlimited funds—organized by laundering campaign money through various people, both suspecting and unsuspecting—and they had the full resources of the executive branch. What they didn't have was any idea what they were doing. For the "expertise" in espionage that they lacked, the group hired a man whose name would soon become famous the world over, splashed across the pages of the *Washington Post* under one of the most famous bylines in the history of American journalism.

For several years, G. Gordon Liddy had been an FBI agent, learning the skills of espionage under J. Edgar Hoover himself. After leaving the FBI, Liddy became a prosecutor, but could never seem to let go of his obsession—one that often seemed comical to those around him—with dirty tricks and the craft of spying. He also had a tendency to act out. Once, using prosecutorial methods that he would later describe as "unorthodox but effective," Liddy fired a gun at the ceiling of a courtroom during his closing argument, believing that showing the jury how the alleged murder weapon worked would be better than simply telling them.[15] (To any aspiring lawyers who might be reading this, please know that the chances of success with this approach are slim, to say the least.) Around the same time, Liddy was also fond of bragging that he could "hold his hand over a flame without flinching." He also "claimed to be able to kill a man with a pencil."[16]

It should go without saying that by the time Liddy joined the Special Investigations Unit, the Treasury Department—where he had been working as a special assistant for guns and narcotics—was more than happy to see him go.

"I was under no illusion about…legality," Liddy would later write in his memoir. "Although spies in the enemy camp and electronic surveillance were nothing new in American presidential politics, we were going to go far beyond that. As far as I was concerned, anything went."[17]

For the next few months, Howard Hunt and G. Gordon Liddy embarked on the kind of demolition derby that you don't usually see outside of screwball comedy films. Short of lighting themselves on fire, I'm not sure they could have messed things up any more than they actually did. As their first trick, having already asked the CIA to write them a fake psychological profile of Daniel Ellsberg—by this point, the main objective was to prove that Ellsberg was insane, and therefore not trustworthy—they decided to break into the office of Ellsberg's actual psychiatrist, which was in California, and search for incriminating files themselves.

During a scouting trip, Hunt took a photograph of Liddy posing outside the building. They were both wearing CIA disguises, and Hunt took the picture using a CIA camera. Then, a few days later, they brought the film to the CIA to get it developed, and they made copies, which they placed in the White House's files. When it was finally time for the break-in, they enlisted a group of Cubans that Hunt had met during the botched Bay of Pigs invasion, broke in, and ransacked the office. The plan, according to their later testimony, was to make the whole thing look like a run-of-the-mill, drug-related crime. The plan failed. They did not find the files they were looking for, returning home having done nothing but destroy a poor shrink's office and leave a whole lot of incriminating evidence in their wake.

In the Oval Office a few days later, John Ehrlichman told Nixon, "We had one little operation. It's been aborted out in Los Angeles, which, I think, it is better that you don't know about. But we've got some dirty tricks under way."[18]

The other dirty tricks, as it turned out, were legion. Just a few months earlier, in the fall of 1971, G. Gordon Liddy had given a presentation to Attorney General John Mitchell, complete with charts and graphs prepared by the CIA, about something he called Operation GEMSTONE.

Again, the details defy belief.

The plan, such as it was, was a collection of several smaller plans, all named after different gemstones: RUBY, EMERALD, QUARTZ, SAPPHIRE, and so on. One of these plans called for a specialized high-tech government airplane that would follow Democratic candidates around the country during their campaigns and record their conversations. Another plan involved hiring mobsters to grab anti-Nixon protestors off the street, pump them full of drugs, and fly them down to Mexico for a few days so they could cool off. There were plans to plant spies in enemy campaigns, to hire prostitutes to seduce high-ranking members of the Democratic Party on a houseboat, and, of course, to break into various buildings around the country. One gets the feeling that Liddy, who seemed to take the opportunity to put all his wildest spy-novel fantasies down on paper, only stopped writing when he ran out of gemstones to name the operations after.

The attorney general objected to this approach, but not because he thought there was anything especially wrong with drugging, kidnapping, or prostitution. He just thought that the plan, which carried a price tag of about one million dollars, was too expensive. He ended the meeting by telling Liddy to cut some of the expenses and come back.

When Liddy did come back a few months later, he had managed to trim the fat off the plan and get the cost down to about $250,000. He couldn't have come at a better time.

Back in the Oval Office, President Nixon's old demons—the belief that everyone was somehow out to get him, and that he couldn't possibly win the next election unless he cheated in some way—were haunting him again. Repeatedly, he asked for something to be done about his potential opponents. Around this time, he arranged for someone to go up to Chappaquiddick, where Senator Edward Kennedy had famously driven his car off a bridge and killed a young woman, to poke around and look for dirt. Nixon believed that Ted Kennedy was very likely to be his opponent in 1972, but he also sent his "tough guys" out looking for dirt on candidates who were less likely to run against him.

Unsurprisingly, none of these operations yielded very much in the way of intelligence. So they thought bigger. If they couldn't get dirt on the individual candidates, they would look to the offices of the Democratic National Committee itself—offices that happened to reside a few floors below the Brookings Institution (which, fortunately, Chuck Colson had never set ablaze), right back in the Watergate complex.

Third-Rate Burglars

The first time they broke into the Watergate, on May 26, 1972, the burglars—James McCord, Liddy, Howard Hunt, and six Cuban men—had a rough time. The police came after only a few minutes, and the would-be burglars had to wait in the building for several hours until they left. Howard Hunt, waiting in a closet on the sixth floor, was forced to urinate into an empty bottle of scotch until he knew the coast was clear. During the second break-in, a few days later, they managed to take some photographs and plant a few listening devices, but later found out that they'd tapped the phones of a few low-level staffers who didn't have much of interest to say. If they were going to break the law, apparently, these men wanted more to show for their efforts than a few conversations about printer paper and grocery lists.

So, on June 17, they went in yet a third time, believing they could either remove the listening devices or plant newer and better ones. To this day, oddly enough, no one is quite sure why they broke in again. Anyone interested in the competing theories, of which there are several, would do well to read *Watergate: A New History*, which analyzes them all in some detail.

This, however, was the night that they got caught—rather infamously, it would turn out. Shortly after midnight, a squad of plainclothes police officers who'd been called about a disturbance came upon some tape that the burglars had left on all the doors they had passed through at the Watergate. It didn't take long for these officers to follow the trail that these bumbling burglars had inadvertently left in their wake, leading anyone who followed it right to the sixth floor, where they were rifling around looking for listening devices.

The sight, I'm sure, must have been ridiculous: six men, all wearing suits and latex gloves, carrying black bags full of burglary tools and big stacks of hundred-dollar bills. The cash, as the world would later learn, was to bribe the cops if they got in trouble—which, obviously, didn't quite work out the way they wanted it to. The scene would later be immortalized in the opening minutes of *All the President's Men*.

Soon, this small burglary would blossom into the political scandal of the century. The Nixon White House would work behind the scenes to cover the whole thing up, going so far as to pay off each of the burglars in cash, using campaign money, so they would keep quiet about the White House's involvement. These payments were massive, and there were so many that no one at the White House quite knew how many were going out at any one time.

Most notoriously, President Nixon used the machinery of the government to cover up the crimes his men had ordered. In the midst of the scandal, he learned that the FBI, which after the retirement of J. Edgar Hoover was being led by a man named L. Patrick Gray, was looking into the burglary. If Nixon had allowed the investigation to continue, he might have been able to save his presidency. Several aides would have gone to jail, of course, particularly the men who had actually committed the burglary. But Nixon might not have been forced to resign.

But that's not what he did. In several conversations captured by his hidden White House taping system, President Nixon cooked up a plan. He would have Richard Helms, the director of the CIA, call the FBI and suggest that the burglary had been a CIA operation all along, demanding that they stop the investigation.

This would prove to be his fatal mistake.

Clearly, Richard Nixon had not learned the lesson that he had written down in *Six Crises*: the cover-up is always worse than the crime.

Even so, that didn't stop him from reminding the American people of that insight several times on national television.

On August 29, for instance, Nixon spoke to reporters about an investigation that the House Committee on Banking and Finance was doing into the Watergate burglary and the White House's involvement in it. Speaking with all the confidence of a man who had done absolutely nothing wrong, he said, "I think that under these circumstances, we are doing everything that we can to take this incident and to investigate it and not to cover it up. Now, what really hurts in matters of this sort is not the fact that they occur, because overzealous people in campaigns do things that are wrong. What really hurts is if you try to cover it up."[19]

Empty Chairs

Looking back on Watergate, one tends to assume that things moved swiftly—that the burglars were caught, the White House covered it up, and everyone was caught red-handed soon after. But that wasn't remotely what happened.

In reality, it took several years for all the dominoes in Watergate to fall. And for much of that time, Richard Nixon remained extremely popular—more popular, in fact, than he had been at any other point in his presidency.

There was good reason for this. In February 1972, amid the growing scandal, President Nixon had traveled to China, effectively ending a long period of isolation and opening the Chinese market to the world. Newspapers would soon dub the week that he spent there attending cultural events and meeting with leaders as "the week that changed the world." In May, he had traveled to the Soviet Union for the Moscow Summit, a meeting with Leonid Brezhnev that many hailed as a defining moment in the Cold War. During the trip, President Nixon argued the merits of capitalism over communism with Brezhnev, the leader of the Soviet Union, and managed to come out on top. Back home, the economy was rebounding, and inflation was remaining steady, something many did not believe Nixon would be able to achieve.

In 1972, Nixon won reelection by the largest margin since Franklin Delano Roosevelt in 1937, winning every state in the country but Massachusetts.

Still, there were people who knew something was up. When it comes to corruption at the highest levels of government, there always are. One of the earliest men to believe that something wasn't quite right about the Watergate narrative was a dignified, elderly congressman from the great state of Texas named Wright Patman. Having been elected just a few years before the Great Depression, Congressman Patman was already one of the longest-serving members of Congress in the early '70s, when he began looking into Watergate. Given that Patman was chairman of the House Committee on Banking and Currency, he believed that his committee had the power to look into the Watergate burglary because of the finance angle. Someone had paid these men, and he wanted to know who'd done it and how. Congressman Patman had also been a good friend of Jerry Voorhis, the man Richard Nixon had defeated early in his career by accusing him of being a Communist, so the investigation had a personal angle as well.

Right away, Patman and his team noticed a few things that were off. For starters, there was the $89,000 check from a Mexican bank that had been given to one of the Watergate burglars. Patman's team knew this unusually large amount must have come from some person—or some organization—with deep pockets. Most interestingly, especially for a finance expert, the serial numbers on the hundred-dollar bills that the burglars carried were in sequential order. That meant that they had probably never been in circulation—that they had likely come, in other words, straight off the presses at the United States Mint.

Who, they wondered, would have access to that much cash in perfectly ordered hundred-dollar bills?

Over time, it became clear that the answer was the Committee to Re-Elect the President, the organization that had served as a front for Nixon's dirty tricks since the early '70s, when it hired G. Gordon Liddy, Howard Hunt, and others. In time, it would come to be known by the cheeky acronym CREEP.

After he had marshaled enough evidence, Congressman Patman and his committee began discussing subpoenas. If Patman could issue subpoenas, then he could get everyone who might have been involved in the Watergate scandal into Congress to testify under oath, where even the slightest lie would be considered perjury, a felony that any rational person would want to avoid.

But there was a problem.

In order to issue the subpoenas, Patman needed a majority of congressmen on his banking committee—twenty-one Democrats and fourteen Republicans—to vote for them. Given that the Democrats were passionately opposed to Richard Nixon, getting a majority in the committee seemed simple at first. But in the White House, a small team was working to ensure that it didn't happen.

All along, President Nixon had been doing everything in his power to make sure the Patman investigation never got off the ground. Shortly after the investigation was announced, Nixon ordered John Dean to look at every Democrat who served on Patman's committee to see whether any of them might have committed any campaign finance violations that could be used to blackmail them into voting against the subpoenas. Even if they hadn't committed any violations, the threat of investigation would have been enough. President Nixon also tapped Gerald Ford, who was then the House minority leader, to make sure all the Republicans on the committee voted his way. This frivolous use of campaign finance law, as we'll see in the pages to come, is another tool that has repeatedly been used by corrupt presidents to intimidate their political enemies. For a while, these cloak-and-dagger tactics worked. Congressman Patman was not able to issue a single subpoena. When it came time to have the big televised hearing he had envisioned to catch the Nixon White House in a cover-up, there were no witnesses for him and his fellow congressmen to investigate. Patman "invited" four people to testify anyway, but they were not compelled by law to show up, and therefore did not.

On October 12, the date the hearing was supposed to take place, having been foiled by the White House and rebuffed by his party, Congressman Patman set up four empty chairs in the cavernous hearing room of the House Banking Committee, each one standing for a witness that he had invited to testify. Before hurling questions at the empty chairs for just under an hour, Congressman Patman called the whole Watergate affair "a massive cover-up," proving that he knew before just about anyone else what was going on behind the scenes. He persisted even when it seemed the evidence, and the powers that be, were against him.

As someone who has repeatedly pressed for investigations into presidential abuse of power—most notably by President Barack Obama, who blatantly politicized the administration of justice and repeatedly rebuffed congressional efforts to hold him accountable—I understand the frustration that men like Patman must have felt, especially when much of the American public thought he was wasting his time.

The Saturday Night Massacre

Throughout the spring of 1973, the walls kept closing in on Richard Nixon. The men he had been paying off weren't going to keep quiet forever. Howard Hunt, in particular, had threatened to talk several times already, demanding more money to pay for his family's comfortable lifestyle. G. Gordon Liddy was growing even more agitated, saying that prison was inevitable, and the six Cuban men who'd actually done the break-in were getting restless.

In the meantime, nearly every major White House official had become involved in the plot. By June 1973, H. R. Haldeman had personally approved almost $500,000 in campaign funds to make the hush money payments.

In May, Nixon's new attorney general, Elliot Richardson, appointed Archibald Cox, a former U.S. solicitor general under John F. Kennedy, to investigate the Watergate burglary as a special counsel. It was an investigation that would only build on the massive information that had already been released about the scandal. The CIA had obtained the photographs of Liddy and Hunt from their trip to break into the office of Daniel Ellsberg's psychiatrist. During his confirmation hearings to become the new FBI director, Pat Gray had described how John Dean had tried to interfere with the Bureau's Watergate investigation on the president's behalf. In March, a judge had read a letter from James

McCord, one of the burglars, aloud in court, making headlines all over the country.

"There was political pressure applied to the defendants to plead guilty and remain silent," it read. "Perjury occurred during the trial....Others involved in the Watergate operation were not identified."

As one political henchman after another lied, it became clear to the nation—if not to Nixon—that he was going to be caught eventually. He had already tried and failed to pin the cover-up on everyone he possibly could. On April 29, he called H. R. Haldeman and John Ehrlichman, his two closest aides—and also the closest thing he had to friends in the administration—to Camp David and fired them. Ehrlichman had begged Nixon to resign and end it all that very night. But Nixon, almost delusional by this point, refused.

That's when he grew desperate.

On Saturday, October 20, 1973, Nixon called Attorney General Richardson into the Oval Office and directed him to fire Cox. Richardson refused and resigned on the spot. Shortly afterward, Nixon called Deputy Attorney General William Ruckelshaus and gave the same order.

He, too, refused and resigned.

So the job fell to a brilliant former Yale Law professor named Robert Bork, who had been named United States solicitor general just a few months earlier. Faced with a direct order from the president of the United States, Bork fired Archibald Cox. As a legal matter, there is no doubt that Bork had the authority to do this. Under Article II of the Constitution, all executive power is vested in the president, and that includes the authority to fire executive branch officers. But morally and ethically, there is a good argument that Bork should not have carried out the order. I've always admired Bork as a jurist and as a legal thinker, but for the rest of his life, Bork would pay for following Nixon's orders that fateful day. In 1987, when President Reagan nominated him to the Supreme Court, the Democratic Senate torpedoed his nomination after a brutal hearing. The proceedings were so nasty, and the accusations leveled against him so vicious, that his name would become a verb: to "Bork" a confirmation hearing became a disgraceful pattern that Democrats would repeat years later with Justice Clarence Thomas and then again with Justice Brett Kavanaugh.

Almost immediately, the events of October 20 became known as the Saturday Night Massacre. It was, according to several books about Watergate, when Richard Nixon finally began to realize that he was alone. The Republican Party would not support him—nor would his closest aides in the White House, who had all either resigned or been fired.

Of course, there were also the Senate hearings, which were particularly damning. Held from May 1973 to June 1974 and covered on every television station in the country, these sessions became like a soap opera to the tens of millions of Americans who watched them play out in their living rooms. Speaking to Dick Cavett—the television host who'd been one of President Nixon's earliest enemies, one of those he'd spoken about on the morning of his daughter's wedding—the writer Gore Vidal famously admitted to "needing his Watergate fix every morning."

It was during these hearings that the walls began to crumble. The cover stories did not stand up to congressional scrutiny. Former attorney general John Mitchell, who had insisted all along that he did not have advance knowledge of the Watergate break-in, was proven to be a liar time and time again as other witnesses testified about the truth of what had occurred. The Senate Judiciary Committee, a committee on which I proudly serve today, subpoenaed hundreds of hours of Nixon's White House tapes, which told the story plainly. Although Nixon hadn't himself ordered his goons into the Watergate, his role in the cover-up was enough to end his presidency. And as my mom told me growing up, Nixon's hateful foul language on the tapes and manifest racism understandably soured her and the American people on him as a person.

During his own turn on the stand, Mitchell was faced with his own involvement in Nixon's schemes—not only the Watergate break-in, but also the crazy plans that G. Gordon Liddy had detailed during his presentation about Operation GEMSTONE. Reflecting on his involvement,

Mitchell said he should have "thrown [Liddy] out of the window" before he could even begin the plan.

But it was too late.

Listening from home to lurid tales of prostitution, kidnapping, and drugging, the American people formed the opinion that most Americans hold today about Richard Nixon and his men: they were corrupt, and they deserved to be punished.

For many of these men, including John Mitchell and John Dean, punishment meant public humiliation, and, eventually, prison. Chuck Colson, who served a seven-month sentence, later underwent a remarkable transformation; he became a born-again Christian and ended up founding Prison Fellowship, which spreads the Gospel and ministers each year to more than 300,000 prisoners nationwide.

For President Richard Nixon, who always maintained that he did not know about the Watergate break-in before it happened, it meant resignation in disgrace. On August 8, after a group of Republican senators visited him at the White House to let him know it was all over, Richard Nixon strode out of the White House and boarded Marine One for the last time, flashing his trademark "V for victory" symbols for the cameras.

His letter of resignation, addressed to Secretary of State Henry Kissinger, took effect while he was still in the air.

A Matter of Luck

For the remainder of the twentieth century, and for the early years of the twenty-first, President Richard Nixon was one of the most reviled figures in modern American history. If you were to ask the average citizen to name a corrupt president, it's likely that only moments would elapse before they said his name. In large part, this reputation is deserved. Nixon earned it. He tolerated, and at times directed, the outright corruption of our justice system. Whatever his achievements in the realms of domestic and foreign policy—the opening of China to the world, for instance, or the creation of the Environmental Protection Agency—the dark shadow of Watergate is unlikely to lift from his legacy anytime soon.

Today, most Americans know what happened during Nixon's presidency. They know about the spy campaigns, the burglaries, the shredding of documents, and the dozens of illegal moves he made to cover it all up. But few people comprehend the scale of what didn't happen. It is amazing, for instance, that even J. Edgar Hoover, now considered one of the most fearsome and amoral officials in American history, actually refused to carry out many of the more sinister tasks assigned to him by the Nixon White House. Likewise, the IRS, asked repeatedly to audit and harass various political enemies of the Nixon White House, actively rebuffed him.

In other words, in substantial parts, the system worked during the Nixon administration. Things worked the way they are supposed to work. The IRS refused to act as the president's enforcer as he requested, believing correctly that the agency—along with the DOJ, the FBI, the CIA, the NSA, and others—was supposed to be apolitical, doing its job without fear or favor, acting the same way no matter what party controlled the White House.

This is a standard that the agency would hold, for the most part, until the early years of the twenty-first century, when a law professor from Chicago named Barack Obama—who had made more than a few enemies of his own during his short, shadowy career in public service—won the White House in 2008.

CHAPTER TWO

THE IRS COMES KNOCKING

In the summer of 2008, Catherine Engelbrecht and her friends started getting together to talk politics. The world seemed to be falling apart, and they wanted to do something about it.

Over the past several months, the race between John McCain and Barack Obama had been heating up. The housing market had just crashed, and the economy was on the verge of a serious recession. It was becoming clear that no matter who won the election, many Americans were going to suffer. For Engelbrecht, a tall, elegant, blonde woman from Houston, Texas, who ran a small business with her husband, the consequences were going to be especially severe. If there was ever a time to be getting more involved in politics, this was it.

So Engelbrecht and her friends signed up to watch the polls on election day. This is an important job, and it's done every four years by dedicated volunteers from all over the country. These volunteers make sure that everyone who shows up that day to vote is supposed to be there, and that they're only allowed to vote one time. The job should have been relatively simple. After all, Engelbrecht was watching the polls in the United States of America, not Venezuela or some Third

World banana republic. She was not prepared to guard against widespread voter fraud or intimidation.

Sadly, that's exactly what she ended up seeing.

"The veil was pulled back on what I thought was a very simple process," Engelbrecht would recall later. "I saw for the first time the mass confusion. I saw what can only be described as out-and-out election fraud. People were coming in with multiple registration cards. They were coming in and being allowed to vote without showing any ID whatsoever."[1]

The experience left Engelbrecht with a lingering question—one that remained in the back of her mind well into the next day, even as she heard the news that Barack Obama had won the White House by a healthy margin.

If this is what they're doing when people are watching, she wondered, *what are they doing when no one is looking?*

She had good reason to be concerned. In the past two decades, the integrity of American elections—something that few people had seriously thought to question since Rutherford B. Hayes prevailed over Samuel Tilden in the infamous "stolen election" of 1876—was in doubt. It had only been eight years since the tumultuous election of 2000, when former vice president Al Gore and his legal team had refused to concede the race to George W. Bush, the clear winner. During the hard-fought legal battles that followed, Vice President Gore attempted to convince the nation that if we could only count a few more votes in Florida, again and again, digging for lost ballots until we found enough with his name on them, then he would somehow emerge victorious. It was not going to happen, of course. But his persistence kept the election and the country in chaos for thirty-six long days.

I was deeply involved in the fight to preserve that election's integrity. As a twenty-nine-year-old lawyer, I had spent the preceding year and a half on the George W. Bush campaign, advising Bush on domestic policy. When Gore challenged the election results in Florida, I was sent to Tallahassee to help with the legal effort. Through serendipity, I ended up being part of the team directing the entire litigation; it just so happened I was the only practicing litigator on the campaign team, and had specialized in constitutional litigation prior to going to work for the campaign. What came together in *Bush v. Gore* was, I believe, the finest collection of legal talent that has ever been assembled—titans of the legal profession, from James A. Baker III, to Ted Olson, to Mike Carvin, to Fred Bartlit and Phil Beck, to John Roberts. Having just passed the bar a few years earlier, I was incredibly privileged to help assemble that team and to work alongside them (with an amazing cadre of younger lawyers as well, including my dear friend and future U.S. solicitor general Noel Francisco).

Gore's legal team was similarly star-studded, but the positions they were called to advance bordered on the frivolous. The votes were counted *four* times, and every time George W. Bush won. Vice President Gore refused to accept that, and his insistence to the contrary did serious damage to his reputation. Indeed, protestors outside the Naval Observatory (the official residence of then Vice President Gore) held signs aloft directing a biting pun at the Gore-Lieberman ticket: Sore-Loserman.

The shenanigans of the contested election—featuring partisan re-counters holding up punch-card ballots with "dangling," "dimpled," and "pregnant" chads and miraculously finding more and more votes for the Democratic ticket—seriously degraded the faith that the American people had in our electoral process, the bedrock of our democracy. I was dismayed at the time by how little many seemed to care about making sure our elections were safe, free, and secure.

In the years that followed, my dismay only grew. I was shocked, for instance, to learn that a community organizing group called ACORN was engaging in brazenly illegal voter registration practices. I was...well, let's say, *not* so shocked to learn that their "mistakes" only ever seemed to go in one direction, or that the organization had deep ties to then Senator Barack Obama. In the years leading up to the 2008 election, the Obama campaign paid an ACORN affiliate some $800,000, claiming on their FEC disclosure forms that the money was for "staging, sound, and lighting." For the next few months, ACORN employees worked tirelessly to register hundreds of thousands of voters in Democratic districts. By the time the registration deadlines rolled around, they claimed to have registered 1.3 million people to vote.

But there was a problem.

According to investigations done by CNN and the *New York Times*—which, clearly, had not yet fully embraced their role as the PR arm of the Democratic National Committee—fewer than half of those 1.3 million registrations were legitimate. The rest, as it turned out, were fraudulent in ways that were almost comical. In one county of about 5,000 people, Drew Griffin of CNN reported that 2,100 forms were "registered to a dead person, registered as a person who lives at a fast-food shop…or, amazingly, all of them done in the same hand."[2] In an article published on October 23, around the same time that Catherine Engelbrecht and her friends began talking politics in Houston, the *New York Times* reported that around 400,000 of the registrations collected by ACORN were rejected "for a variety of reasons, including duplicate registrations, incomplete forms, and fraudulent submissions from low-paid field workers trying to please their supervisors."[3]

Under pressure from the public and news organizations, the Obama campaign had amended its filing, admitting that the roughly $800,000 it had paid to ACORN was, in fact, for "get-out-the-vote efforts." By that time, there had been enough red flags about election integrity to make many Americans nervous about the upcoming race. To many observers, it seemed that the deck was stacked on behalf of Democrats. I'm sure this idea was reinforced on election day of 2008, when several members of the New Black Panther Party stood outside polling places in Philadelphia holding batons and baseball bats, almost daring people to vote against their preferred candidate. In the months that followed, of course, the Obama Justice Department would refuse to prosecute anyone involved in this naked voter intimidation.

In the aggregate, there wasn't sufficient evidence in 2008 to conclude that voter fraud actually altered the outcome of the race, but the appearance of impropriety was almost impossible to deny. Many Americans wondered, as they would for years to come, whether our elections were sufficiently secure. They saw what was going on around them, observing the fraud that occurred out in the open, and wondered whether there was more going on in secret.

And they had the same thought as Catherine Engelbrecht: if this was going on in plain sight, what were partisan operatives doing when no one was looking?

For the next two years, Engelbrecht and a few close friends made it their mission to find out. Together, they formed a group called True the Vote, a nonpartisan group dedicated to finding fraud in our election system, exposing it, and rooting it out. Unlike the King Street Patriots, another group Engelbrecht had formed during the first days of the Tea Party movement, True the Vote did not advocate for any one party or candidate. They did not consider whether fraudulent votes might be Republican or Democrat; they just started digging, and then told the world what they found.

In the beginning, that would prove to be quite a lot. During the first few months of its existence, True the Vote found thousands of potentially fraudulent ballots in the greater Houston area. Using the resources that national media companies chose not to deploy, they dug deeply into the voter rolls of cities all around the country, attempting to clean up the rolls in advance of the 2012 presidential election. For a while, they were successful. Shortly after their first investigations concluded, Engelbrecht and her team announced that they had uncovered several vacant lots that happened to have a few hundred "ghost voters" living somewhere on the land; they had also found thousands of double registrations, dead voters, and people who were registered in multiple states at once.

In a functioning political system, both parties would have been happy to hear this news. But in *this* political system, one party seemed concerned—even downright angry—that True the Vote had uncovered so many potential instances of fraud. In fact, the Democrats seemed upset that anyone was even *looking* for fraud. In the eyes of the Obama White

House, any attempt to clean up our voter rolls was an attack on democracy. They argued that if fraud did exist, it was so rare as to be completely inconsequential, and that if it did not exist, looking for it was a waste of time, and (surprise, surprise) also racist.

This hadn't always been the case. In fact, just five years earlier, President George W. Bush had formed a bipartisan commission to study the integrity of our elections. The commission was co-led by Jim Baker, a Republican who had served as Ronald Reagan's chief of staff and George H. W. Bush's secretary of state (and who had brilliantly led our legal team in *Bush v. Gore*), and President Jimmy Carter, a die-hard liberal. Despite their massive political differences, they had managed to reach a conclusion that in 2005 did not seem scandalous or racist to anyone. Baker and Carter found that the American people had very little confidence in U.S. elections—so little, in fact, that they titled their final report "Building Confidence in U.S. Elections"—and that there were "five pillars" we could build to make sure people's confidence increased.

According to their findings, the government needed to build a national system to connect state and local voter registration lists, thereby reducing the possibility of fraud; needed to institute voter identification based on universally available REAL ID cards; needed to improve voter access with new technologies; needed to develop stronger efforts to combat fraud in absentee voting; and needed to produce auditable paper backups for all voting machines.

For a while, the United States took their advice. We implemented several of these steps during the presidency of George W. Bush. But as soon as President Obama took office, things changed. Any discussion of voter ID laws was shut down, and anyone who raised concerns about voter fraud was quickly labeled a conspiracy theorist. Clearly, American citizens who were concerned about the integrity of our elections were deemed enemies in the eyes of the Obama administration.

Catherine Engelbrecht found that out the hard way.

In the fall of 2010, the Internal Revenue Service contacted Engel-brecht in her capacity as the leader of True the Vote. A few months earlier, in July, she had written to the agency seeking permission to operate True the Vote as a 501(c)(3) organization. This designation, reserved for groups that are not organized for profit and are, in the words of the IRS, "operated exclusively to promote social welfare," would have allowed Engelbrecht to take in outside donations and expand into other states. True the Vote met all the criteria for operation as a 501(c)(3). The application should have been accepted quickly.

Instead, the IRS came back with demands. *Hundreds* of them. Ana-lysts from the agency wanted to see copies of every tweet Engelbrecht had ever sent, as well as every Facebook post she had ever made. They wanted to see a detailed list of every speaking engagement she had done since the group was founded and another list of every speaking engage-ment she planned to do in the future. Short of her private diary, I'm not sure there was any scrap of paper in the Engelbrecht household that the IRS *didn't* ask for.

But that wasn't the end. Far from it, in fact.

For the next two years, just when True the Vote had been planning to expose more fraud in the lead-up to the 2012 presidential election, the full force of the executive branch came crashing down on them. The FBI opened multiple lines of inquiry into their activities, going so far as to interview several of Engelbrecht's friends about her. The Bureau of Alcohol, Tobacco, and Firearms opened an investigation concerning several guns that her husband, Bryan Engelbrecht, had sold years earlier for less than $200. Then, around the same time, the Occupational Safety and Health Administration (OSHA) came after the couple's other business—a small manufacturing firm which, on paper, had nothing to do with True the Vote. The Texas Commission on Environmental Quality (the state agency that works closely with the federal EPA) showed up a few days after that for a "surprise" inspection due to "a complaint being called in." In the end, the OSHA audit resulted in $25,000 in fines, and the TCEQ forced them to pay $42,000 for improvements on their property. And the IRS found it owed them a refund.[4]

I'm sure that for a while, all of this might have seemed like a monumental stroke of bad luck. As the government bureaucrats moved through Engelbrecht's offices, sporting their acronym-ridden windbreakers and hats, trying to dispense violations everywhere they went, she might have wondered whether she and her family might have crossed paths with an evil witch or an angry leprechaun in the old country.

Soon, though, Engelbrecht would realize exactly what had happened to bring Obama's enforcers to her front door.

The trouble began for Catherine Engelbrecht, as it would for so many other Americans who had dared to express conservative views in public, in July 2010—the day she sent her company's paperwork to the IRS.

The Enforcers

For almost a century, the Internal Revenue Service has been housed in a gray stone building on the corner of Constitution Avenue and 12th Street in Washington, D.C. When this building was unveiled in the early 1930s, several newspapers noted with amazement that its offices contained a system of 837 mechanical clocks, all of which were wired to tick at precisely the same time. This system, the first of its kind in the world, served almost as a metaphor for the way the IRS was supposed to operate: with efficiency, precision, and simplicity. No matter what was going on outside the building, employees of the IRS were meant to be calm, rational actors: writing and amending tax policy, collecting taxes, and...well, that was pretty much it.

But over the years, political bias crept in, as it often does in government bureaucracies. Presidents who had made enemies on their way to the White House indulged the urge to punish those enemies with audits, harassment, and coordinated leaks of their private financial information.

This shadowy practice is almost as old as the agency itself. Nixon did not invent abuse of the IRS; multiple Democrats before him had perfected the art.

In the 1930s, for instance, shortly after the staff of the IRS—then known as the Bureau of Internal Revenue—moved into its new home in the capital, President Franklin Delano Roosevelt spent quite a lot of time on the phone with them. At the time, he was trying with all his might to pass the New Deal, a raft of controversial legislation that would dramatically expand the size and scope of the federal government. These bills were expensive, and they were deeply unpopular at the time, especially with conservatives who preferred the government to remain relatively small and under the control of the people.

Occasionally, some of these conservatives would air their objections in public. That's when Roosevelt came after them.

When Senator Huey Long, a populist from Louisiana who was contemplating a run for the presidency, began speaking out against the New Deal in the early '30s, President Roosevelt looked all around the federal government for a weapon to use against him. He considered the FBI, which dug up some dirt on Senator Long. Finding that nothing was quite having the effect he wanted, Roosevelt settled on the Bureau of Internal Revenue, which fell under the control of the Treasury Department. A few months earlier, President Roosevelt had installed Henry Morgenthau, one of his best friends and closest confidants, as the head of the Treasury. Morgenthau owed him a favor.

Roosevelt called in that favor during the autumn of that year, and soon hundreds of federal agents were combing through every financial transaction that Huey Long had ever made, rifling through his tax returns and making sure to make a lot of noise as they did it. Soon, news of the search was everywhere, especially in the local Louisiana papers. Senator Long, of course, was infamously corrupt, and had engaged in multiple kickback schemes and backroom deals in his home state. This made President Roosevelt's plot quite easy to carry out.

It went so well, in fact, that he pushed even further. The next year, Roosevelt had the IRS start going after anyone who had ever been associated with Senator Long, prosecuting several of them for tax evasion. At one point during this madness, there were thousands of audits open;

many had been started only because of the president's personal vendettas. Eventually, Roosevelt's goons cut a deal with Huey Long and his team: he would drop the IRS investigations if they would all agree to support him when he ran for a second term. I'm sure that the threat carried special weight. After all the harassment from the federal government, these local cronies knew that if they promised to support Roosevelt and then didn't do it, he would find out, and the surprise visits from IRS agents would pick up again.

The intimidation tactics worked. Roosevelt was re-elected two years later in a landslide. He had also found a bright, shiny new weapon to pummel his enemies with, and he was not shy about using it.

The press was next. Shortly after the Huey Long affair, the legendary newspaper publisher William Randolph Hearst (the inspiration for *Citizen Kane*) wrote in the *New York American* that Roosevelt was "carrying out a Marxist agenda" by passing the New Deal, likening him at various points to a communist, a socialist, and a Bolshevik. Soon after, President Roosevelt called up his friends at the IRS, and within days, Hearst was tied up in audits and federal investigations. Fortunately for Hearst, his books were much cleaner than Huey Long's, and he gave the IRS no real ammunition to work with. The whole affair was particularly awkward for President Roosevelt's son Elliott, who'd just been hired as an editor at the *Los Angeles Express*, a newspaper owned by Hearst, whom Elliott considered a friend.

In a book titled *As He Saw It*, Elliott Roosevelt would write that his father "may have been the originator of employing the IRS as a method of political retribution," joking that "other men's taxes...fascinated him" throughout his time in office.[5] Looking back on Roosevelt's list of other targets, this certainly seems to have been the case. During his unprecedented twelve years in the White House, President Roosevelt went after well-known figures such as Father Charles Coughlin, Hamilton Fish, Nucky Johnson, and many others. If the IRS couldn't do the job, he would hand things over to the FBI, as he did in the case of Hamilton Fish. But the IRS was usually the first stop. The message was clear: if you mess with the president, make sure your finances are in perfect order, because if they're not, you might be heading to federal prison.

When John F. Kennedy took office, the abuse became even more brazen. Alongside his brother Robert Kennedy, whom he had installed as his attorney general, JFK worked hard to make sure that those who dared to express conservative views in public were punished. They would work primarily, they decided, through the IRS. In a memorandum entitled "The Ideological Organizations Audit Project," the attorney general laid out in clear, incriminating prose his plan to go after any organization that seemed even remotely conservative. If these organizations had nonprofit status, they would take it away; if they were applying for nonprofit status, they would deny it. Sound familiar? Eventually, the brothers Kennedy would make a show of expanding this scrutiny to far-left organizations as well. But in 1976, a Senate investigation into the matter would find that this was a lie. President Kennedy, much like the liberal heroes after him, wanted to shut down conservative speech, and he was willing to do so by any means necessary.

By the time Richard Nixon took office, the practice of using the IRS to get even with your enemies was woefully well established in the executive branch. For Nixon, a man who had so many enemies that his chief of staff needed to hire people just to keep track of them, this must have been like a dream come true. Finally, after all these years of fuming quietly in the corner, creating fantasies of getting back at the people who had wronged him, he had a massive government machinery to harass and intimidate them.

During his first term in office, Nixon worked with his aide Arthur Burns to convince the IRS to begin investigating his enemies, a diverse list that included leftist political organizations, campus groups, and Democratic politicians who had spoken out against him over the past few decades.

"What we cannot do in a courtroom via criminal prosecutions to curtail the activities of some of these groups," one of his aides wrote in a memo, "the IRS could do by administrative action."[6]

Soon, the IRS created a special, secret team of operatives known as the Special Services Staff. This team was tasked with looking into any political enemies of the White House, a job they attacked with zeal. In the end, they compiled dossiers on 8,585 people and 2,873 organizations, organizing the research so that it could be weaponized at any time. But when it came time to act on that information, the IRS was thankfully hesitant, much to the dismay of President Nixon. In the early '70s, Nixon pressured the IRS to audit reporters who wrote negative stories about him, but most of these audits never occurred. When the Nixon White House began sending physical copies of its lengthy enemies lists over to the IRS, the commissioner, Donald Alexander, knew that something needed to be done.

A graduate of Harvard Law School who had served in the army during World War II, Alexander had been named head of the IRS after a successful career as a tax lawyer. When he got to the IRS in July 1973, he found the organization in the midst of a crisis—one that it might not survive. With the Watergate hearings airing constantly on national television and the White House embroiled in scandal after scandal, it was becoming clearer every day that the time for dirty tricks and political hit jobs was almost over.

"The IRS was under particular attack," Alexander would recall later in an interview at Harvard. "It was called an evil organization and part of the Nixon political apparatus. And I was determined to help the IRS get through that and prevent any misuse of IRS people and powers."[7]

In August 1973, Alexander announced that he had disbanded the Special Services Staff and discontinued all improper investigations. That evening, he recalled, President Nixon made his first of three attempts to fire him. It was only when George Shultz, the head of the Treasury Department and Alexander's boss, threatened to resign if Alexander was fired, that Nixon decided to drop the matter and pause his political vendettas. It was a brave stand that might have saved the credibility of the IRS, at least for a time. But it also left a mark. Asked years later what his time as the head of the IRS had been like, Alexander responded curtly: "Pure hell."

Alexander was vindicated, at least to some degree, when the impeachment articles against Richard Nixon were released. They contained, among other charges, the following sentence:

"He has, acting personally and through his subordinates and agents, endeavored to…cause, in violation of the constitutional rights of citizens, income tax audits or other income tax investigations to be initiated or conducted in a discriminatory manner."

In the aftermath of that impeachment proceeding—and Nixon's resignation, and the raft of Watergate prosecutions that followed—the nation took a long, hard look at the powers of the executive branch, focusing primarily on the possibility of corruption. Congress held multiple hearings that attempted to investigate the weaponization of federal agencies against political enemies—not only by President Nixon, but by Hoover, Roosevelt, and Kennedy as well. What they found shocked the world. In 1975, for instance, a committee led by Senator Frank Church uncovered an array of abuses that showed the FBI, CIA, and NSA had been all too willing to act as a mob enforcement squad for the White House. The findings of the Church Committee, as it would come to be known, soon made headlines all over the country.

Reading these headlines, Americans were horrified to learn that the FBI had often infiltrated civil rights groups in a series of illegal operations known as COINTELPRO. They learned of clandestine CIA programs to surveil journalists and assassinate foreign leaders, and to conduct illegal experiments with drugs and mind control in a program known as MK-Ultra. This program began in the 1950s and included giving LSD to mental patients, prisoners, drug addicts, and prostitutes—"people who could not fight back," in the words of one CIA officer. LSD was also administered—often without the subject's knowledge—to CIA employees, military personnel, and other government employees. In one operation, dubbed "Midnight Climax," the CIA set up and operated multiple brothels in San Francisco to film unsuspecting men from behind one-way mirrors. They, too, were unknowingly dosed with LSD.

The backlash, rightly, was severe. In this new political climate, at least for a time, future presidents managed to temper their worst instincts. Given that the American public had become disillusioned about the presidency during Watergate, no chief executive wanted to be seen as being even remotely like Richard Nixon. The accusation alone was enough to cause problems. So, for the next couple of decades, no president seriously attempted to use the IRS—or any other agency, for that matter—as a weapon to attack his political enemies. That doesn't mean there weren't accusations and small improprieties, of course, but nothing happened that remotely matched the scale of Nixon's political hit jobs (or those of his predecessors).

But still, no laws were passed that made it formally illegal for a president to target his political enemies based on their politics. Other than the constitutional charges of "high crimes and misdemeanors" that could be brought during an impeachment trial, there was nothing that a president who wanted to bring the full force of the federal government to bear on his enemies needed to fear. Such a president would need only to install a friendly person at the head of the agency he wished to use, and then direct that person to attack his enemies in a way that was unlikely ever to be uncovered. As long as he did not get caught, that president would be able to achieve what even Richard Nixon could not: the brutal silencing of political opposition by the machinery of the federal government.

In 2008, the United States elected that president, and he and his team got to work quickly.

The Power of the Tea Party

During his inaugural address on January 20, 2009, President Barack Obama addressed a nation divided. But he didn't see it that way.

Speaking from the steps of the United States Capitol, President Obama suggested rather boldly that his election proved that the citizens of the United States had "chosen hope over fear, unity of purpose over conflict and discord."[8] He droned on about a new liberal consensus and an end to political division.

Coming from a man who seemed to have done little but divide Americans from the moment he emerged onto the national stage, this statement seemed rather ridiculous. For the past several months, I had watched as President-elect Obama talked down to conservative Americans, mocking them as "bitter and angry" for wanting to "cling to their God and their guns."[9] His tendency to ripping open long-healed racial wounds was similarly concerning. I knew that he was about to take the United States of America down a slippery slope that could lead right to socialism.

As the son of a man who had been imprisoned and tortured for his politics in Cuba, fleeing to the United States in search of freedom from tyranny, I knew I had to do something. When Kay Bailey Hutchison, the senior senator from Texas, announced that she would not seek re-election in 2012, I saw my opportunity. On a conference call with conservative bloggers in January 2011, I launched my campaign for the United States Senate.

Unfortunately, so did eight other people.

Most of my opponents in the Republican primary were about as well known in Texas as I was. That is, not at all. But there was one candidate who posed a real threat. His name was David Dewhurst, and he had been the lieutenant governor of Texas for eight years. His name recognition was off the charts, especially compared to no-name candidates like me. He controlled the state senate, and every lobbyist and special interest group in the state had no choice but to side with him. It also didn't hurt that he had a personal net worth of over $200 million, $35 million of which went straight into his campaign.

During the first few months of the race, I was a hopeless long shot. Most observers believed I had no chance whatsoever. At the time we launched, I was polling at 2 percent. Literally. The margin of error in that poll was 3 percent, which led my wife, Heidi, to helpfully point out that, technically, I could have been at negative 1 percent.

But I soon learned that the nation was ready for a change. All across Texas, people had grown fed up with the Obama administration. They saw that we were hurtling quickly toward a radical and dangerous future, and they wanted out.

So, I set out to talk to every single one of them.

I had never been elected to anything important—the last thing I had been elected to was student council—but now I was running for office in a massive state of 26 million people. (Today, ten years later, we've grown to 29 million.) For the next two years, I traveled to hundreds of towns and spoke to virtually any political group that would have me. Along the way, I heard the concerns of thousands of American citizens who wanted to upend Washington and make the government work for the people again. At the same time, thousands of these citizens had been organizing themselves into groups, recruiting new members and attempting to make their voices heard. They called themselves the Tea Party, named for the immortal colonial protest that occurred in 1773, and they were just as hard to ignore as their namesake.

Well before my campaign launched, I had gotten to know Catherine Engelbrecht, the dynamic leader who had formed a group called the King Street Patriots in 2010. In a crowded sea of Tea Party groups and their leaders, Engelbrecht and the King Street Patriots stood out. From the moment we first met, I knew that Engelbrecht had a deep love for her country, and that she was going to make a difference in our political system one way or another.

One night, after an event we had done, she mentioned to me the widespread harassment she had endured at the hands of the Internal Revenue Service. At the time, this was not a well-known phenomenon. The Obama administration was systematically denying requests from conservative groups for nonprofit status, sending agents to their doorsteps and making outrageous demands, but those groups had not yet begun speaking to one another about their experiences. Many of them assumed, as Catherine Engelbrecht had during the IRS's harassment of True the Vote, that they were alone.

I resolved to do something about it if I ever got the power. All I had to do, I thought, was get elected to the United States Senate, which, at the time, was looking more difficult than ever.

Despite a relentless event schedule, my team was having trouble breaking through the noise. We were low on cash, which was especially dangerous in a race against a man who had virtually unlimited funds. So we decided to fight him on the issues—and, most memorably, on his unwillingness to show up and speak to the people. As the primary progressed, I had participated in more than forty candidate forums, and Dewhurst had skipped every single one of them.

At one Tea Party candidate forum in North Texas, a grassroots activist arrived with a milk carton with Dewhurst's picture on the side, emblazoned with the query *Have you seen this man?* We did all we could to amplify that rather amusing message. Because our campaign had virtually no money, we had to rely on nontraditional means of communication. We launched a website called DuckingDewhurst.com, emphasizing that Dewhurst was ducking all of the debates. Indeed, for several months I sent a campaign staffer dressed as a duck to attend many of his campaign events. After an event with local firefighters, for instance, when the Dewhurst campaign was hoping to get a headline about their candidate's support for the fire department, they would instead get one along the lines of: "Man dressed as duck greets David Dewhurst at campaign event." In general, when it comes to negative attacks on political opponents, it's usually more effective to have a light touch. You never want to be too over the top, instead gently poking fun with a smile.

After a few months, the ribbing succeeded. Since the beginning of the race, our aspiration had been to come in *second place*. As I explained to countless confused supporters, if we could make sure Dewhurst got less than 50 percent of the vote and we came in second, then we could force a runoff and have a real chance of winning.

On May 29, that's exactly what happened. The race for the Republican nomination narrowed to just me and Dewhurst, and the fight intensified.

Shortly afterward, the Dewhurst campaign dramatically escalated their attack ads on me—and they did not use a light touch. Quite the opposite. At some point, Dewhurst's campaign team had learned that when I was a lawyer in private practice, my firm had represented a tire company in a trademark dispute against another tire company. Both companies manufactured their tires in China, but the one that had hired the firm where I worked was also based there. I didn't argue the case, but the Dewhurst campaign used my firm's involvement in this trademark case to suggest that I was secretly a traitor to the United States, loyal instead to Communist China. The campaign went so far as to print fake currency with my face on it, discolored and altered to make me appear Chinese, which they handed out at their events. It was a move that could have come straight from the dirty-tricks handbook of Richard Nixon, a man who loved nothing more than falsely alleging his political enemies were Communists and smearing their names in the press. The Dewhurst campaign followed it up by spending millions of dollars on television ads and campaign mailers that showed me in front of a Chinese flag. One of these mailers was delivered to my father, a man who knew a thing or two about the evils of communism.

A few weeks after that, not long before the runoff election was set to occur, I met David Dewhurst on a debate stage in Houston. The debate was a Tea Party event, attended by hundreds of concerned citizens and hosted by my friends Catherine Engelbrecht and the King Street Patriots. It would be my last chance to confront the lieutenant governor before the ballots were cast. Fortunately, I had something of a home-field advantage. Not only was Houston my hometown, but the audience was filled with the very people I had been traveling around Texas to speak with for months—the people who were hungry for change.

Midway through the debate, I reached into my jacket pocket and pulled out the mailer that had been sent to my father's home.

The crowd went silent.

I pointed out that my father, who'd been surprised to get the mailer suggesting I was a Communist, had been imprisoned and tortured in Cuba.

"Governor," I said, "there are few worse things you can do than to impugn a person's patriotism." At this point, I held the mailer aloft so the audience could see it, then turned to the lieutenant governor. "Governor," I continued, "you're better than this. Do you stand by the attacks in this mailer?"

At that moment, the debate was over. Dewhurst stammered, unsure of what to say. The crowd in the room and watching on television was firmly with me. On the day the runoff ballots were counted, I beat the lieutenant governor by fourteen points and then went on to win the general election by sixteen points.

Catherine Engelbrecht and the King Street Patriots played an important part in our victory. Not only did they host the debate that allowed me to corner the famously elusive David Dewhurst in front of the people I would go on to represent, but they also helped to amplify my message throughout the campaign. On election day in 2012, the country learned that there was nothing more powerful than groups of concerned citizens who were willing to invest their time, energy, and what little money they had to make sure their voices were heard. All over the nation, the Tea Party helped to elect anti-establishment candidates who would soon go to Washington and attempt to stop the Obama administration from implementing its worst ideas. Together, we had proven that nothing—not attack ads, political connections, or enormous sums of money—were going to stop We the People from making ourselves heard.

For the Obama administration, this was troubling news—and not only because this small band of Tea Party congressmen was about to jam up the gears of President Obama's liberal agenda. For the past two years, the Obama administration had been using federal agencies—the IRS, the FBI, and several others—to try to muzzle the Tea Party and other conservative groups that sought to expose their wrongdoing. Now that there were even more people in Congress who weren't afraid to investigate such wrongdoing, their dirty tricks were about to be exposed.

Pleading the Fifth

When I got to Washington, I didn't forget about what I had heard on the campaign trail. I knew that the IRS had been harassing groups like True the Vote and the King Street Patriots, and I intended to find out how many other groups had been victimized.

Already, we were beginning to hear reports from conservative groups all over the country who had applied for nonprofit status and had been denied. Although they amply satisfied the statutory criteria for granting that status, the IRS repeatedly denied them because they were conservative. Before denying them, the IRS had asked hundreds of invasive questions and made unreasonable demands for information. Catherine Engelbrecht's experience with True the Vote had not, in fact, been as unusual as it had first seemed. It was happening all over the country. Clearly, the Obama administration had sensed that the Tea Party was going to be a problem for them, especially during the 2012 election, and they had attempted to do everything they could to make sure that those citizens could not raise money, expand, or make too much noise.

Just like Richard Nixon, they had found their enemies, written down their names (perhaps even on yellow pads), and sent the government after them.

Over the next few months, congressional investigations would reveal the shocking timeline of events. Soon, the nation learned that in the spring of 2010, shortly after the midterm elections that had resulted in startling victories for Tea Party candidates, officials at the IRS began looking out for groups whose names included words like "Tea Party" and "patriot." In July of that year, around the same time that Catherine Engelbrecht was filing her paperwork to have True the Vote designated a nonprofit entity, managers from the IRS's tax exemption division instructed their specialists to "be on the lookout (BOLO)" for groups that seemed conservative.

In 2012, likely aware of the immense influence that Tea Party groups were having on races such as my own, the tax exemption division of the IRS again updated its search criteria, instructing its agents to single out "political action type organizations involved in limiting/expanding Government, education on the Constitution and Bill of Rights, social economic reform/movement." Pause and reflect on that: our federal government was explicitly deeming—in writing, no less—a group's commitment to the Constitution or the Bill of Rights as politically suspect and subject to investigation and official harassment.

Several times throughout this process, the IRS was asked about what it was up to. Concerned lawmakers sent multiple letters asking outright whether the IRS was targeting the Tea Party. In every response, the IRS insisted it was not.

But the reports kept pouring in. Hundreds of Tea Party groups who were seen as enemies of Obama had been singled out for targeted harassment. During my first months in office, I heard once again from Catherine Engelbrecht. The harassment of her nonpartisan group True the Vote had continued during the intense 2012 election season. Plainly, the Obama administration was worried that it might lose its re-election bid. By the time the election came around, President Obama's approval rating had fallen from 67 percent when he first took office to the low 40s.[10] The economic recovery he had promised had been one of the slowest in American history. The Tea Party had risen up in direct opposition to his agenda, and so he and his team attempted to shut the Tea Party down. Working all around the country at various processing centers, the Obama administration was able to do what even the Nixon administration could not: successfully use the IRS to harass, intimidate, and silence its enemies.

Luckily, the Tea Party movement was strong enough to withstand an all-out assault by the Internal Revenue Service. There had been enough committed patriots during the 2012 election to raise awareness about the Obama administration's misdeeds, marshal grassroots support, and send candidates like me to Washington to represent their interests. They did this even as they were being shaken down by Obama's enforcers in the IRS. Their hard work had helped send us to Washington, and I was determined to fight for them with all my might. So were many of my colleagues.

In May 2013, the Treasury Department's inspector general released a bombshell report that explicitly concluded, "the IRS used inappropriate criteria that identified for review Tea Party and other organizations applying for tax-exempt status." The next day, a visibly embarrassed Obama was forced to address the scandal at a White House press conference. He admitted the conduct was "inexcusable" and claimed to be "angry" about it:

> I've reviewed the Treasury Department watchdog's report, and the misconduct that it uncovered is inexcusable. It's inexcusable, and Americans are right to be angry about it, and *I am angry about it*. I will not tolerate this kind of behavior in any agency, but especially in the IRS, given the power that it has and the reach that it has into all of our lives. And as I said earlier, it should not matter what political stripe you're from—the fact of the matter is, is that the IRS has to operate with absolute integrity. The government generally has to conduct itself in a way that is true to the public trust. That's especially true for the IRS.

The next week, the House Oversight and Government Reform Committee questioned the IRS Exempt Organizations director Lois Lerner about the improper targeting carried out by the bureaucrats under her direction. Normally, when government officials testify before Congress, they try to explain or justify their conduct. Or, if the questioning becomes uncomfortable, they may try to be evasive and dodge the issue. Lerner did far more. Each time, when she was asked about the IRS targeting Tea Party groups, she asserted her Fifth Amendment right, refusing to answer because doing so could incriminate her personally in criminal conduct.

It is extremely unusual for a government employee to plead the Fifth before Congress. But, despite her refusal to testify, Lerner was not fired. Instead, she was placed on administrative leave, and several months later she was allowed to retire (with pension) from the IRS. The next year, she was called by the House once more to testify about the scandal, and yet again she pleaded the Fifth. As a result, the House voted 231–187 to hold her in contempt of Congress for defying a duly issued subpoena. Congress asked the Department of Justice to pursue criminal charges against her.

The Obama Department of Justice, under enormous public pressure after the Treasury inspector general report, announced that it was "investigating" the matter. And whom did the DOJ put in charge? A prosecutor named Barbara Bosserman, who public records show had given $6,750 in personal donations to Obama and the DNC. When I demanded that DOJ put a prosecutor in charge who was not a partisan Obama donor, the department responded in Orwellian fashion: "It is contrary to department policy and a prohibited personnel practice under federal law to consider the political affiliation of career employees or other non-merit factors in making personnel decisions," said the DOJ in an official statement. In other words, "We put a partisan Democrat in charge (and of course we damn well knew her politics), but now we can't remove her...because of her politics."

When it became apparent that the DOJ investigation was a sham—that DOJ had put a Democratic donor in charge to ensure that the investigation went nowhere—I went to the Senate floor and called on the attorney general to appoint a special prosecutor who was not an active political supporter of President Obama. And if he refused to appoint a special prosecutor, the House should impeach the attorney general. Here's what I argued:

> When an attorney general mocks the rule of law, when an
> attorney general corrupts the Department of Justice by

conducting a nakedly partisan investigation to cover up political wrongdoing that conduct by any reasonable measure
constitutes high crimes and misdemeanors....Attorney General Eric Holder has the opportunity to do the right thing. He
could appoint a special prosecutor with meaningful independence who is *not* a major Obama donor.

Predictably, DOJ did nothing. Holder refused to appoint a special
prosecutor. And the House did nothing, declining to impeach Holder.
(Of course, the Democrats' brazen partisanship contributed powerfully
to the Republicans' tidal wave election in 2014, retaking the Senate and
electing the largest House majority since 1928.)

And what were the final results from the Obama DOJ? Despite
Obama's laughable assertion that he was personally "angry" about the
misconduct, the Justice Department refused to prosecute Lerner. As the
U.S. Attorney for D.C. wrote to Congress, "We respectfully inform you
that we will...not bring the Congressional contempt citation before a
grand jury or take any other action to prosecute Ms. Lerner for her
refusal to testify."

Unlike Richard Nixon, who famously tried and failed to pin Watergate on every low-level member of the executive branch who came within
shouting distance of him, President Obama succeeded. Not only had he
fulfilled the Nixonian dream of turning the IRS on his political opponents, he had also pulled off the cover-up that Nixon could never get
right. Still, many of us continued to fight to hold his lawless administration accountable.

Abolish the IRS

In October 2013, I returned to the King Street Patriots in Houston.
Just weeks earlier, I had spoken for twenty-one hours and nineteen min-
utes continuously on the Senate floor, the fourth-longest filibuster in
Senate history. Obamacare was rendering health care unaffordable for

millions of Americans, and I was doing everything in my power to fight against it. (That included reading Dr. Seuss's *Green Eggs and Ham* aloud at bedtime, so that my five- and three-year-old daughters could hear the good-night story on C-SPAN.) The King Street Patriots had arranged a celebration to welcome me home to Texas, and over 2,000 patriots greeted me raucously. That night, I spoke with hundreds of members of the organization, several of whom asked me about the ongoing IRS scandal. They had filed a lawsuit seeking damages. When I was leaving, Catherine Englebrecht gave me a copy of Leo Tolstoy's *War and Peace* signed by many of those in the room that day, suggesting that I read aloud from it during my next filibuster.

I returned to Washington ready for war.

Two months later, during a session of the Senate Judiciary Committee, citing the pattern of abuse from the IRS, I introduced two amendments that would have made it illegal to target American citizens based on their politics. The first amendment would have prohibited an IRS employee from intentionally targeting individuals or groups based on political views. It would have made it a federal crime for any IRS employee to willfully discriminate against groups based solely on the political beliefs or policy statements held, expressed, or published by that organization. The second amendment would have amended the tax code to use the bipartisan, independent Federal Election Commission's definitions to determine whether an organization is engaging in political activity. In other words, the IRS should focus on taxing people, ensuring that everyone is following the tax laws, and nothing else. The language was simple. There was nothing inside that anyone from either political party should have objected to.

That is, of course, if we hadn't been dealing with the Democratic Party of 2013. I could have introduced a bill that instituted a one-time free ice cream party, funded by me, for all senators, and they would have rejected it.

On February 27, my Democratic colleagues on the Judiciary Committee voted unanimously against both of the amendments I had proposed. Despite Obama's feigned "anger," Democrats were willing to do nothing to prevent future abuse of the IRS. To the contrary, they wanted more of it.

In the years since it was first formed, the IRS has ballooned, shooting up from around 20,000 employees in 1932 to more than 75,000.[11] As it grew, so did the laws the agency was meant to enforce. In 1955, for instance, the Internal Revenue Code—the set of laws governing the amount we as Americans pay in taxes, and the manner in which we must pay them—was about 400,000 words long. Today, it's around 2.4 million words, or 70,000 pages. For reference, the copy of *War and Peace* that I'd been given by the King Street Patriots is only a quarter of that length; the Bible is less than half as long.

Inside the Internal Revenue Code, you'll find hundreds of thousands of rules and regulations that even the most advanced supercomputers in the world have trouble working through. If you're an adult person in the United States, it's entirely possible (likely even) that you've violated some obscure provision of this code without even knowing it. That is why the IRS does not seek to track down every small violation and punish those who commit those violations. Instead, it conducts routine and usually random audits of certain taxpayers, reviewing that person's tax returns to make sure that he or she hasn't done anything wrong.

Officially, the IRS is supposed to decide whom it audits based on a complex and semi-random computer algorithm. There is a points system for violations, and if a taxpayer gets a certain number of "points," that person gets audited. If the IRS goes after a person for anything other than those reasons, it is in violation of the law.

Of course, there are so many potential violations—more than 70,000 pages of them—that it often isn't hard for an IRS employee to get an investigation going.

So, if another president—say, Joe Biden, who has already advocated for a new law that would empower the IRS to track every single banking transaction over $600—wanted to sic the IRS on his political opponents, he wouldn't need much justification to do so. The tax code is so complicated that it can be weaponized against virtually anyone at any time.

And clearly, most of the government bureaucrats who carried out operations against the Tea Party have not left the agency in the years since. In 2021, for instance, the Biden IRS leaked details of the tax returns of numerous wealthy Americans, including Jeff Bezos, Peter Thiel, Rupert Murdock, and Elon Musk. The aim seemed to be to prove that these people paid relatively little in taxes, although without their full returns, it would be impossible to be certain. I'm sure it wasn't a coincidence that several of these people tend to lean Republican—or, at least, that they lean away from the radical left.

Leaking individual tax returns was a gross abuse of power, and it suggested that the Biden administration is more than willing to pull the same dirty tricks that the Obama administration did. It should be indisputable that whoever leaked these documents should be fully investigated, prosecuted, and, ultimately, sent to jail. But it's impossible to have any confidence that we'll ever know exactly what happened, at least not with the Biden administration leading the "investigation."

The best answer, I believe, would be to abolish the IRS completely. In the years since President Obama used the agency to attack conservative Americans, the IRS has become even more bloated and politicized than it was before. It's also become more brazen. Whereas the scandal during the Obama administration pertained mostly to nonprofit groups that had sent their paperwork to the government, the Biden IRS has shown that it's willing, at any time, to potentially leak the private tax documents of any American citizen who has crossed it. And if you think that the leaks will stop with billionaires—perhaps the class that the Biden administration claims it hates the most—then you are mistaken. It is only a matter of time before the leaks of ordinary conservative taxpayers begin coming out, too.

That's why, in my 2016 presidential campaign, I proposed a simple, flat tax for everyone. Here were the key elements:

- For a family of four, no taxes whatsoever (income or pay-roll) on the first $36,000 of income
- Above that level, a 10 percent flat tax on all individual income from wages and investment
- No death tax, no alternative minimum tax, and no Obamacare taxes
- Elimination of both the payroll tax and the corporate income tax, to be replaced by a 16 percent business flat tax. This would tax companies' gross receipts from sales of goods and services, less purchases from other businesses, including capital investment. Simple, efficient, fair.
- A Universal Savings Account, which would allow every American to save up to $25,000 annually on a tax-deferred basis for any purpose

History has shown us that cutting taxes—and dramatically simplifying the tax code—produces extraordinary economic results. After Ronald Reagan passed historic tax reform, the economy boomed, growing 4.4 percent a year from 1983 to 1989. John F. Kennedy did the same thing, and it produced annual growth of 5.3 percent. Likewise, Harding and Coolidge in the 1920s, whose tax cuts produced 4.7 percent annual growth. In contrast, Obama raised taxes, made the tax code more complicated, increased regulations, and produced an anemic 1.2 percent average annual growth. Millions of Americans suffered under the Obama economic stagnation.

The nonpartisan Tax Foundation scored my plan, and found that it would produce extraordinary results for the economy: 4.9 million new jobs, average wages rising 12.2 percent, and capital investment going up 43.9 percent. And it benefits everyone: at every single income decile, from the very poorest to the very richest, Americans would enjoy *double-digit percentage increases in after-tax income.*

But as important as economic growth and prosperity is, that's not the most important part of my flat-tax plan. The most important part is that everyone fills out their taxes on a simple postcard (we produced the actual postcard), and so we abolish the IRS. Sure, there will still need to be an office to process the postcards and enforce the tax laws, but the vast array of laws, rules, and regulations that today's army of IRS agents enforces would be gone. Eliminated altogether. And with it, much of the ability of presidents to abuse the IRS by using it as a political weapon to destroy their enemies.

We didn't get that accomplished in 2016. But I continue to believe that the issue resonates powerfully with the American people, and that we *will* get it done. We will padlock the IRS.

In the meantime, the machinery exists for unscrupulous presidents to politicize and weaponize the IRS. And in the end, the Obama administration learned its lesson.

Of course, that lesson was not: Do not harass your political enemies with the machinery of the United States government. Rather, the lesson seemed to be: If you're going to harass your political enemies using the machinery of the United States government, make sure you use the FBI, the CIA, and the Department of Justice to do it, and then work very, very hard to cover it up; and if anyone accuses you of doing something wrong, make sure you tell them that they are crazy.

Toward the end of their eight years in power, that's exactly what they did.

CHAPTER THREE

CROSSFIRE HURRICANE

The Big Lie

When the definitive account of Donald Trump's historic four years in office is finally written, the story might very well begin on January 6.

On that day, I walked onto the floor of the United States House of Representatives and found the chamber as tense as I had ever seen it. Republicans sat on one side of the room, Democrats on the other. There was no cross-party mingling, no jovial handshakes or small talk among colleagues. Several people in attendance seemed ready to begin openly weeping.

Shortly after one o'clock, a line of clerks entered the chamber, carrying the results of the Electoral College in a battered leather briefcase. The vice president stepped up to the dais and gave us our mission for the day.

"Pursuant to the constitutional law of the United States," he said, "the Senate and the House of Representatives are meeting in a joint session to verify the certificates and count the votes of the electors of the several states for president and vice president of the United States."

I sat back in my chair and braced for what we all knew was coming. This had been the most bitter, partisan election of my lifetime, and it was not going to be certified without a fight. According to the rules that govern our elections, members of Congress may submit objections to a state's election results in writing; debate on those objections begins if, and only if, a United States senator and a representative have both signed the objection. To my knowledge, in this election cycle, that hadn't yet happened.

But that wasn't going to stop the objections.

One by one, Members of Congress lined up at a microphone in the center aisle of the House chamber.

Clearly, it was going to be a long afternoon.

The first objection came from a representative from Alabama. As the vote totals from that state were being read aloud, as was customary during the certification proceedings, he began talking about illegal tampering in our elections by a foreign power. The vice president, cutting him off, asked if a senator had joined his objection. The congressman replied that no, no one had yet signed the objection, but if he could just—

The vice president banged the gavel, and the congressman from Alabama sat down. Five minutes later, a representative from Maryland raised similar objections, citing an arcane law from the state of Florida. He, too, was cut off and asked to sit down.

As the vice president read the vote totals, moving in alphabetical order from state to state, six more representatives stepped to the microphone to voice their objections.

Not one of them was joined by a senator.

These representatives, many of whom shook with emotion as they spoke, were grasping at straws. They told wild tales of election meddling, voter suppression, and *even a strange conspiracy theory involving the possible corruption of our voting machines by a foreign power.* One of them objected simply because, in her words, "People [were] horrified."

The day was January 6; the year, 2017. The objectors were Democrats. And Donald J. Trump, the brash billionaire from Manhattan who'd been given a 2 percent chance of victory on the morning of the election, was now just a few minutes away from officially being named president-elect of the United States.

In the weeks since his election, Democrats and the corporate media had used every weapon in their arsenal to try to stop this from happening. Members of the Electoral College had seriously considered breaking their oaths—and the law—to ignore the election results in their respective states and vote for Hillary Clinton instead. The media had begun pushing a strange narrative about Russian meddling in our elections, suggesting without evidence that the Trump campaign had somehow "colluded" with Russia to win the presidency. This theory had been in the air for a few months now, though no one was quite certain of the details.

In October, Senate Minority Leader Harry Reid—who was, shall we say, a "real piece of work"—had sent a letter to James Comey, the tall, sanctimonious, incandescently ambitious director of the FBI, claiming that the Bureau possessed "explosive information about close ties and coordination between Donald Trump, his top advisors, and the Russian government," adding that he believed the public "had a right to know the information." Again, Senator Reid had no evidence that his claims were true. He had been briefed about an open FBI investigation, and he was shamelessly using that classified information to wage a political vendetta. It was not the first time Reid had leveled baseless partisan accusations.

In 2012, channeling Nixon's attempted abuse of the IRS, Reid had stood on the Senate floor and assailed the then Republican nominee for president: "So the word is out that [Mitt Romney] has not paid any taxes for ten years. Let him prove he has paid taxes, because he has not." Reid knew that his statement was false, and it wasn't an accident that he chose the Senate floor to launch his attack. Ordinarily, if you level false charges against someone, you can be sued for defamation, but Article I, Section 6, of the Constitution states that members of Congress shall "be privileged from arrest during their attendance at the session of their respective

Houses, and in going to and returning from the same; and for any speech or debate in either House, they shall not be questioned in any other place." That meant Reid could slander Romney with impunity and face no legal liability. Even the hard left-wing "fact checkers" (who usually just spout Democratic talking points dressed up as objective "facts") were forced to call out Reid's lie; the *Washington Post* gave him "4 Pinocchios," and PolitiFact gave him a "Pants on Fire."

Reid, however, didn't care. Years later, when asked about his deliberate false smear of his fellow Mormon, he cynically replied, "They can call it whatever they want. Romney didn't win, did he?"

In the same spirit, whether or not the Democrats truly believed that the Russian government had stolen the presidential election, after the election they saw it as their only real hope of getting Donald Trump out of the White House. Despite multiple failed attempts to find proof of these allegations—notably, in October 2016, the *New York Times* explicitly admitted that the FBI had found "no clear link" between the Trump campaign and Russia—the narrative stubbornly stayed alive.

Several Democratic representatives had already cited the off-the-wall collusion theory during their objections, but they all ended the same way.

In a fact that drips with irony (and is consistently ignored by the corporate media), one of those Democratic objectors raising spurious Russia collusion charges in 2017 was newly elected representative Jamie Raskin of Maryland, who would later be named the House's lead impeachment manager for the second impeachment of Trump, concerning the events of January 6, 2021, just four years later.

Finally, after nine Democrat objections and a full forty minutes had transpired, Representative Maxine Waters of California stepped up to the microphone for the tenth. Unlike the other representatives, she admitted outright that she did not have the signature of any senator on her letter of objection. It was the same move she'd pulled when she objected previously during the certification of the 2000 election, the last presidential race that had ended in something other than victory for the Democrats. No senator had been willing to join her then, either.

Frantically waving the letter above her head, Representative Waters made one last plea to the chamber, giving no reason for her objection beyond what had already been said by her colleagues.

"I wish to ask," she said, "is there one United States senator who will join me in my letter of objection?"

At this point, Vice President Joe Biden banged the gavel and called the race. Republican lawmakers applauded as he did.

"There is no debate," he said. "It's over."

Shortly after Biden spoke those words, three protestors in the gallery stood up, walked to the railing, and began to scream. Everyone in the chamber, me included, struggled to make out what they were saying. From what I gathered, they were yelling something about Russia, collusion, and God knows what else. One of them seemed to be reciting a few lines from the United States Constitution as he was dragged out of the Senate chamber by the Capitol Police. His two comrades soon met the same fate, and the chamber fell silent again.

Now, if we had lived in a functioning democracy in the year 2017, those screams from the balcony might have been the last things anyone heard about Russia, a stolen election, or hacked voting machines. The corporate press might have removed their tinfoil hats and moved on to other, more pressing issues. The Democratic Party might have taken the next four years to analyze their defeat and figure out exactly why the American people had decided to vote for Donald Trump, a political outsider with considerable personal flaws, over the credentialed establishment candidate that the Democrats had thought could not possibly lose.

But we were *not* living in a fully functioning democracy at the time. The "Resistance" to Donald Trump was already entrenched in place. By the time my colleagues and I had finished certifying the results of the Electoral College at two o'clock in the afternoon, it was already too late to stop the Russia Hoax from sweeping the country.

Fewer than twenty-four hours earlier, Vice President Joe Biden had met with President Obama and the heads of our intelligence agencies in the Oval Office. Deputy Attorney General Sally Yates had also been in attendance. Their objective, at least on paper, had been to discuss what the intelligence community had been able to find out about Russian efforts to interfere in our elections, and to decide what to do about it.

After settling on yet another round of sanctions—which, as we now know, had little to no effect—they had moved on to the real purpose of the meeting. About half of the initial group left the Oval Office. Only James Comey, Joe Biden, Sally Yates, and President Obama remained.

The conversation, according to memos and contemporaneous notes, turned quickly to Donald Trump.

For about six months, a team of special agents at the FBI had been conducting a secret investigation into the Trump campaign. These agents, nearly all of whom harbored deep personal grudges against the future president, had exhausted almost every possible avenue to sabotage his administration before it could even begin. They had sent spies to conduct surveillance on members of the campaign, combed through several decades' worth of financial transactions, and interviewed hundreds of people in multiple countries trying to find something. And they had done it all, as the world would soon learn, based on evidence so flimsy that the FBI would spend the next several years attempting to hide it.

But they hadn't expected him to win. Now, with less than two weeks to go before Donald Trump placed his hand on the Bible and succeeded Barack Obama to become the forty-fifth president of the United States, the government officials who'd gathered in the Oval Office had a decision to make. Should they let the investigation against Donald Trump die, accepting that it was probably a mistake from the start, and give the new president a chance to govern? Given how nonexistent the evidence was, this would have been the responsible thing to do. But then, of course, there was option two: should Obama and Biden do everything possible to keep the ridiculous investigation alive, setting the machinery of the federal government on their political enemies once more and ensuring that this time, the attacks would continue long after they were no longer in office?

I don't need to tell you which one they picked.

During this ill-fated Oval Office meeting, Comey brought up the subject of Lt. General Michael Flynn. A few weeks earlier, General Flynn, the decorated war fighter who would serve as President Trump's national security advisor, had participated in conversations with a Russian ambassador named Sergey Kislyak. As the incoming national security advisor, whose job would involve speaking to foreign leaders every day, this was a perfectly normal thing for General Flynn to do. Every incoming national security advisor, from both parties, does exactly the same thing as they come into office. Still, the FBI had listened in on the call, as they do with all calls between future government officials and foreign leaders, and found reason to be suspicious. Comey was wondering how to handle the general from this point on.

According to FBI notes, it was Vice President Biden who raised the idea of prosecuting General Flynn under the Logan Act, a little-known law from the 1800s that was written to forbid private citizens from conducting foreign policy. The law has always been of dubious constitutionality. In its more than two hundred years of existence, the Logan Act had been invoked only twice—once in 1802, and again in 1852—and never successfully. The notes do not specify how Joe Biden, a man who at times seemed to have trouble remembering his own name, had managed to recall the details of this obscure and never-enforced statute.

Taking up the conversation, President Obama asked openly whether his administration should refuse to "pass sensitive information as it relates to Russia to Flynn." Comey, according to a memo written by National Security Advisor Susan Rice on her last day in office, responded "Potentially." It is interesting, considering what we know now, that Rice saw fit to write the memo at all. In it, she takes pains to note that Obama had not directed James Comey to do anything against the Trump campaign, making sure to say that Obama wanted everything done "by the book." It isn't explicitly entitled "CYA," but it's the sort of memo that the CFO of Enron might have written, knowing full well that someday—maybe not tomorrow, maybe not the next day—the world would find out about the various crimes they were committing.

By the end of the meeting, the team had decided to let the investigation continue. Vice President Biden had explicitly raised the possibility of a criminal prosecution for Michael Flynn, the decorated three-star general who at that point was not even under investigation. The Russia Hoax was under way, and for all anyone in the Oval Office that day knew, it was going to destroy the Trump presidency before it could even begin.

I suspect that as Vice President Joe Biden stood before the joint session of Congress on January 6, 2017, he may not have believed that Donald Trump, the man he had just formally named the next president of the United States, would remain in office for long.

Which might explain why he seemed so untroubled at 1:58 p.m. as he banged the gavel once more and ended Congress's certification of the presidential election results. He knew full well that whatever went on in that room, the intelligence community's war against Donald Trump was aggressively under way, and it was far too late for anyone to do anything about it.

As one long-respected Washington political columnist, eyebrow raised, wryly observed to me at an inauguration party in 2017, "Has anyone ever won a war with the intelligence community?"

The Drop

That same afternoon, no more than an hour before we began certifying his Electoral College victory, President-elect Trump welcomed James Comey into a conference room on the fifth floor of Trump Tower. Officially, Comey had come to give the president-elect the same briefing he'd given Obama and Biden fewer than twenty-four hours earlier. He was supposed to detail the Russian attacks on our elections, discuss our responses to those attacks, and then leave. The heads of other intelligence agencies, including John Brennan of the CIA and James Clapper, director of national intelligence, had also come along. Both Brennan and Clapper were extreme leftists; Clapper had repeatedly been caught lying to

Congress, and Brennan had publicly admitted that, in 1980, because he thought Jimmy Carter wasn't liberal enough, he had cast his own vote *for the Communist Party's candidate* for president of the United States.

But Comey had also brought something else—something that would soon upend the Trump presidency, making it nearly impossible for them to govern effectively. I have long believed that James Comey fancied himself the modern incarnation of J. Edgar Hoover, full of grandiose ambition and replete with blackmail files illicitly obtained. (I don't know if he also favored women's lingerie and red pumps.)

In that dubious tradition, for several months, the FBI had been in possession of a shady group of documents about Donald Trump and Russia. These documents would soon come to be known collectively as the Steele Dossier. At the time Comey carried them into Trump Tower, the details on where exactly the dossier had come from were hazy at best (in large part because the FBI did not want to know). It's only after years of thorough investigative work that we know for certain how they came about—and *that* is a story that makes Watergate seem tame by comparison. In fact, the details of this story are so strange that if a Hollywood screenwriter had come up with them, he'd probably have his script rejected all over town as too farfetched (and stupid) to be true.

The story, most of which you probably know by now, goes like this. During the early stages of the 2016 presidential campaign, when there were more Republican candidates in the race than there are genders in the Biden White House, a conservative website called the *Washington Free Beacon* hired a company called Fusion GPS to dig up dirt on Donald Trump, who was then polling in the low single digits. The principal funder of that website was aggressively supporting one of the other Republican candidates who was running against both Trump and myself. The *Free Beacon* wanted to attack Trump from the right, claiming he wasn't conservative enough. Fusion GPS—an opposition research firm run by a former *Wall Street Journal* reporter named Glenn Simpson—hired a former British spy named Christopher Steele, who had contacts in Russia, to help them do some of the heavy lifting on the job.

For three years, Steele had run the Russia desk at the London head-quarters of MI6, the British intelligence agency made world famous by Ian Fleming's suave superspy, James Bond. Unlike that fictional char-acter, though, Steele did not jump out of airplanes or make daring escapes from the headquarters of supervillains. Nor do we know how he takes his martinis. Instead, for the most part, he stayed behind his desk. After an unremarkable career at MI6, Steele left to start a private intelligence firm called Orbis in 2009. By that time, according to research done by Real Clear Investigations, Steele "hadn't traveled to Russia in decades and apparently had no useful sources there."[1]

As the Republican primary was nearing its close, the funding for Fusion GPS shifted to the Hillary Clinton campaign and the Democratic National Committee. Over time, Hillary's campaign and the DNC fun-neled more than one million dollars into trying to dig up (or manufac-ture) dirt on Donald Trump.

As soon as Orbis was hired by Fusion GPS in the spring of 2016, Steele got to work making phone calls. Among the people he spoke with was Igor Danchenko, a former employee of the Brookings Institution who was born in Russia but spent most of his time in the United States. During his time here, Danchenko had become a heavy drinker. He'd also been arrested several times. Like Steele, he didn't have many friends who actually lived in Russia; most of them were drinking buddies who'd been born in Russia but spent all their time stateside.

Danchenko, soon to become world famous as Steele's "primary sub-source," told Steele about some "rumors" that had been cooked up by Danchenko's drinking buddies—namely that Donald Trump had been an asset of the Russian government for decades. He was party to some shady business deals, and, most infamously, was allegedly the star of an amateur sex tape produced by the KGB and Vladimir Putin himself—a tape which supposedly showed Trump in a hotel room ordering prosti-tutes to urinate on him in bed. Steele listened to these wild accusations, typed them up as if they were facts, and sent them over to the folks at

Fusion GPS, where some of the firm's employees got to work sorting through them.

In a later interview with the FBI, Danchenko would say that he "never expected Steele to put [his] statements in reports or present them as facts." He also called the information he'd passed on to Steele as nothing more than "conversations" that he'd had with his friends "over beers."

But Fusion GPS didn't know that (or care to know that) at the time. Instead, they took everything Steele wrote as fact, believing that he was out doing the work of a real spy rather than sitting behind his desk making phone calls.

Among those Fusion GPS employees digging for dirt on Trump was a woman named Nellie Ohr, who in turn was married to Bruce Ohr, an associate deputy attorney general in the Justice Department. (In 2001, I held the same post, an "ADAG" in DOJ parlance.) Bruce Ohr was a career lawyer at the DOJ, and he knew both Steele and Simpson as well. Steele had previously been a paid informant for the FBI, until they fired him in the fall of 2016 for repeatedly leaking information harmful to Trump to the press. When that happened, Bruce Ohr became the back-channel conduit between Steele and the FBI, circumventing the department's strict rules for handling confidential informants. And Ohr did all that without informing his superiors of his massive conflicts of interest, including his wife's literally being on the payroll of the firm Hillary Clinton had paid to target Trump.

For several months in 2016, Fusion GPS attempted to shop the dossier around to multiple news outlets. Most of these outlets passed, assuming (correctly) that the dossier was made up of rumors, speculation, and nothing more. But Fusion did have a few minor successes. During the early campaign, *Mother Jones* and *Yahoo! News* both published pieces that referenced the dossier and hinted at some of the salacious material that could be found inside. But those stories were minor compared to what was coming.

By the time James Comey entered Trump Tower with the dossier, CNN had been holding onto a copy, waiting only for a "news hook" to make it public. The same, no doubt, was true of several other "news" organizations at the time.

Toward the end of his meeting with President-elect Trump, Comey placed the dossier on the table and began telling him about the bizarre allegations inside.

That evening, miraculously, the gossip website *Buzzfeed* published the dossier in full, lending its questionable weight to the ridiculous allegations, and (as intended) it soon spread to every corner of the Internet. Other "news" organizations, even those that had been somewhat reputable at the beginning of the whole affair, behaved as if they had no choice but to report on the leak and the unfounded material inside the dossier.

Within a few days, the whole country was wrapped up in the Russia collusion narrative. It would soon come to be known as "Russia-gate," with Democrats painting Donald Trump, the political outsider who had shocked the world by winning the election, as the return of Richard Nixon. In the middle of Trump's presidency, the website *Slate* launched a podcast called *Slow Burn*, which told the story of the Watergate scandal in great detail. In the first episode of the show, the host of the podcast compared the actions taken by President Nixon and his men to the Russia scandal that was unfolding around them at the time, asking his listeners in a grave voice: "If we were living through the next Watergate, would we know it?"

Obviously, the answer was no. While the corporate media and the Democratic Party establishment were fixated on the Trump campaign's nonexistent ties to Russia, attempting to manufacture another scandal out of thin air, they ignored the much greater scandal that had been right there for all to see. During the final days of the Obama administration, the FBI—with virtually no credible basis—had launched an investigation directly targeting the sitting president's principal political opponent.

Doing so is a big damn deal, and in any properly functioning DOJ the evidence necessary to initiate such a blatantly political investigation should have been required to be overwhelming. But it was not. Not even close. Instead, this investigation was carried out by a team of agents who seemed to want to go after President Trump for reasons that had nothing to do with his possible crimes and everything to do with their deep personal dislike of the man.

For the entirety of the Trump administration, as my colleagues in Congress and I attempted to get to the bottom of the Crossfire Hurricane affair, those involved in this investigation would lie, obfuscate, and attempt to hide their complicity in what might be the greatest crime ever committed by the U.S. government against a sitting president. Every day, as the evidence against them became stronger (and stranger), the nation learned just how far Obama, Biden, and the rest of that administration had been willing to go to smear, attack, and destroy their political enemies.

Investigations

From the moment the first allegations of Russian collusion emerged in the press, I was skeptical. There seemed to be no real evidence of collusion between the Trump campaign and the Kremlin, as anyone who was looking at the situation with any degree of honesty could tell. But it wasn't until I started digging that I realized quite how brazen—and how absolutely *strange*—the radical left had acted in their attempts to take down President Trump.

As I've said, part of my duty as a senator is to conduct oversight of government agencies, including the Department of Justice, the FBI, and the other agencies that were ultimately tied up in the Crossfire Hurricane affair. During my early preparations for these oversight hearings, I learned that the story of the federal government's attempt to stop Donald Trump at all costs had been much more widespread—and, thankfully, much more inept—than I had imagined.

It began, strangely enough, with a conversation in a London wine bar. There, a twenty-eight-year-old low-level volunteer from the Trump campaign named George Papadopoulos told Alexander Downer, an Australian diplomat, that he'd heard that Russia might have a slew of emails from Hillary Clinton that could be damaging to the Clinton campaign. The information was passed along as idle chatter, not unlike the other boozy information that had gone into Christopher Steele's dossier. But Downer, sensing that something might be off, repeated the interaction to the FBI.

Based on nothing more than this rumor, the FBI launched an operation to uncover any links between the Russian government and the Trump campaign. The investigation, which was code-named Crossfire Hurricane and led by James Comey and his hyper-partisan deputy, Andrew McCabe, also comprised several smaller investigations. In this respect, it was not unlike the insane Operation GEMSTONE plan that G. Gordon Liddy had cooked up for Richard Nixon. In the case of McCabe and Comey, however, the names were much less entertaining. Crossfire Razor was an investigation designed to look into Michael Flynn, President Trump's incoming national security advisor; Crossfire Fury would look into Paul Manafort, President Trump's onetime campaign manager. A furious razor in a hurricane, that's how the DOJ approached the incoming Trump administration.

Almost as soon as they opened the investigation, McCabe and Comey authorized the use of spying. To do this, they needed to file an application with the Foreign Intelligence Surveillance Court, or FISA Court, making the case that the target of their investigation was worth the effort of wiretapping and intelligence gathering they were proposing. At first, when they attempted to obtain a FISA warrant to spy on Carter Page (a professor and foreign policy advisor loosely affiliated with the Trump campaign), the FISA Court came back and said that the evidence—or, rather, the lack of evidence—they had submitted was insufficient. So they went back to the FISA Court with the Steele Dossier. Thanks to the lurid accusations contained therein, they soon had warrants to spy on Carter Page.

Repeatedly, the strained efforts of the FBI revealed no evidence of collusion between the Trump campaign and Russia. Every time they attempted to make a link, they failed. Yet they continued to renew their FISA warrants, hoping that eventually, they would be able to nail President Trump on something.

Why? The answer is simple. The intelligence community saw President Trump as an existential threat—someone who would come from the outside and shake things up. He needed to be taken down at any cost.

Anyone who doubted the deep hatred that organizations like the FBI harbored for President Trump needed only to look at the long series of text messages between FBI agent Peter Strzok, a major figure on the Crossfire Hurricane team, and Lisa Page, an FBI lawyer with whom Strzok was having an adulterous affair at the time. Reading through these texts, the nation would soon learn just how deep the hatred for President Trump ran.

In one text, sent in August 2016, shortly after Strzok had begun working on the Crossfire Hurricane investigation, Page said, "[Trump's] not ever going to become president, right? Right?!" Strzok, who knew exactly what was going on behind the scenes, replied "No. No he won't. We'll stop it."

The rest of these conversations have been well reported, so they don't bear much repeating here. But the point is clear. These two partisans—like much of the senior leadership of the DOJ and FBI—loathed Donald Trump, and they would do anything to stop him from becoming president. In addition to revealing a strange proclivity for pillow talk involving Donald Trump (which I, along with most of America, found quite odd), they also reveal a government bureaucracy that was dead set on keeping Trump out of office. In one of these texts, sent in March 2016, Strzok asked Page whether Donald Trump might potentially be "a worse president than Cruz," to which she responded in the affirmative, calling Trump "awful" and "an idiot."[2] Given that I was also running for president at the time, I think it's safe to assume that "Cruz" referred to me.

If Peter Strzok and Lisa Page didn't like me at the time, I must have been doing something right.

By the time President Trump took office, the Crossfire Hurricane investigation was already quite public. This is largely thanks to a disclosure that James Comey made in front of Congress in March 2017, shortly after he dropped the dossier on the conference room table in Trump Tower and brought the whole Russia Hoax mainstream.

For the remainder of President Trump's time in office, numerous lawmakers did their best to bring the corruption of the Obama administration to light. These included my good friends Jim Jordan and Mark Meadows, then congressmen who stayed on the Russia beat almost full time, and Devin Nunes, whose staff worked tirelessly to expose the various lies surrounding the fake collusion narrative.

In 2019, DOJ inspector general Michael Horowitz released a detailed look at the Crossfire Hurricane investigation, finding, among other things, that the FBI had made seventeen significant errors in its application for a FISA warrant against Carter Page. On page 254 of this report, Horowitz found that Kevin Clinesmith, a senior lawyer at the FBI during the time the Crossfire Hurricane investigation was conducted, deliberately altered an email about Carter Page. The basis for the FBI's scrutiny of Page was that he was having conversations with some shady Russian characters. That was understandable. However, if Page was doing so *on behalf of the CIA*, those conversations would not be suspicious, but rather would be actively furthering our national security. So the FBI sent an email to the CIA asking if Page was a CIA source. Much to the dismay of the partisans at the FBI, the CIA responded *yes, Page was a CIA source.*

Instead of relaying this vital fact, Clinesmith edited the inconvenient CIA email to make it say that Carter Page was "*not* a source." In other words, he fraudulently changed a government email so that it would say *exactly the opposite* of what it actually said, hoping all the while that the alterations would increase the chances that Carter Page could be legally surveilled by the FBI. And he submitted that counterfeit email to the federal FISA Court.

In the fall of 2020, I had the chance to grill James Comey and Andrew McCabe—virtually, of course—about the origins of the Crossfire Hurricane investigation. Time and time again, they obfuscated, stumbled, and refused to give a coherent account of why they had allowed the investigation to continue for so long.

During questioning, I asked James Comey whether having seen all the evidence—the sloppy applications for FISA warrants, the blatant political bias of his team—he still believed the FBI had acted in a "competent and honest way." He ducked the question. I asked whether he believed Kevin Clinesmith had been acting according to FBI policy when he created a fraudulent document to submit to the FISA Court, and he refused to admit that such a thing had even taken place. He gave similar evasions when it came to the Steele Dossier, Steele's primary sub-source—who had been under investigation by the FBI—and leaks.

Clearly, these people had something to hide. They know that the FISA warrants used to surveil the Trump campaign were obtained through illegal means. They know that the entire Trump-Russia collusion narrative that took up millions of column inches and countless hours of airtime on cable news was built on nothing but opposition research funded by the Hillary Clinton campaign. But they were counting on the outlets of the corporate press—many of which played a major role in pushing the fake dossier in the first place—to give them cover until the narrative simply faded away, pushed down the same memory hole as the Obama administration's abuse of the IRS, Hillary Clinton's illegal private email server, and the many crimes committed by people whose politics aligned with the left.

Consider the way the press has treated the explosive findings of John Durham, the veteran federal prosecutor who has been looking into the corrupt origins of Crossfire Hurricane since he was appointed by Attorney General Bill Barr to do so in the late spring of 2019. Unlike the investigation of Michael Horowitz, the Durham probe was not simply a fact-finding mission. His mandate was to find those responsible and make sure they were held accountable. Despite (frustratingly) taking longer than expected to act on that mandate, the findings of his investigation so far have been stunning—although the press continues to downplay them.

In September 2021, for instance, Durham's team indicted Michael Sussmann, a cybersecurity lawyer at Perkins Coie, a law firm retained by the Clinton campaign, for lying to the FBI. Almost exactly five years earlier, Sussmann had met with officials at the FBI and given them "evidence" that the Trump campaign was being aided by Russia. This evidence, as it would later turn out, was based on nonpublic Internet traffic data to which the firm had gained access.[3] But the source of the data—which proved nothing—was not the biggest problem. The problem, rather, was that during the meeting, Sussmann had claimed that he was not working on behalf of a client, even though his client was clearly the Clinton campaign (which he billed for every minute he spent talking to the FBI). According to the indictment, Sussmann's claims "led the FBI general counsel to understand that Sussmann was acting as a good citizen merely passing along information, not as a paid advocate or political operative."[4]

The press, of course, played down the severity of these charges. In an article published shortly after the court filing, the *New York Times* published a news analysis piece claiming that the outrage that came with its findings was the result of "conspiracy theories from [President] Trump and his allies."[5] To them, the real story was not that a lawyer representing a political campaign brought fake evidence of collusion against a rival campaign and then lied about his intentions to the FBI, it was that reporting on such information honestly might be good for President Trump.

Unfortunately, Durham had to bring the Sussmann charges in D.C. federal court. There, he drew an Obama-appointed district judge who proceeded to issue a legal ruling excluding much of the evidence (including almost anything that might incriminate the Hillary Clinton campaign directly). As *Politico* reported at the time,

The ruling spares the Clinton campaign and the Democratic National Committee the potential embarrassment of a federal judge finding they were part of a coordinated effort to level since-discredited allegations that candidate Donald Trump or his allies maintained a data link from Trump Tower to Russia's Alfa Bank.[6]

And the jury pool was drawn from D.C. voters, who voted 91 percent for Clinton over Trump. Despite the unequivocal evidence, in May of 2022 that D.C. jury voted to acquit, a decision that raises real questions about a partisan double standard.

Mind you, the corporate press remain in active collusion with Biden's and Obama's dishonest partisans. Both the *New York Times* and the *Washington Post* were awarded Pulitzer Prizes for their exhaustive reporting on the fraudulent Steele Dossier and the Russia Hoax. Neither has had the journalistic integrity to return those celebrated prizes when their reporting was revealed to be overwhelmingly false. And, as of the time of this writing, Hillary Clinton's campaign manager just testified that *Hillary personally approved* the campaign's pushing those bogus Russia stories to be amplified by their friendly media stooges.[7]

In fact, given that Durham was appointed by President Trump, chances are relatively high that Attorney General Merrick Garland will ultimately try to discontinue his investigation on the grounds that it is expensive or not yielding enough in the way of results. (These odds have risen even higher with the Sussmann acquittal.) With the corrupt corporate press acting as cover, the chances of Durham being shut down continue to rise. But, if these initial court filings are any indication, the findings of Durham's investigation will be vital. I consider it my duty to make sure he is allowed to finish his work, and that the American people are allowed to learn about the true roots of the left's war on President Trump.

CHAPTER FOUR

CRITICAL RACE THEORY

Racist Babies?

In March 2022, a large box arrived in my office in the United States Senate. It was full of children's books—or, at least, books that are typically shelved in the children's section at your local Barnes & Noble.

A few days earlier, during initial discussions about the upcoming confirmation hearings of Judge Ketanji Brown Jackson, President Biden's nominee to fill the Supreme Court seat left vacant by the impending retirement of Justice Stephen Breyer, I had asked a few members of my staff to look into the curriculum at Georgetown Day School, a private school in Washington, D.C., on whose board Judge Jackson was a current trustee. The board of trustees was chaired by Judge Jackson's college roommate, who would personally introduce her the next week at her Senate confirmation hearing. My office had received reports that the curriculum and assigned reading at the school was wildly left-wing, and we figured we should check it out.

Three years ago, just before Justice Ruth Bader Ginsburg passed away, I wrote a book titled *One Vote Away: How a Single Supreme Court Seat Can Change History*. It became a number-one Amazon bestseller, and it brought the reader behind the curtain to understand what really happens at the Supreme Court. Rather than a dry academic treatise, it told war stories about my litigating some of the biggest land-mark cases at the Court—protecting free speech, religious liberty, the Second Amendment—many of which were decided 5–4...leaving us just one vote away from keeping or losing our fundamental rights.

In researching more than two centuries of Supreme Court cases, studying the arguments that surrounded them, I became even more convinced of my main thesis: the simple act of nominating a justice to the Supreme Court—something that nearly every president in our history has done more than once—can drastically alter the course of history, not only for the people who are alive to witness the nomination, but for their children and grandchildren too.

Having spent the last decade on the Senate Judiciary Committee, I have the solemn constitutional responsibility to "advise and consent," that is, carefully to examine and evaluate the records of people nomi-nated to become federal judges and, in particular, Supreme Court jus-tices. It is a task, as I'm sure you can tell, that I do not take lightly. For weeks before a confirmation hearing, I try to read almost every critical opinion that the nominee has written. I comb through the decisions they've made as a judge, and I study their biography, attempting to find out how they view the role of a Supreme Court justice. And I read their speeches and the law review articles they have written.

When President Trump had three Supreme Court vacancies to fill, he spoke to me directly about whether I had any interest in serving on the Court. For each, I told him no. He didn't formally offer me a seat, but he leaned in vigorously in our discussions. At his request, I had agreed that Trump could put my name on his public list of potential Supreme Court nominees, but he did so only after I told him explicitly that I was *not* willing to accept an appointment. Many are surprised by that, given my decades of legal background and training. Before I was in the Senate, my career was arguing Supreme Court cases. I revere the Court—it mat-ters immensely—but principled judges stay out of political and policy fights. If I were ever a federal judge, that is precisely what I would do. But I don't want to stay out of political and policy fights; I want to lead them. And the elected branches of government are the proper arena to wage those battles.

For that reason, when President Trump nominated Neil Gorsuch, and then Brett Kavanaugh, and then Amy Coney Barrett to serve on the Court, I led the fight in the Senate to confirm all three. These are likely not the nominees I would have put forward—I think the nominees who have served the best (like Scalia and Thomas and Rehnquist and Alito) are those who have built long and proven records of defending constitutional principles, and enduring the ferocious crucible of criticism that inevitably results. I urged President Trump to nominate someone like my colleague Senator Mike Lee to the Court, because I am absolutely certain that Mike would remain faithful to the Constitution no matter the political pressure to do otherwise. But the three choices Trump put forward are good and honorable people, and all had serious and distinguished records that merited confirmation. I very much hope, in the fullness of time, that they will each prove to be principled constitutionalists for decades to come.

Examining her record, I could not have the same confidence about Judge Jackson.

To be sure, she and I have known each other a long time. We were both students at Harvard Law School; Ketanji was one year behind me, and we were editors together on the *Harvard Law Review*. Ketanji and I were not close, but we were friendly. I always liked her personally. She's smart, charming, and very talented; she's affable and has a powerful, inspiring personal story.

But I was not being called upon to assess whether I liked her personally, but rather whether she should be confirmed as a Supreme Court justice. And her record over the past three decades raised serious questions as to whether she would protect or undermine our constitutional liberties.

So I decided that it would be best to do some supplemental research that might give me a clearer picture of her thinking. This included interviews and law school speeches she has given over the years and articles she had written. And it included the curriculum at Georgetown Day School. Some of the books were what you'd expect students of that age to be reading—nice stories about dogs who go out on adventures, didactic tales of children who learn various lessons by meeting new friends.

But many of the titles were strange, to say the least. I was first struck by a book for young children called *Antiracist Baby*, written by the radical scholar Ibram X. Kendi. Many Americans know very little about Kendi or his work. His name is often mentioned in the same breath as the writer Ta-Nehisi Coates and Nikole Hannah-Jones, the radical *New York Times* "journalist" who led the revisionist history 1619 Project (more on that later).

Now a left-wing celebrity, Kendi, born Ibram Rogers, is best known for bringing the term "antiracism," a made-up word once confined to academic seminar rooms, into mainstream political discourse. He, along with several of the other "serious thinkers" mentioned above, is one of the main proponents of a doctrine known as Critical Race Theory. In short, this explicitly Marxist set of ideas posits that every social and political interaction should be viewed through the lens of race. The world, in the eyes of people like Kendi, Robin DiAngelo, and others, is all about battling power differentials. History, to them, is an eternal struggle between oppressed people (usually those who are gay, transgender, Black, queer, or members of some other self-described victim group) and their oppressors (who are almost exclusively White males). In their view, the main job of government officials—a group that presumably includes Supreme Court justices—should be to fight on the side of the oppressed people, bringing about equality of outcome for all by means of racial privileges, referred to as "equity."

And here, language matters. CRT does not fight for equality; it fights for "equity." Equity sounds similar to equality, but it means the opposite. Rather than oppose discrimination, CRT mandates discrimination. It teaches that White people must be discriminated against (as must Asian

Americans), that property rights are inherently evil, and that capitalism must be overthrown and replaced with socialism.

If that sounds ridiculously convoluted to you, don't worry. We'll get to the actual theory soon enough. There is a reason that popular proponents of such theories do not come right out and say these things off the bat. If they did, people might begin to think, quite rightly, that they are unhinged.

Instead, they use simple, almost storybook-like language to smuggle these ideas into popular culture.

Ibram Kendi is a perfect example. According to his writings, it is not possible for a person to be neutral—i.e., *not racist*—when it comes to race. Either someone is actively engaged in the fight against racism, talking about race every second of every day, actively discriminating against the "oppressors" and making sure everyone else is, too, or that person is racist. There is no in between. If you think this is an exaggeration, or perhaps an unfair summation of what Kendi has to say, consider the following passage from his book *How to Be an Antiracist,* which shot to the top of bestseller lists during the civil unrest that followed the death of George Floyd in Minneapolis:

> What's the problem with being "not racist"? It is a claim
> that signifies neutrality: "I am not a racist, but neither am I
> aggressively against racism." But there is no neutrality in the
> racism struggle. The opposite of "racist" isn't "not racist."
> It is "antiracist."

I must admit that when I first encountered the term "antiracism," I felt a subtle pang of admiration for Kendi's facility with language. Clearly, he was trying to come up with a term that no one could possibly raise any serious objection to, and it worked. How, after all, could anyone seriously claim to be *anti*-antiracist? Surely, that would make them racist!

According to this deliberately overbroad definition, anyone who is not "aggressively against racism" is necessarily racist. And "aggressively against racism" is in turn defined as embracing left-wing, extreme policies...like widespread government discrimination, destruction of the nuclear family (mom, dad, and kids), universal redistribution of wealth, and abolishing the police. Indeed, if you look at the website for the organization Black Lives Matter (a group that was founded by three avowed and trained Marxist organizers), it expressly calls for "defunding the police" and also explicitly demands "disrupt[ing] the Western-prescribed nuclear family structure" (until that latter language was magically scrubbed from the site in September 2020). And if you disagree with Kendi's and BLM's radical agenda, that's their justification for labeling you a racist.

Today, the word "racist," a word that once held immense meaning, the mere accusation of which was, quite rightly, enough to end a career or cause serious reputational harm, has been co-opted to mean...well, really anything the radical left thinks it should mean.

Elsewhere in the same book, Kendi claims that "to love capitalism is to love racism. To love racism is to love capitalism." He elaborates:

> these conjoined twins are two sides of the same destructive body.... *Capitalism is essentially racist; racism is essentially capitalist.* They were birthed together from the same unnatural causes, and they shall one day die together from unnatural causes. Or racial capitalism will live into another epoch of theft and rapacious inequality, especially if activists naively fight the conjoined twins independently, as if they are not the same.[1]

Bad prose aside, this claim is profoundly wrong. If you care about social justice, if you care about racial equality, you should be an enthusiastic advocate of capitalism, because free enterprise—and the American free enterprise system, in particular—has lifted more people out of poverty than any economic system in the history of humanity. There is a reason that millions of people come to America every year. There is a reason that people risk their lives to come here. Because, even if you start with nothing—as my father did in 1957, when he came from Cuba as a penniless teenage immigrant—there is no place on earth where you have a greater chance of achieving prosperity and abundance.

Realizing the American Dream should not depend on your race, ethnicity, wealth, or who your daddy was; rather, it should depend, as Dr. Martin Luther King, Jr. powerfully put it atop the steps of the Lincoln Memorial, "not on the color of your skin, but on the content of your character."

In 2019 and again in 2020, I joined a half dozen of my colleagues, both Republican and Democrat, in reading aloud on the Senate floor Dr. King's historic *Letter from a Birmingham Jail*. Most of us have read the letter before, perhaps in school, but speaking those words out loud is altogether different. The power, the eloquence, echoes throughout the ages. In particular, I was struck again by Dr. King's serious, sober-minded commitment to equality for *all people*. When he spoke, he invoked the law of God, not the crackpot theories of injustice that are being pushed today. He sought to live in a world where all people were equal under one law, not one in which every policy needed to be analyzed according to some new Marxist theories of "antiracism."

Kendi, on the other hand, is obsessed with race; it's the only thing he sees. In 2003, writing for the student newspaper at Florida Agricultural and Mechanical University, he launched into a diatribe in print about White people. "Europeans," he writes, "are completely different from Asians who are completely different from Hispanics and so on and so forth." The rest is worth quoting at length:

> Europeans are simply a different breed of human. They are
> socialized to be aggressive people. They are taught to live by
> the credo "survival of the fittest." They are raised to be racist.
>
> Caucasians make up only 10 percent of the world's popu-
> lation and that small percentage of people have recessive

genes. Therefore they're facing extinction. *Whites have tried to level the playing field with the AIDS virus* and cloning, but they know these deterrents will only get them so far. This is where the murder, psychological brainwashing and deception comes into play.

Europeans are trying to survive and I can't hate them for that. However, I'm not going to just sit back and let them physically, mentally, socially, spiritually and economically destroy my people.[2]

Now, unlike Ibram Kendi, I do not have a Ph.D. in African American studies. I have not attended graduate-level courses in antiracism, and I have not written any of the major works of Critical Race Theory that have suddenly become in vogue in our culture. However, I do feel relatively safe in asserting that when you're trying to determine who is and is not racist, it might be a good idea to check whether the person in question has ever...well, let's see, *accused an entire race of creating and deliberately spreading the AIDS virus.*

As usual, a little cursory Googling of Kendi's name reveals something important about modern leftism, which is this: almost every time you find someone who is obsessed with calling everything racism, it is usually because they have a deep, complicated relationship to the issue themselves. These preening, virtue-signaling liberals are often far more racist than the people they spend their days attempting to label as such.

Take the Democrats. Today, there is virtually no issue in the Democratic Party platform that has not been twisted to align with the far left's views on race. When it was time for the Biden administration to unveil its plan to provide COVID-19 relief, they made sure to say that they wanted to help "business owners of color" who had been affected first, and then everyone else. Astonishingly, the Biden Health and Human Services Department announced (before retracting it in the face of overwhelming backlash) that—in the name of "racial equity"—the federal government would provide free crack pipes to drug addicts. So much for antiracism.

They never seemed to tire of labeling President Trump a racist and a White nationalist, despite his economic policies that produced the lowest African American and Hispanic unemployment in U.S. history. And before the hearings about Judge Ketanji Brown Jackson even started, there were whispers that anyone who opposed her confirmation could only be doing so in the name of racism. The Democrats have co-opted the struggles of minorities and the concept of racism—which, again, was once a real word with a real meaning—to further their own pursuit of power.

By now, it's well known—though not nearly as well known as it should be—that the Democratic Party's history on racism is nothing short of horrific. From its founding days, this party has been an edifice of racism. It was Democrats, after all, who founded the Ku Klux Klan, and Democrats who wrote the Jim Crow laws that terrorized African American people well into the twentieth century. Indeed, Nathan Bedford Forrest, the ignominious founder of the Ku Klux Klan, was a national delegate to the 1860 Democratic Convention in Charleston, South Carolina. Virtually every leader of the KKK throughout history has been a Democrat.

Anyone who thinks that this legacy of vicious racism stopped sometime in the 1950s or '60s should consider that the final member of the Klan to serve in Congress did not leave office until his death in 2010. His name was Robert Byrd, and he was, of course, a Democrat. As a young man, Byrd—who would eventually rise through the ranks of the Democratic Party to become the Senate majority leader—had not only been a member of the KKK, but a top officer in the group. By the time he left the group to run for higher office, Byrd was known around Klan headquarters as an "Exalted Cyclops," one of the many ridiculous titles that these racist goons in white sheets conferred upon themselves. He earned that title by going around his home state of West Virginia and recruiting other young racists to join the KKK. Once Byrd was elected to the Senate, he vigorously opposed passing the Civil Rights Act of 1964, and stalled other major civil rights legislation.

This man was not some fringe character. In fact, by the time he died, Byrd was the longest serving United States senator in history. He was also revered by his Democratic colleagues. Just over a decade ago, President Joe Biden called him "a friend." Hillary Clinton likewise called him "a true American original, my friend and mentor."[3] When Robert Byrd died in 2010, Joe Biden gave his eulogy. During that speech, Biden explicitly referred to Byrd as a "*mentor* and a friend," saying that he "elevated the U.S. Senate." Many prominent Democrats, from Chuck Schumer, Nancy Pelosi, and a little-known Democratic figure named Barack Obama also showed up to pay their respects. As soon as Joe Biden was done speaking, Obama took to the podium, saying that Byrd was "a party leader," "an elder statesman," and "my friend."

Now, if you want to pontificate on race as the Democrats insist on doing whenever they get the chance, few people in United States history have entirely clean hands. But there are several questions you might want to ask yourself. One of the first, I think, should be: *Have I ever given the eulogy for an Exalted Cyclops of the Ku Klux Klan? Have I ever called a Klansman a personal "mentor"?* If the answer is yes, you might consider sitting down and shutting the hell up.

There is no shortage of supposedly "antiracist" Democrats today who, subjected to even a tiny amount of scrutiny, end up revealing themselves as deeply hypocritical on race. One of my colleagues on the Judiciary Committee, the junior senator from Rhode Island, is a current member of an elite country club that apparently still does not admit African Americans. In 2022. When asked about it last year by a local reporter, here was the exchange:

> Reporter: "Back in 2017, you had expressed concerns about the membership of the all-White Bailey's Beach Club, you hoped it would become more diverse. Now your family's been members, your wife has been one of the largest shareholders, has there been any traction in that? Are there any minority members of the club?"

Democratic senator: "I think the people who are running the place are still working on that, and I'm sorry it hasn't happened yet."

Reporter: "Do you have concerns in 2021…your thoughts on an elite, all-White, wealthy club again in this day and age, should these clubs continue to exist?

Democratic senator: *"It's a long tradition in Rhode Island,* and there are many of them, and I think we just need to work our way through the issues, thank you."

I do not doubt that excluding Black people is "a long tradition in Rhode Island," and in the Democratic Party too. In the aftermath of that disastrous interview, the club tried to do damage control, insisting that it actually had admitted at least one "non-White member" (Egyptian? Asian? Italian?). Demanding no more facts or details, the corporate press yawned and moved on. And the Democratic senator remains a member of the discriminatory club to this day.

And I'm sure you remember when Ralph Northam, the Democratic governor of Virginia until 2022, ran into his own trouble involving the Ku Klux Klan. In February 2019, Governor Northam admitted that he was, according to an account by the *New York Times,* "one of the two men in a racist photograph that had been published in a medical school yearbook about thirty-five years earlier."[4] The photograph, which the corporate press did everything in its power to bury, showed two men; one of them was in blackface, and the other was dressed in the full regalia of the Ku Klux Klan. During his initial speech, Northam said he wasn't sure which of these two men was him. Then, fewer than twenty-four hours later, he held a press conference to declare that he was not, in fact, either of the men in the picture. It is a curious thing that when this picture came out, several prominent Democrats in Virginia almost immediately admitted to having themselves dressed in blackface in the past. And what they and the corporate media refused to acknowledge was that, by saying initially that he could have been "either of the men" in the photograph,

Northam was implicitly admitting that he could well have dressed either in blackface *or* as a member of the KKK in the past.

Now, for the first fifty-one years of my life, I have found it quite easy to avoid dressing in blackface. And even more so for dressing as a member of the KKK. Blackface wasn't really a thing in Texas, at least among the folks I grew up with. And I was always raised with the knowledge that the Klan were and are evil, vicious, bigoted idiots. Perhaps things were different among Virginia Democrats. But I find it amazing that Governor Northam, who regularly made a point of lecturing people about the evils of racism in public, still has not been able to say with any certainty that he has never dressed as a Klansman. Again, maybe I have not subscribed to the proper Marxist views, but I think that if you, as an aspiring public figure, cannot say definitively that you have never donned a white sheet and pranced around town dressed as a member of the Ku Klux Klan, you might want to shelve your plans to become a candidate for public office. At the very least, you should avoid giving condescending diatribes to your fellow citizens about your racial enlightenment.

Of course, Northam joins a crowded club of liberals who have been outed as hypocrites on race. Think of Howard Stern, who performed a comedy skit spewing racial epithets while wearing blackface. Or Jimmy Kimmel, who in 2020 had to apologize for wearing blackface while doing an impression of the NBA player Karl Malone. (He may be able to dress as an NBA player, but his game doesn't match. Kimmel regularly insults me on his late-night comedy show, and when he blamed me for my Houston Rockets losing the 2018 Western Conference finals, I challenged him to one-on-one to raise money for charity. He accepted. What transpired was terrible basketball—the ESPN announcer said, "If Dr. Naismith had seen what happened here tonight...he would have invented a different game!"—but I beat Kimmel 11–9.)

So perhaps I should not have been so surprised upon learning that Ibram X. Kendi, one of the reigning high priests in the new religion of wokeness, had a long history of blatant racism as well. Indeed, Kendi seems to have made a career out of attacking the "Europeans" he railed against in college. The only difference is that now he simply labels them "racists" and moves on.

Sitting in my office reading *Antiracist Baby*, Kendi's book for children that had ended up on the suggested reading list at Georgetown Day School, I was stunned once again by just how far this dangerous ideology had spread into our schools. It was one thing for consenting adults who had paid $28 to read Kendi's thoughts in hardcover to be exposed to these vile, racist ideas, but having them foisted upon unsuspecting children was another matter altogether. I had also ordered a copy of *Stamped (for Kids)*, an amended version of Kendi's book *Stamped from the Beginning*, wondering if it was filled with the same strange, hateful garbage that characterized his other writings.

It was.

For the next few days, I had my staff pull together all the quotes we had discussed from *Antiracist Baby*, *How to Be an Antiracist*, and a few other so-called "children's books" that were on the reading list of Georgetown Day School. I read the entirety of some of these books myself and made notes in the margins. I was particularly struck by this passage, which appears in *Stamped (for Kids)*:

> The idea that we should pretend not to see racism is connected to the idea that we should pretend not to see color. It's called colorblindness.... Here's what's wrong with this. It's ridiculous. Skin color is something we all absolutely see.... So to pretend not to see color is pretty convenient if you don't actually want to stamp out racism in the first place.

On its face, this book argues precisely the opposite of what Dr. Martin Luther King, Jr. advocated for during his historic "I Have a Dream" speech. Elsewhere in the book, Kendi suggests that rather than making sure that all laws apply to all races equally, we should create a federal Department of Antiracism, which would explicitly take race into account when making policy. He, like the rest of the Critical Race Theorists, seems to believe that the only remedy for discrimination in the past is explicit, state-sanctioned discrimination in the present and in perpetuity.

If a potential Supreme Court justice sat on the board of an institution that taught children this nonsense, I believed it was important that the American people find out about it. Did she believe, for instance, that "to love capitalism was to love slavery," as Kendi advocated in his books? Did she believe that Europeans were "a different breed of human?" Did she believe that babies should "confess to being racist" as part of their developmental process?

Given that the Supreme Court is certain to hear cases that involve charges of racism, both real and alleged, these were important questions to ask Judge Jackson. So, in the days before she was set to appear before the Judiciary Committee, I went over my notes about the various articles she'd written and speeches she had given. I noticed that she had told the alumni magazine at Georgetown Day School that she was proud in particular of the institution's "commitment...to social justice," which suggested that the CRT being taught there to students was something she personally embraced. I also read through some more of the books from Georgetown Day School's reading list for older kids, just to make sure I hadn't misjudged their content during my initial research.

Reading a little further, I quickly discovered that no, I had not. The school's curriculum was overflowing with Critical Race Theory. In one book, titled *The End of Policing*, the writer Alex S. Vitale argues—not convincingly—that "police exist primarily as a system for managing and even producing inequality by suppressing social movements and tightly managing the behaviors of poor and nonwhite people: those on the losing end of economic and political arrangements." Elsewhere in the same book, he explicitly states that the police do not exist to protect people; rather, they exist to perpetuate a system of White supremacy that disadvantages some racial groups and benefits others. This kind of garbage, with its half-baked Marxism and reliance on long-debunked strands of political theory, has no place in a classroom of adolescent children.

If Judge Ketanji Brown Jackson thought otherwise, I thought she should have to explain why to the American people.

So, on March 22, I asked Judge Jackson about Critical Race Theory. I noted that the theory had been invented largely at Harvard Law School, an institution we had attended together. Judge Jackson fumbled around for an answer. She insisted that although she had some vague idea what Critical Race Theory was, the ideas did not come up in her work as a judge. This, however, directly contradicted statements she had made in the past.

In 2015, for instance, Judge Jackson gave a lecture on federal criminal sentencing policy, during which she said that

> sentencing is important for all lawyers, even if criminal law is not your thing, because, at bottom, the sentencing of criminal offenders is the authorized exercise of the power of the government to subjugate the free will of individuals...sentencing is just plain interesting on an intellectual level, in part because it melds together myriad types of law—criminal law, of course, but also administrative law, constitutional law, *critical race theory*, negotiations, and, to some extent, even contracts.[5]

The emphasis, of course, is mine. All of the other elements she listed—"criminal law," "administrative law," "constitutional law," "negotiations," and "even contracts"—are undoubtedly part of sentencing. But Critical Race Theory is not. Criminal justice should be blind to race; the law should apply equally to all Americans, regardless of skin color, just as the Equal Protection Clause in the Fourteenth Amendment requires.

And criminal sentencing was the area where Judge Jackson's record was the most extreme. Overall, in her time as a federal district judge, she sentenced all criminal defendants to an average sentence of 29.9 months, which was 34 percent lower than the average judge nationally (45.1

months). But her leniency veered furthest from the mainstream when it came to sex offenders. Judge Jackson's average sentence for possession of child pornography was 29.2 months, which is 57 percent less than the national average (68 months). And for distribution of child pornography, her average sentence was 71.9 months, which is 47 percent less than the national average (135 months).

At her confirmation hearing, I gave her the chance to explain her record, walking her through each of the roughly dozen child pornography cases she had decided. She had no good explanation for this persistent pattern. Over and over again, with defendants who possessed or distributed hundreds or thousands of truly horrifying videos of very young children (often toddlers or younger) being sexually assaulted, Judge Jackson imposed consistently light sentences on these predators. In one of the most egregious cases, a defendant named Wesley Hawkins pleaded guilty to possessing multiple videos of boys as young as eight being sexually assaulted; in that case, the sentencing guidelines called for ten years in prison, the prosecutor asked for two years, and Judge Jackson sentenced him to just three months. A slap on the wrist.

In the aftermath of Judge Jackson's confirmation hearings, I was attacked by the corporate press with a ferocity that was slightly above average. While I have grown accustomed over the years to being labeled a racist by Democrats, particularly when I dare to point out the hypocrisy of their positions in public, the incoming fire that came after the Jackson hearings was more vociferous than usual.

This was particularly true on Twitter, where criticism of Judge Jackson for anything—her leniency on child sexual predators, for instance, or her (frankly hilarious) inability to say for certain what a woman was—was deemed racist and therefore impermissible. I would reprint some of the worst Twitter insults here, but I'm sure you'd have no trouble finding them on your own. I should point out, of course, that the vilest comments came, as always, from the tolerant, anti-hate, antiracist left.

For the most part, the corporate press was outraged that I would question the first African American woman nominated to the Supreme

Court about Critical Race Theory. They suggested that these doctrines, which explicitly state that everything in the world—our legal system included—is intimately connected to race, have nothing to do with Judge Jackson's work as a Supreme Court justice. Some outlets took a familiar track, suggesting that Critical Race Theory was, in the words of the *Guardian*, "the right's new boogeyman." Not only is it not being taught in our schools, they laughably claim, but it does not, in fact, exist at all.

In the *New Republic*, journalist Alex Shephard called Critical Race Theory "a mash-up of a clutch of right-wing tropes," writing that it was nothing more than "a reaction to students being taught the actual history of America—warts and all—instead of a puffed-up faux-patriotic rendition that passes for the truth in the works of Dinesh D'Souza and Bill O'Reilly."

These are the same kinds of outlets, of course, that continually print articles saying that Critical Race Theory is vital, especially to young minds. Shortly after the *Guardian* called CRT "the right's new boogeyman," for instance, it referred to attempts to ban Critical Race Theory as "a fight to whitewash U.S. history." The same publication also wrote in glowing terms about all editions of Nikole Hannah-Jones's 1619 Project, reacting with horror when its author was denied tenure at the University of North Carolina in 2021. In March 2022, the *New Republic* published an article about how attempts to ban Critical Race Theory would make "teachers afraid to teach history."[6]

So, according to the left, Critical Race Theory is a) an immensely important set of ideas that everyone should know—so important, in fact, that we should be handing out copies of the 1619 Project in every classroom in America, and simultaneously b) not real at all, so please move on. This dichotomy is so strange that whenever I speak seriously about the issue with someone on the left, I half-expect them to wave their hand over my face, look into my eyes, and proclaim, Obi-Wan Kenobi–style, that "these aren't the droids you're looking for."

Fortunately, I happen to know that Critical Race Theory is very real. In fact, I was there when it started.

Critical Race Theory: A *Real* Introduction

By the time I arrived at Harvard Law School in the early 1990s, the institution had already galloped far to the left. Numerous professors on staff were proud devotees of Karl Marx, the nineteenth-century writer and philosopher who laid the intellectual groundwork for communism. This was troubling, to say the least. Anyone who's ever studied the work of Marx, or the work of the many acolytes he's accumulated throughout history, knows why.

To Marx, and the academics who've made it their life's work to interpret everything in the world according to his theories, history is simple, and it can be described like this: There is an eternal struggle going on between the haves and the have-nots, or the "bourgeoisie" and the "proletariat." Workers, according to the Marxist view, will always be kept down by "capitalists," the people who own factories and make money. When workers do not have a stake in the "means of production," the upper classes will exploit them, paying them the lowest wages possible for the highest amount of work. The system will never be fair until the workers of the world "unite," rise up, and take control of the means of production, ushering in a communist revolution and a new age of peace for all mankind. The goal, as always, is a massive and forcible redistribution of wealth.

To eighteen-year-old college students taking their first seminars in political theory (and, occasionally, to fully grown idiots), this can sound like a good idea. After all, who wouldn't want the poor working classes to make more money if such a thing were indeed possible? Who *wouldn't* want the world to be fairer? The problem, of course, is that Marx's ideas were a lot of jumbled, important-sounding nonsense. They don't work in practice. Ever. Students need only turn a few more pages in their textbooks to find out that every single government that has ever attempted to implement these ideas has failed miserably. Indeed, Marx's philosophy is responsible for more death and human suffering than any other set of ideas in the history of mankind. Anyone who doubts this need only look up the Soviet famines that occurred between 1921–22 (which killed five million people), 1930–33 (six to nine million people), and 1946–47 (one million people); the soul-crushing poverty today in Cuba and North Korea and Venezuela; or the more than 100 million mass murders carried out in the name of communism, including by Stalin (more than twenty million people), Mao (more than forty-five million people), and Pol Pot and the Khmer Rouge in Cambodia (two million people). A great resource chronicling these atrocities is the Victims of Communism Memorial Foundation, which was created by a unanimous act of Congress in 1993.

Despite this bloody history, many Western academics—the ones who have never seen a person starve because their food has been taken by the state for redistribution, who have never been forced to report their own parents to the government for subversive thoughts or hidden religious faith—maintain a deep affinity for Marx and his ideas. For a while, these ideas were contained primarily in departments of English literature and economics. But in the latter half of the twentieth century, they began infecting law schools, too.

And like all viruses, the Marxist philosophy mutated as it moved to new hosts.

By the 1960s and 1970s, when Marxism reached the faculty offices and lecture halls of Harvard Law School, it had undergone a series of strange mutations, accumulating influences from different departments until it became something altogether new. From the humanities, it picked up a bit of New Age literary theory, including the work of the French "post-structuralist" Jacques Derrida. In short, Derrida believed that language was meaningless, and that…well, I'll just quote him here, in saying that:

> If writing is no longer understood in the narrow sense of linear and phonetic notation, it should be possible to say that all societies capable of producing, that is to say of obliterating, their proper names, and of bringing classificatory difference into play, practice writing in general. No reality

or concept would therefore correspond to the expression "society without writing." This expression is dependent on ethnocentric oneirism, upon the vulgar, that is to say ethnocentric, misconception of writing.

Now, I think I'm pretty good when it comes to reading comprehension. During my career as a lawyer, I was forced to make my way through some of the most convoluted, so-boring-you-could-scratch-your-eyes out legal prose ever written. Yet I have to admit that I would have real trouble telling anyone what in the world Jacques Derrida means in this passage. Keep in mind, by the way, that this comes on page 110 of the French philosopher's landmark work *Of Grammatology*, and it was selected almost completely at random; there are thousands more sentences that I'm sure are even more complex and verbose.

But for the professors who infiltrated the ranks of Harvard Law School in the '70s, this word salad apparently made perfect sense—enough sense, clearly, for them to cite Derrida in countless articles about the inherent meaninglessness and disutility of the law. One of these professors, a man named Duncan Kennedy, wrote his philosophy down in a short book called *Legal Education and the Reproduction of Hierarchy*, which argued, among other things, that the law served no real purpose other than to perpetuate the interests of the ruling classes. The book, which was printed privately at Professor Kennedy's own expense, contains several citations to Karl Marx and other Marxist theorists of the day. (Kennedy, like many Marxists, enjoyed the trappings of material wealth; each day, on campus, his green Jaguar sat parked outside his office.) As a law student, I took Professor Kennedy's class, and read his academic writings and those of the other Marxists professors at Harvard; I didn't agree with what they were preaching, but I wanted to do my very best to understand and appreciate the possible repercussions if their ideas became more widespread.

In time, Professor Kennedy's philosophy came to be known as Critical Legal Studies, and it spread throughout the 1980s from Harvard

University to other top law schools all over the country. Its proponents argued, in explicitly Marxist fashion, that the law was merely an instrument used by the powerful to keep the lower classes subservient. The "Crits," as they came to be known, then "deconstructed" the law, attempting to show that it, like language, was completely meaningless and served no real useful purpose in society. In articles on everything from criminal justice to taxation, these adherents of Critical Legal Studies spread a new, virulent strain of Marxism throughout the American legal system. Somehow, Harvard Law School, a place that was already so left-wing that President Richard Nixon famously referred to it as the "Kremlin on the Charles," had lurched even further leftward.

Thankfully, Critical Legal Studies began dying out around the late 1980s, as dumb, half-baked theories often do. As it turns out, there are only so many ways you can say "everything is bad and meaningless, especially the law" before the intellectual well runs dry. If nothing else, you simply run out of ways to keep arranging the same words. For a few years, it looked as if the world had seen the last of Critical Legal Studies forever.

But that began to change in the early 1990s, about the same time I arrived on the campus of Harvard Law School to find a student body and a faculty bitterly divided. It was during those years that another group of left-wing radicals, now obsessed with race, gender, and sexuality rather than just economics, attempted once again to re-engineer the virus of Marxism and spread it all over the world. This time, they mixed it with a strange cocktail of race and gender theory made popular by feminist scholars like Judith Butler, a woman whose work remains influential on the left today, as well as scholars in a new field known as "Whiteness studies."

During my time at Harvard, I heard students and professors regurgitating the dead talking points of Critical Legal Studies. Only this time, there was a twist. Instead of attacking capitalism and the ruling classes by themselves, proponents of the New Marxism would talk about sexism, homophobia, and, most importantly, racism. They cited thinkers such as Peggy McIntosh, who had written an article called "White Privilege: Unpacking the Invisible Knapsack," in which she unveiled a theory of "interlocking oppressions." According to this theory, people effectively earned points based on how many victim groups they belonged to: Black people were oppressed, sure, but Black women who also happened to be gay were *three times* as oppressed, and even more deserving of praise.

Again, few of these academics came right out and said this. Back then, they dressed up their ideas in strange, impenetrable sentences and published them in academic journals.

Take this one by Judith Butler, for instance, which would later go on to win first prize in a "world's worst writing" competition hosted by the left-wing British newspaper the *Guardian*:

> The move from a structuralist account in which capital is understood to structure social relations in relatively homologous ways to a view of hegemony in which power relations are subject to repetition, convergence, and rearticulation brought the question of temporality into the thinking of structure, and marked a shift from a form of Althusserian theory that takes structural totalities as theoretical objects to one in which the insights into the contingent possibility of structure inaugurate a renewed conception of hegemony as bound up with the contingent sites and strategies of the rearticulation of power.[7]

If you had to Google "Althusserian," as I did, you might be surprised to learn that Louis Pierre Althusser was a Marxist professor in France, beset by mental illness, who murdered his own wife, strangling her in a moment of madness. Clearly, a weighty authority.

At first glance, you might think that left-wing academics like Judith Butler need to use this dense language because they are discussing really deep, complicated ideas. Perhaps they cannot express themselves in simple, clear language like the rest of us because their thoughts are simply too highbrow for short sentences and monosyllabic words.

But this isn't the case.

In his excellent book *The Madness of Crowds: Gender, Race and Identity*, British journalist Douglas Murray investigates the roots of modern leftist ideologies such as radical feminism and Critical Race Theory. In discussing the writing of Judith Butler, Kimberle Crenshaw, and other prominent leftists whose ideas gained currency among law professors in the early '90s, Murray notes that one thing these people all have in common is that their work is "unreadable."

"Their writing," he continues, "has the deliberately obstructive style ordinarily employed when someone either has nothing to say or needs to conceal the fact that what they are saying is not true." After quoting the passage from Judith Butler above, Murray notes that "prose this bad can only occur when the author is trying to hide something."

Remember, this wasn't nuclear physics. What Butler and others were trying to hide, of course, was that their ideas were nonsense. When subjected even to the mildest scrutiny, all that jargon comes tumbling down like a house of cards. This is exactly what happened in the late 1980s, when Critical Legal Studies fell apart. People realized that there was really no substance to all this impenetrable language and began letting the theory die on its own. But this time around, the repackaged ideas were now immune to criticism. Anyone who attempted to argue with them was quickly labeled a racist or a sexist, foreshadowing tactics that the left would take for decades to come.

By February 1993, shortly after I arrived at Harvard, the campus had become so divided over this new identity politics that the magazine GQ published a piece titled "Beirut on the Charles," a reference to bitter fights that occurred among professors and students. This article, written by journalist John Sedgwick, described some of the more ridiculous actions that Critical Race Theorists (although they weren't called that at the time) were taking on campus. He writes, for instance, about a mock trial of Christopher Columbus that was held in early 1993. The event, in Sedgwick's telling, "had all the levity of the Nuremberg trials."

During this mock trial, which featured students playing the roles of prosecutors, defense attorneys, and, of course, Christopher Columbus himself, fake prosecutors leveled charges of "racism, genocide, greed, and peer exploitation" at the student playing Columbus. "Two witnesses," he writes, "then spoke for the Black and Native American peoples and gave stone-faced accounts of their many sufferings."[8] Anyone who has read about the ridiculous scenes that often play out at modern universities—students shouting down conservative speakers over false charges of racism, for instance, or holding protests because of "cultural appropriation" in the dining halls—will surely recognize these activities at Harvard Law School in the '90s as the beginning of something quite sinister. Soon, it would spread everywhere.

Bear in mind, by the way, that every student who got up to accuse a fake Christopher Columbus of crimes in the year 1993 was an enrolled student at Harvard Law School. Presumably, they went on to become lawyers and judges, bringing their warped belief in Critical Race Theory with them. During my three years at Harvard Law, which intersected for two years with those of a young Ketanji Brown Jackson, Critical Race Theory metastasized even further, spreading among the faculty to other graduate schools at Harvard University, and eventually other law schools as well.

The question, of course, is how CRT managed to get from law schools and humanities departments into classrooms and corporate boardrooms all over the country. Even though I was there for the inception of Critical Race Theory, I confess that for a while, I didn't fully appreciate how dangerous it was. I thought that surely, once this nonsense got beyond the sheltered campuses of our elite universities, it would die out in the same manner that Critical Legal Studies had a few years earlier.

But that didn't happen.

Instead, the virus of CRT spread all over the university system, including to our graduate schools of education. This time, there was virtually no one who stood up to oppose it. Anyone who even tried would be quickly labeled a bigot, and those charges, particularly in university culture in the early 2000s, were enough to kill academic careers before they had even begun. In his book *The Critical Turn in Education: From Marxist Critique to Poststructuralist Feminism to Critical Theories of Race*, scholar Isaac Gottesman lays out exactly what happened.

"In the mid-1990s," he writes, "scholars in the field of education began drawing upon CRT as a framework to make sense of racism and inequality within educational systems. This was a landmark moment in the field. As was the case with the emergence of Marxist thought and postmodernist and poststructuralist feminist theory, the emergence of CRT radically transformed educational inquiry and discourse."

Professor Gottesman outlines in painstaking detail how the work of critical race theorists such as Kimberle Crenshaw became not only popular, but required, in schools of education. The same goes for the work of Derrick Bell, another foundational thinker in Critical Race Theory. (Judge Jackson, in a speech to the University of Michigan Law School, described in depth how foundational Derrick Bell's writing was for her personally.) For the next two decades, these graduate schools of education trained the future teachers of America to view the world through the lens of race and nothing else. They taught young educators that White people were at the top of a racial hierarchy that kept people of color oppressed. Soon, the buzzwords emerged: *White privilege, spirit murder, systemic racism, Whiteness, oppressor, oppressed, equity, anti-racism, collective guilt, affinity spaces.*

Then, those young teachers went out into the world and began teaching this nonsense to students. They also filled the administrative staffs of our schools and other educational institutions. These young teachers did not, of course, teach children as young as three and four years old to read the work of Judith Butler, Kimberle Crenshaw, or other jargon-laden articles from law reviews. But they did take those concepts and adapt them for young minds. Rather than the dense prose of Derrick Bell, for instance, they used the simplified work of the new antiracist movement—people like Ibram Kendi, Robin DiAngelo, and Nikole Hannah-Jones, writers whose work just so happened to be available in formats especially made for young readers.

It was Nikole Hannah-Jones who led the 1619 Project for the *New York Times*. That project was explicitly revisionist history; its goal was to "revise" U.S. history so that our nation did not start in 1776 with the Declaration of Independence, or in 1789 with the ratification of the Constitution, but rather in 1619 with the first arrival of slaves from Africa on U.S. soil. Moreover, the 1619 Project asserted that "one of the primary reasons the colonists decided to declare independence was because they wanted to protect the institution of slavery."

This incendiary claim emerges directly from Critical Race Theory. It also is a lie. So much so that numerous acclaimed historians, like Princeton's James McPherson and Brown University's Gordon Wood, called it out as historically inaccurate and deceptive. McPherson said the 1619 essays were "a very unbalanced, one-sided account, which lacked context and perspective"; Wood elaborated, explicitly rebutting Hannah-Jones's revisionist claim that the Revolution occurred to try to preserve slavery as "so wrong in so many ways," and contrary to the radical ideas upon which our nation was founded, such as "all men are created equal." Indeed, the scholarly refutation was so overwhelming that, sheepishly, the *New York Times* was forced to issue a correction deleting that false claim.

Leftists claim that anyone criticizing the 1619 Project is trying to erase slavery from our history. That, of course, is a straw man. Slavery was the original sin of America, a grotesque abomination that enslaved, tortured, and murdered countless African Americans. Slavery was evil, and America fought a bloody Civil War—where more than 600,000 Americans lost their lives—to expunge that sin. And, in the century and a half since then, our journey toward civil rights and equal justice has been halting and imperfect. No reasonable person denies that.

But what is unique about America is not slavery; tragically, societies throughout history, for millennia, employed the brutal practice of slavery.

What is unique about America is emancipation, and that our founding ideals put us on the path toward it. The Declaration proclaimed, "We hold these truths to be self-evident: That *all men* are created equal." Was there hypocrisy in the fact that the author of those words, Thomas Jefferson, was himself a slave owner? Of course. But the powerful ideals his pen memorialized set us on the path to liberation.

The 1619 Project maintains that America is irredeemably racist. That is false. It claims that our founding documents were written to perpetuate slavery. That is a lie. It erases the heroic work of countless abolitionists—including many among our framers—who fought tirelessly to end the scourge of slavery. It argues that our founding principles were corrupt from the outset. That's precisely the opposite of the approach taken by civil rights champions from Frederick Douglass to W. E. B. Du Bois to Dr. King—who explicitly appealed to our founding principles, arguing (rightly) that we needed to do a better job of living up to their nobility. As Frederick Douglass put it in his immortal "What to the Slave Is the Fourth of July" speech, delivered in 1852 (before the Civil War) and excoriating the horrific evil of slavery that still existed:

> Allow me to say, in conclusion, notwithstanding the dark picture I have this day presented, of the state of the nation, I do not despair of this country. There are forces in operation, which must inevitably, work the downfall of slavery. "The arm of the Lord is not shortened," and the doom of slavery is certain.
>
> I, therefore, leave off where I began, with hope. While drawing encouragement from "the Declaration of Independence," the great principles it contains, and the genius of American Institutions, my spirit is also cheered by the obvious tendencies of the age.

But appealing to America's "great principles" in our long journey toward justice—as Dr. King put it, "the arc of the moral universe is long, but it bends toward justice"—is the opposite of what Marxist proponents of CRT teach. Instead, they argue that America is irredeemably racist, and our institutions and laws and "great principles" exist to perpetuate that racism.

When it came to the 1619 Project, Judge Jackson gave a speech at the University of Michigan Law School embracing it, expressly praising "acclaimed investigative journalist Nikole Hannah-Jones" and her "provocative thesis that the America that was born in 1776 was not the perfect union that it purported to be."

And the 1619 Project was always intended for indoctrination. Indeed, in the years since the original magazine piece was published, Nikole Hannah-Jones has appeared at several events with educators who have, in the words of her publisher, "incorporated the original '1619 Project' issue of the *New York Times Magazine* in their classrooms in creative and compelling ways."[9] In 2021, Hannah-Jones published *Born in the Water*, a children's story that takes the main ideas of the 1619 Project and smuggles them into the brains of children in a pretty, colorfully designed picture book. The very same strategy was used to produce Ibram Kendi's *Antiracist Baby*.

Indeed, the Pulitzer Center's 2020 annual report assessed that the pernicious and discredited 1619 curriculum is currently being taught in more than 4,500 classrooms across America.

Not long ago, during an episode of my chart-topping weekly podcast *Verdict with Ted Cruz* (you should subscribe!), I spoke with a journalist and documentary filmmaker named Christopher Rufo about the pernicious phenomenon of Critical Race Theory. For several years, Rufo, who lives in the liberal hub of Seattle, has been following and carefully chronicling the development of this twisted ideology. Looking back, it is clear that he saw the warning signs long before most other people.

When I asked Rufo what it looked like when Critical Race Theory entered schools, he made an interesting point, noting that it all comes back to Marxist theory:

Like all Marxist ideologies, you have theory and praxis—general ideas and then the practical implementation of those ideas. That's embedded in Critical Race Theory. What it looks like in a scholarly paper—obviously, they're not teaching kindergarteners how to read the *Harvard Law Review*, what they are teaching kindergarteners can be thought of as applied Critical Race Theory.

So, you might wonder, what does Marxist "praxis" look like when it's done to our children? Keep reading if you dare.

Praxis

Two years ago, at an elementary school in Buffalo, New York, a kindergarten teacher announced to her class that today, instead of doing their ordinary lessons, they would be watching a video. I'm sure the children rejoiced, at least for a few seconds. Perhaps they thought they were about to watch a cartoon about talking animals or an episode of *VeggieTales*. Why, after all, would it be anything else? These children were in kindergarten.

But that's not what showed up on the screen.

Instead, the children were subjected to a long video of animated Black children speaking to them in solemn voices. These children, the kindergarteners learned over the course of the video, were dead. They had been murdered by "racist police and state-sanctioned violence."

Now, it's been a long time since I was in kindergarten. It's been several years since I've even had a child in kindergarten. But I do not remember hearing anything about horrific videos of murdered ghost children from when my daughters were in school. Perhaps that's because I wasn't paying enough attention. But I think a better explanation is that something has changed in American education since then—something that urgently needs to be reversed.

According to lesson plans that were leaked to Christopher Rufo, the students in that kindergarten class in Buffalo were watching such strange videos because they needed to learn about "systemic racism." Five years later, when the students reached the fifth grade, they would be taught that the United States of America—an irredeemably racist place that makes Black people suffer for no good reason—"had created a 'school-to-grave pipeline' for Black children and that, as adults, 'one million Black people are locked in cages.'"[10]

This, it turns out, was all part of a plan developed by Fatima Morrell, the "diversity czar" of Buffalo Public Schools. One of the many teachers who was trained at Marxist-influenced schools of education—including a stint at Harvard, the birthplace of Critical Race Theory—Morrell made it her mission to make Buffalo schools more "woke." According to Christopher Rufo's analysis of her documents, she "created a new curriculum promoting Black Lives Matter in the classroom and an 'antiracist' training program for teachers...[pushing] 'radical politics,' [which], in practice, become a series of 'scoldings, guilt-trips, and demands to demean oneself simply to make another feel empowered.' Teachers must submit to these 'manipulative mind games' and express support for Morrell's left-wing politics, or risk professional retaliation."[11]

Sadly, Morrell was not alone. She is one of thousands of similarly educated left-wing radicals who have taken control of our education system and attempted to twist it to suit the political needs of the modern Democratic Party.

The same thing happened at the William D. Kelley School in Philadelphia, where students were told to celebrate Angela Davis, the activist who gained notoriety in the '60s and '70s working with the Communist Party and the Black Panthers. "Investigators," according to Fox News, "linked [Davis] to the purchase of weapons later used by three inmates who took a judge and juror hostage during their trial in 1970 for killing a prison guard. Law enforcement officials responded with a barrage of bullets, and the inmates and judge later died."[12] Six decades later, a teacher in Philadelphia "led the ten- and eleven-year-old students into the auditorium to 'simulate' a Black Power rally to 'free Angela Davis' from prison, where she had once been held while awaiting trial on charges of conspiracy, kidnapping, and murder. The students marched on the stage, holding signs that read 'Black Power,' 'Jail Trump,' 'Free Angela,' and 'Black Power Matters.'"[13]

All this while the William D. Kelley School, whose students are mostly disadvantaged children of color, keeps its spot as one of the worst-performing schools in Philadelphia. "By sixth grade," according to Rufo, "only 3 percent of students are proficient in math, and 9 percent are proficient in reading. By graduation, only 13 percent of Kelley students will have achieved basic literacy."[14]

Once again, these left-wing radicals are harming the very students they purport to want to help. The same is true of elementary and secondary educators all over the country. Thanks to the bravery of whistle-blowers and the work of investigative reporters such as Christopher Rufo, Andy Ngo, and others, a few minutes of Internet research now reveals just how far Critical Race Theory has spread into our education system. Elementary school students all over the country now participate in "privilege walks," an exercise that requires White children to acknowledge their roles as oppressors and Black children to embrace their roles as the oppressed. Children are told that the United States is a hopelessly racist place, and that Dr. King's dream of a colorblind society is nothing but a tool of oppression to be used against people of color.

The children in Philadelphia were instructed to march holding "Free Angela Davis" signs. In addition to her active involvement in multiple violent acts of terrorism, Angela Davis was also the Communist Party's vice presidential nominee in both 1980 and 1984. (John Brennan, Obama's CIA director, cast his own vote for Gus Hall and Davis in 1980.) And here's how Kendi's *Stamped (for Kids)* ends its final chapter:

> From the beginning, racist ideas have been stamped into the United States—into the Constitution, laws, policies, practices, and beliefs of segregationists and assimilationists. Antiracists

continue their work in helping us become tied to antiracist ideas and to use them to lift people up. Turning potential into power. *People like Angela Davis*. Like [BLM founder and avowed Marxist] Patrisse Cullors. And, *perhaps, like me and you.*

Parents Rise Up

Isaac Newton taught us that, for every action, there is an equal and opposite reaction. Well, the insanity of CRT is producing its reaction across the nation.

Just north of Fort Worth, Texas, lies the small, affluent town of Southlake. Hardly where one would imagine a major CRT battleground. Yet, on July 31, 2020, the Southlake school board quietly released the agenda for the next school board meeting, just three days later, and on it was a seemingly minor reference to the consideration of their "Cultural Competence Action Plan (CCAP)." The thirty-four-page CCAP was a radical document, which would have:

> created "an equity and inclusion grievance process system";
> expanded the district tip-line to include equity and inclusion;
> conducted an "equity audit" of curriculum and policies;
> established a diversity and inclusion week "and/or" diversity
> and inclusion day; mandated diversity and inclusion training
> for students; instituted mechanisms to "hold staff account-
> able for equity and inclusion work"; added "diversity into
> teaching materials and instruction in all classrooms";
> audited every student group on diversity-and-inclusion
> grounds; and on and on....
>
> Indeed, the most insidious part of the plan proposed to
> "[s]trengthen wording and consequences" in the student
> code of conduct "for microaggressions and discriminatory
> behavior." It called for creating "a process for campus
> administrators to include incident notes to document

microaggressions and discriminatory behaviors in the discipline offense history for students.[15]

Although many Southlake families were on vacation then, and the school board had given just three days' notice, word spread like wildfire throughout the community. Community activists Leigh Wambsganss and Tim O'Hare began organizing a petition to try to stop the CCAP; within hours, more than 2,600 people signed the petition—out of a town of just 32,000 people. Many of them showed up at the school board meeting and spoke out; the board paused the plan. Then, the activists filed public-information requests, and they found out that "an assistant superintendent had traveled to events and spoken on social-justice themes and bad-mouthed the community. The administration spent $15,000 for a staff-training talk by a motivational speaker named Adolph Brown; his website boasts 'The actualization of diversity and inclusion is Dr. Brown's life's work.'"[16]

Realizing they had a bigger problem, the parents formed a PAC and, in the coming weeks, raised over $250,000.

And then they began interviewing people to run for school board.

There were two seats up for re-election on the seven-member school board. One of the organizers explained the parents' approach:

> We wound up interviewing six candidates, and these interviews were about two hours each…and they all had the same questions, and it was a very organized effort. We had seventeen people in the room. [We] led the questions so that everyone got the same questions, but then at the end we opened it up to anyone on the committee who wanted to ask additional questions.

Because a candidate only needed a plurality to win, the parents agreed not to run multiple candidates and split the vote; instead, they decided to unite around one candidate for each seat. Together, they coalesced around Hannah Smith and Cam Bryan. Smith is a mom of four young kids, a lawyer, and a former law clerk for Justice Clarence Thomas and Justice Samuel Alito. Bryan is a dad of two young kids and a successful businessman who spent a decade coaching youth football and who is beloved in the community. The two ran as a ticket and conducted more than seventy meet-and-greets over three months.

Typical turnout in a school board election is very low, often 10 percent or less. This time, on election day in May 2021, over 40 percent of the citizens showed up to vote. And the parents won with nearly 70 percent of the vote.

Shortly thereafter, another school board member quit, and in November 2021 the Southlake families elected a third board member with 66 percent of the vote.

Then, in May 2022, the Southlake families elected two more board members, this time with over 70 percent of the vote. The parents now hold a 5–2 majority. All since the summer of 2020.

These parents in Southlake sparked a movement. In that same May 2022 election, three other Tarrant County school districts—in Keller, Grapevine-Colleyville, and Mansfield—all followed the Southlake model. Parents ran conservative candidates in each district, vigorously campaigning against CRT. Every single one prevailed, beating multiple incumbents and flipping control of the boards.

The same thing happened in Houston (where I backed several insurgent candidates), in Spring Branch (a Houston suburb), and in communities across the nation. And we are seeing the same pattern replicated all across the nation.

When parents stand up and speak out, they can beat Critical Race Theory.

* * *

The children whose parents care enough to educate them about real American history might make it out of school unscathed. But those whose parents are okay with left-wing ideology, or who are (quite understandably) too afraid to resist, might do serious damage to their children—and, in the process, to our justice system. It is these children, after all, who will cast ballots for district attorney races across the country; it is these children who will serve on juries during criminal trials, and it is these children who will run for office, deciding what the justice system—and the United States—will look like long after we're gone.

This, as we have learned during the past few years, can be a very dangerous thing. One need only read the news from around the country to learn how dangerous it can be when half-baked ideas like Critical Race Theory, once confined to the halls of universities and left-wing think tanks, begin to directly infect our justice system.

CHAPTER FIVE

LAWLESSNESS

On November 21, 2021, after more than a year of being kept apart due to concerns about COVID-19, the citizens of Waukesha, Wisconsin, finally gathered again for their annual Christmas parade. The parade, held every year on the Sunday before Thanksgiving, was supposed to kick off the holiday season in joyous fashion. Groups of children in elf costumes danced down the streets to festive music. Their parents held hand-painted signs and sipped hot cocoa from paper cups, watching as the floats and community groups marched slowly down Main Street. One of these groups, a dozen or so octogenarian women known as the "dancing grannies," drew the usual hoots and bursts of laughter from the crowd.

Tragically, these festivities would not last long.

A few miles away, a man named Darrell Brooks got into an altercation over a drug deal gone wrong. A thirty-nine-year-old aspiring rapper who'd spent almost enough time in court to earn a seat with his name on it, Brooks was no stranger to senseless violence. In 1999, when he was only seventeen years old, Brooks had pleaded guilty to inflicting substantial bodily harm against another person. A few years later, during a routine traffic stop, a police officer had been forced to climb into Brooks's car to stop him from fleeing the scene, wrestling him for control of the steering wheel. In July 2020, he had fired a gun at one of his relatives and a friend, resulting in "two felony counts of second-degree recklessly endangering safety and possession of a firearm by a felon." For those charges, Brooks was brought before a judge, who set bail at $10,000, then quickly lowered it to $7,500.

At the time, a program known as "bail reform" was sweeping the nation. Proponents of the policy argued that charging money to be released from prison before trial was unfair to criminals, particularly criminals of color. John T. Chisholm, the district attorney in Milwaukee County, where Brooks had been arrested, had been one of the first public officials in the nation to implement such policies. During his campaign in 2007, Chisholm had promised to remake the county's justice system so that it better served the aims of racial "equity" (that CRT code word). He had vowed during his speeches to make it much easier for criminals, including violent ones, to get out of jail while they awaited trial. He had also promised to "divert" drug offenders from prison to treatment centers. Asked during an interview about the danger that such policies might pose, Chisholm had answered with a cold, detached certainty.

"Is there going to be an individual I divert," he said, "or I put into a treatment program, who's going to go out and kill somebody? You bet. Guaranteed. *It's guaranteed to happen.* It does not invalidate the overall approach."

For the next decade, Chisholm and his team implemented these policies with devastating results. In 2020, a year when riots broke out across America and homicides in major cities rose at a shocking rate of 32 percent nationwide, the murder rate in Milwaukee rose at *three times* that rate. To make matters worse, the criminals who committed these acts were often shuffled into courtrooms, given outrageously low bail, and then released back onto the streets once their bond was paid.

Despite the carnage going on in cities like Milwaukee, which had adopted these policies earlier than most, Chisholm was roundly praised by the liberal media. In 2015, CNN's scandal-ridden legal analyst, Jeffrey Toobin, wrote that Chisholm had "stuck his neck out there and started saying that prosecutors should... be judged by their success in reducing mass incarceration and achieving racial equity."[1] Chisholm was similarly praised in the op-ed pages of major newspapers all over the country.

After reading this praise, far-left prosecutors and government officials in other cities sought to implement similar reforms. In 2018, the state of California passed a bail reform law. In 2019, spurred on by Congresswoman Alexandria Ocasio-Cortez, New York City did the same thing. As of this writing, Chisholm's website brags that "progressive prosecutors in Philadelphia, Boston, St. Louis, and San Francisco have followed in John's footsteps," which is certainly true. Whenever they met resistance from rational people, these leaders claimed that although overall crime might rise, these policies were worth it because they would further the goal of racial "equity."

There will be consequences, they seemed to say. *We just don't care.*

It was only a matter of time before ordinary citizens paid the price.

In February 2021, after a delay in his trial for firearm charges, Darrell Brooks's lawyer asked for his bail to be lowered again. It was—this time to the measly sum of $500. All Brooks had to do was promise to show up for a sentencing hearing on November 11, more than ten months from the date of his release, and he was allowed to walk right out the door. For the next ten months, he was free to commit as many senseless acts of violence as he wished.

He didn't wait that entire time.

Nine months later, on November 2, just a few days before his hearing on his previous charges, Brooks knocked on the door of a hotel room in Milwaukee. When the woman inside the room answered, Brooks accosted her, stole her cell phone, then drove off with it in his car, a maroon 2010 Ford Escape. A few hours later, he spotted the woman walking toward a gas station and pulled up beside her, asking her to get in his car. When she refused and tried to run away, Brooks ran her over with his car, evidenced by the tire marks that were later found on her pants. Thankfully, the woman survived.

Brooks was again taken into custody.

Surely, you might think, *this* time would be different. Even under his own ridiculously liberal bail policies, the district attorney of Milwaukee County would not allow a man who had repeatedly attacked his fellow citizens with his fists, a gun, *and now his car* to walk free once more.

But that's exactly what happened. Bail was set at just $1,000. Brooks paid it, and then walked free a few hours later.

That is how, on November 21—only nineteen days after being released yet again on bail—and just moments after fleeing the scene of a knife fight, Brooks once more found himself behind the wheel of his red Ford Escape—the very same SUV that he had used to run over a woman just weeks earlier. With grim resolve, he turned the wheel toward Main Street in Waukesha, where the annual Christmas parade had just begun. Finally, after many years of close calls and lucky breaks, the world was about to feel the full wrath of a psychopath like Darrell Brooks.

His car broke through the wooden barricades at 4:39 p.m., just as the "dancing grannies" were making their way down the street. At first, I'm sure spectators assumed that there had been some horrible accident. Perhaps they thought Brooks had fallen asleep at the wheel or had a heart attack while driving. But rather than slowing down, the truck picked up speed. Soon it was clear that Brooks wasn't swerving to avoid people.

He was aiming for them.

For the next few horrible seconds, Brooks's truck made its bloody way up Main Street, striking parade-goers, many of them children, as it went. At one point, Brooks leaned out the window to get a better view of the crowds; his windshield had become too littered with lifeless bodies for him to see. By the time he finally crashed, Brooks had killed five people and injured sixty-two more (including sixteen children). By the time the world learned Brooks's name and began guessing as to his motives for the crime, the death toll had risen from five to six, one of whom was an eight-year-old child.

In reviewing the case, district attorney John Chisholm's office reluctantly admitted that the $1,000 bail on which Darrell Brooks had been released a few weeks before the attack was "inappropriately low."

No kidding.

The report they released said nothing about his bail in the other cases, or the devastating effects of Chisholm's bail reform policies more generally. They seemed to know that in the United States in 2022, devout liberals like Chisholm were effectively immunized from scrutiny. They knew that the corporate press would not ask hard questions about their policies, and that there would be no marches in the streets or riots for the six victims who'd been murdered partly due to their incompetence. All they had to do was keeping preaching "woke" orthodoxy, and they would be politically safe.

Over the next few weeks, the corporate press proved this to be the case. For days after the attack, outlets such as CNN and NPR described how "an SUV" had killed multiple people. The PBS headline on November 22 was typical: "Multiple people killed *by SUV* in Waukesha Christmas parade." Not a violent criminal, improperly released on ridiculously low bail, but rather an inanimate object. Reading or watching these reports, you might have thought that the red Ford Escape had come straight from the pages of a Stephen King novel, acting on its own accord to mow down sixty-seven innocent people.

As the days went on, the reasons for the media's odd grammar became clear.

Brooks, who happened to be African American, did not fit the mold of a deranged mass murderer—at least not the mold you might be used to if you're a frequent reader of the *New York Times* or a viewer of CNN and MSNBC. Even if you're not a regular consumer of those news outlets—congratulations, by the way—I'm sure you're familiar with what terrorists are *supposed* to look like in the year 2022: young, White, usually disaffected and "radicalized" by far-right message boards on the Internet. Preferably wearing a MAGA hat. Usually, we're told, their attacks involve guns that have been purchased legally, and the victims are members of some permanent victim class. When that sort of person attacks, the media is always more than happy to plaster his name all over the place.

Similarly, when White police officers tragically kill young Black men—something that happens far less frequently than the media would have you believe—the incidents receive wall-to-wall coverage on nearly every major media outlet in the country. Usually, the individual who is killed is an armed criminal, actively threatening others or violently resisting arrest, but that fact is ignored or aggressively downplayed in the corporate media. This is because they want to frame the incidents to support the media narrative that was decided on long ago: White people in the United States are oppressors, committing crimes against a permanent victim class, and anyone who says otherwise is racist, case closed.

A few months before the attack in Waukesha occurred, a young man named Kyle Rittenhouse shot two people in self-defense while attempting to protect the nearby city of Kenosha from rioters and looters. When the corporate press got a load of *that* story, they weren't shy at all about immediately labeling Rittenhouse a domestic terrorist, or from attaching a racial motive to the case.

In an opinion piece for *Yahoo! News*, a writer named David Love wrote that "Rittenhouse continues a long tradition of self-deputized White men who believe their job is to police and terrorize Black people."[2] Nowhere in the piece does the author mention that Rittenhouse did not, in fact, shoot *any* Black people. The people he shot were both White—a fact that would be largely ignored by the mainstream media for the next several months.

During their investigation, police plumbed the young Rittenhouse's social media feeds for potentially racist remarks and also scoured his cell phone, which Rittenhouse gave over voluntarily, for evidence that the attacks had been racially motivated. It was only after a lengthy trial, during which a video recording of the incident was played for the jury, that Rittenhouse was found not guilty on all charges. The jury concluded that, based on the evidence, the three people he shot were dangerous rioters (all three with extensive criminal histories), who were directly and violently threatening his life.

With Darrell Brooks, however, the media felt no such obligation to look for a racial motive, although there was certainly one to be found. For years, Brooks had been posting on social media about his desire to harm White people, often explicitly citing ideas that come straight from Critical Race Theory and its proponents. In July, he had posted his passionate support for the Marxist organization Black Lives Matter.

Take, for example, this post from June 9, 2020:

"Learned and taught behavior!! So when we start bakk knokkin white ppl TF out ion wana hear it.. the old white ppl 2 KNOKK DEM TF OUT!! PERIOD.."

Or this one, from May 13, 2017:

"This is not the land of the free and home of the brave. It's the land of the stolen and home of the slave."

Given the obsession in our culture with race and racism, you might think that the media would have pounced on these messages. After all, they represent as clear an example of racism as you're likely to find anywhere. If you don't think so, you might try an experiment: wherever the word "White" appears in those messages, replace it with "Black" or "Jewish," and see whether you still have any doubts.

Of course, reporting on these statements might have presented a problem for the corporate press. After all, many of them sound as if they could have been spoken on a CNN prime-time show without eliciting so much as a sidelong glance from the panelists, nearly all of whom would support the idea that the United States is "the land of the stolen and home of the slave." In August 2019, the *New York Times Magazine* said almost precisely that when it published Nikole Hannah-Jones's 5,000-word introduction to the 1619 Project.

The media also didn't bother to listen to the music that Brooks had produced under his rap name MathBoi Fly, which might also have indicated a tendency toward racism, or at least a propensity for violence. In one of the songs, titled "Gon Kill U," he rapped the lyrics, "Sliding through the city with no safety on," and "f**k the pigs." In another, he raps, "They gonna need a cleaner for the s*** we did/all my killers Gacey where them bodies hid."

Again, this might have been useful information. But the corporate press decided that it would be far better to ignore the man who'd been behind the wheel that day in Waukesha—instead, it was just a self-driving car—attempting instead to sweep the whole thing under the rug and await the next act that could be labeled White supremacist violence.

As of this writing, Darrell Brooks has yet to stand trial for his crimes. There is no indication of how that trial will proceed when it happens, or of whether Brooks will be found guilty when it's over. But one thing is certain. His case is not a one-time event, and he will not be the last career criminal to commit an act of violence that could have been prevented by a stronger, more sensible criminal justice system. For more than two decades, the world got relatively lucky when it came to Darrell Brooks. The people he attempted to shoot survived, literally dodging bullets; the woman he tried to run over with his car got mostly out of the way just in time. Then, one morning in November, our luck ran out and he murdered six people.

This was allowed to happen because a certain kind of prosecutor—one who believes that the United States of America is a hopelessly racist hellscape, where the primary objective of the law should be to bring about racial "equity" rather than punish violent criminals—was allowed to impose his strange, misguided ideology on Milwaukee County. If Darrell Brooks had been held on bail that was even slightly higher than the small amounts he paid to get out of jail, he might not have been able to pay it and the world might have been spared the senseless murders he committed.

But the country did not learn the right lesson from that tragic massacre. As of this writing, the various campaigns for bail and sentencing reform have only gained steam in major cities. Importantly, there's a big difference between reasonable criminal justice reform (which shortens mandatory sentences for *non*-violent offenses and expands drug treatment programs), and these left-wing crusades to release *violent* offenders from jail. Violence is different; and far too many violent offenders predictably re-offend and hurt or kill more innocent people.

If this were the will of the people, that would be one thing. But, as always, what's happening goes much deeper than the ballot box. If you're wondering just how these absurd policies have come to dominate the discourse on criminal justice in the United States, you should take the advice of the ace reporters who managed to unravel the Watergate conspiracy—advice which, admittedly, was added after the fact by the screenwriter of *All the President's Men*, but still applies:

Follow the money.

The Soros Prosecutors

During the lead-up to the 2016 presidential election, massive political donations flowed into the presidential race. This is typical. When I was still in the running, for instance, I raised over $92 million from concerned citizens all over the country—the most money every raised in the history of Republican presidential primaries. That historic support came from more than 1.5 million contributions, averaging $59.90 each. The other candidates were likewise raising tens of millions. When we dropped out, however, leaving only Donald Trump and Hillary Clinton, the money from major donors all went to those two campaigns.

Well, *almost* all of it.

Around that time, the ultrawealthy billionaire George Soros, born in Hungary and radicalized over a decades-long career in hedge funds, began funneling a large chunk of his massive fortune into smaller, less noteworthy races all over the United States. Suddenly, the well-known supporter of radical left-wing causes such as police "reform," reparations, and court packing seemed more interested in local races for district attorney than he was in the most consequential presidential race of his lifetime. An article in *Politico* at the time referred to this effort, quite presciently, as "an under-the-radar 2016 campaign to advance one of the progressive movement's core goals: reshaping the American justice system."[3]

At the time, according to *Politico*, Soros had funneled more than $3 million into seven local district attorney campaigns that year, "a sum that [exceeded] the total spent on the 2016 presidential campaign by all but a handful of super-donors."

It should come as no surprise that all of the candidates Soros supported in those races—none of whom would have had a prayer of getting elected without his massive campaign war chest backing them up—were some of the most far-left prosecutors that the United States had ever seen. These were people who had seen the work of men like John Chisholm in Milwaukee County, applauded, and then said, effectively, "You think *that's* crazy? Hold my latte."

For several months, operating under everyone's radar—which, considering the Republican who was at the top of the ticket at the time, wasn't all that hard to do—Soros and a small group of political foundations in his shady network funneled money into these races, seeing them as their best chance to corrupt the American justice system from the inside.

They were correct.

When it comes to the prosecution of criminals, there are few elected officials with more power than your district attorney. As soon as they're elected, district attorneys have the power to decide what crimes to prosecute in your county and whom to prosecute; there's an old adage that, if a DA asks it to, a grand jury will indict a ham sandwich. Electing radical DAs dramatically increases the chance that criminal prosecutions will be used as partisan weapons to target their political opponents.

But, perhaps even more importantly, DAs have enormous discretion about which cases *not* to prosecute. If a district attorney decides, for instance, that assault with a wrench should not be prosecuted in his county and sends a memo around the office that says so, it effectively becomes legal in that county to run up to people, attack them with a wrench, and run away. This, as several astute commentators have pointed out, represents a direct encroachment upon the powers of the legislative branches of local governments. But, for now, it's perfectly legal.

So, if you were a determined billionaire looking to upend the established order in the United States, this was a good place to begin. While the corporate media was focused on Vladimir Putin and alleged Russian interference in our elections, another rich, foreign-born character was doing the real work of rotting our justice system from within.

And this one paid off.

On election night, while the world was reeling over the election of President Trump, each one of Soros's preferred DA candidates won their races. Either the people who voted in these cities had become extremely liberal and insane overnight, or those millions of dollars played a major hand in the victories. In the span of just a few months, local races for district attorney became battles that unfolded on the national stage. No matter what the people in these counties wanted—no matter how they attempted to make their voices heard—they could now be effectively overruled by enormous amounts of money.

In Philadelphia, for instance, Soros had supported a long-shot candidate named Larry Krasner. For years, Krasner had made a name for himself by suing the police. He also represented Black Lives Matter and Occupy Philadelphia, an offshoot of Occupy Wall Street. There's nothing wrong with that, of course. But it did seem strange that he wanted to use that experience to now take on a law enforcement role. After all, what does someone who has never interacted with the police anywhere other than opposing them in a courtroom know about how to prosecute crimes?

The people of Philadelphia agreed. Even with an eye-popping investment of $1.4 million from the George Soros machine, Krasner didn't initially do terribly well in the polls. With only weeks to go before election night, it seemed as if one of the other six candidates for DA might edge him out. But then, thanks to another last-minute $211,000 donation from Soros, Krasner emerged victorious on election night. Taking stock of the election a few weeks later, representatives from local political groups grew concerned.

"I have a general and growing concern about how we seem to be nationalizing local elections," said David Thornburgh, whose group Community of Seventy keeps an eye on corruption in local politics. "You know, these independent expenditures flowing from elsewhere are kind of Exhibit A of how that's playing out. And if this continues, it starts to feel like Philadelphians lose control of our own elections."

In Chicago, another radical, a woman named Kim Foxx, became the state's attorney.

For the next four years, these "Soros prosecutors" wreaked havoc in counties across the United States. They used their immense discretionary power to achieve their benefactor's goal of remaking the U.S. justice system from the bottom up. They would work not to prosecute criminals and make our cities safer, as such things apparently did not matter to the billionaire donor who supported them. Instead, they would attempt to achieve social and racial "equity" at all costs, working to make sure that as few people went to jail as possible.

For the most part, that involved not doing much of anything at all.

In Chicago, where the rate of violent crime was already shockingly high, Kim Foxx declared that theft cases involving less than $1,000 would no longer be prosecuted by her office. This meant, in effect, that anyone could walk the streets of Chicago and steal up to $999 in cash from anyone, then walk right up to a police officer and wave the cash in his face without fear of arrest. After all, why would the police make the arrest if the criminal is not going to be charged?

In Baltimore, Marilyn Mosby—one of Soros's first handpicked prosecutors, elected in 2015 thanks to millions of dollars in donations from his various foundations—declared that the war on drugs was officially over, and that possession of illegal narcotics would now be effectively legal. Clearly, when this woman watched *The Wire*, she must have rooted for the murderous drug dealers. According to the *Baltimore Sun*, her office also declined to prosecute crimes such as "attempted drug distribution, prostitution, trespassing, open containers, and minor traffic offenses."[4] It was, in essence, the opposite of the "broken windows" approach—the innovative law enforcement strategy pioneered in New York City, which focused first on stopping small crimes of vandalism (graffiti, "squeegee men")—that had transformed crime-ridden Gotham in the 1980s and '90s. The Soros DA's approach seemed to be, "Break all the windows you want, and steal anything you like."

During normal times, these policies would have been disastrous for ordinary Americans. Unfortunately, we were living in anything but normal times.

There was a storm coming.

Summer of Love

On May 25, after months of enforced lockdowns due to COVID-19, the nation watched in horror as a forty-six-year-old man named George Floyd was killed by the police. All of us saw that awful video, as an officer pressed his knee on Floyd's neck for a full nine minutes and twenty-nine seconds. Floyd was incapacitated, handcuffed, and posed no danger to the officer or anyone else. Floyd is in visible distress, begging for help. There was no law enforcement justification—ZERO—for what occurred, and the officer was rightly prosecuted and convicted for his shocking criminal conduct.

This horrible crime could have been an opportunity for unity. Everyone agreed that the officer's conduct was wrong and was criminal. As a nation, we could have had an incredible moment of solidarity agreeing across party lines that this horrific abuse of power should be fully prosecuted.

But the partisan demagogues wanted more. And I knew that the ramifications for public safety would be severe. For years, elements of the radical left had been pushing a narrative that *all* police officers are racist by nature. They claimed that men and women in law enforcement treat Black people differently than White people—that when officers came across a Black suspect, they treat that suspect differently based on the color of his or her skin. This had begun, in significant part, during the Obama administration, when the president had claimed with a straight face that Trayvon Martin "could have been [his] son" and deliberately stirred up racial division for his own political gain.

In the years since, with the appearance of doctrines such as Critical Race Theory and the 1619 Project, the false narrative spread far and wide. By the time George Floyd was tragically killed in May 2020, it had become the de facto lens through which major news organizations such as CNN, MSNBC, and the *New York Times* viewed interactions between police and people of color. It was also popular among some of the far-left district attorneys who had come to power in the years since.

Not only was this ideology dangerous, sure to lead to a dramatic upsurge in violence against the men and women of our police forces, it was also flat-out wrong. Police officers are not, in fact, more likely to kill Black people than White people, and in the rare instances when they *do* kill Black people, they typically do not do so because of some latent racism in their DNA. Sure, with police, as with any sizeable population, there are a handful of bad actors who commit criminal acts for racist reasons. But they are a tiny minority of officers. In the vast majority of cases, police officers are forced to draw their weapons and fire when they believe their lives or the lives of others may be in danger.

According to a widely read op-ed in the *Wall Street Journal* by Heather Mac Donald, the evidence that police are somehow racist against Black people is simply not there. "A solid body of evidence," she writes, "finds no structural bias in the criminal justice system with regard to arrests, prosecution, or sentencing. Crime and suspect behavior, not race, determine most police actions."[5] As evidence, Mac Donald cites several studies, one of which found that the percentage of police homicide victims who are Black—about 25 percent—was "less than what the Black crime rate would predict, since police shootings are a function of how often officers encounter armed and violent suspects. In 2018, the latest year for which such data have been published, African Americans made up 53 percent of known homicide offenders in the U.S. and commit about 60 percent of robberies, though they are 13 percent of the population."

John McWhorter, a self-described "cranky liberal Democrat" professor of linguistics at Columbia University, has also pushed back on the simple, wrongheaded narrative that all police are racist. According to McWhorter, who is Black, the evidence suggests that "racism is less important to understanding police behavior than is commonly supposed." Writing in *Quillette*, he tells the story of Tony Timpa, a thirty-two-year-old man who, like George Floyd, was detained by police and held down by an officer's knee for nearly thirteen minutes, dying of suffocation. There is a recording of Timpa's death, McWhorter notes, during which he can be heard "pleading for his life." For nearly every death of a Black person at the hands of police, there is a comparable case of a person of another race being killed; the difference, of course, is that we know the names of the Black victims but not the White, Latino, or Asian ones.

Why? According to Professor McWhorter, the problem lies with the media's obsession with a false narrative, namely that racist cops kill Black people more frequently than any other race. "Because the killing of Black suspects by White police officers receives more media attention and elicits more outrage, such instances leave us vulnerable to the availability heuristic—a cognitive bias that leads us to form judgments about the prevalence of phenomena based on the readiness with which we can recall examples. Had Tony Timpa been Black, we would all know his name by now."

Similarly, one of Joe Biden's many radical district court nominees, Nusrat Choudhury—who spent her career working at the ACLU in New York and Illinois—gave a speech at Princeton University in 2015 and said, "The killing of unarmed Black men by police happens *every day* in America." This was a brazen lie. According to the *Washington Post* database, in 2021 a total of *six* unarmed Black men were shot and killed by police. Of course, the killing of even one innocent person is tragic—and if a particular police officer committed a criminal act he or she should be prosecuted, as were the officers who killed George Floyd. But six shootings in a year is world of difference from 365, one *every day*. When confronted at her hearing about her blatant falsehood, her only response was, "I was making a comment in my role as an advocate, and I was engaging in rhetorical advocacy." Indeed.

So, whenever a Black person is killed tragically by police, the corporate press gives that murder wall-to-wall coverage for weeks, completely ignoring cases in which the victim was not Black. Then, they cite an "epidemic of police shootings against Black people," which they have invented all by themselves. In a formal logic class, you might call this "circular reasoning." But since we are not in a formal logic class, I'm happy to just call it propaganda. The numbers, as you can see, tell the story. The evidence is there for anyone who wishes to see it.

Still, for those on the left who insist on viewing all things through the lens of race, the numbers can be altered to say whatever they want them to say. They can also make inconvenient data disappear. Shortly after Heather Mac Donald's op-ed in the *Wall Street Journal*, for instance, the authors of one of the studies she cited took the rare step of retracting their findings. Unforgivably, these scientists had gone against the prevailing liberal orthodoxy, and so they were forced to retreat out of fear that their reputations would be permanently destroyed. Following this saga, one is reminded of Galileo, who famously was forced (on threat of torture) to retract his heliocentric model of the universe when the pope informed him that it went against the dogma of the church. In a follow-up article titled, "I cited their study, so they disavowed it," Mac Donald warns that "if scientists must disavow their findings because they challenge reigning orthodoxies, then those orthodoxies will prevail even when they are wrong."[6]

Sadly, this is exactly what ended up happening. As the video footage of George Floyd's murder spread on social media, protestors began taking to the streets in droves. At first, these demonstrations were mostly peaceful. People held hands and marched through the streets holding signs, seeming to enjoy the release after so many months locked in their homes. But that peace didn't last. Spurred on by a media that seemed desperate to prove that there was some epidemic of police killings against Black people, violent looters and rioters began taking over our nation's cities.

In Minneapolis, not far from where George Floyd had been killed, rioters burned down an AutoZone and attacked a police precinct. In New York City, rioters clashed with police in the streets and looted stores across downtown Manhattan. Similar scenes of carnage unfolded in major cities all over the country. Amid broken glass and fires in the streets, protestors screamed, stole, and assaulted people who dared to disagree with them. It was like something you would normally see in the back pages of newspapers, where they report international news from Third World countries in political turmoil.

In the summer of 2020, anarchists took over six square blocks of downtown Seattle, burned the police precinct, and declared an "autonomous zone" alternately known as the "CHOP" (Capitol Hill Occupied Protest) or the "CHAZ" (Capitol Hill Autonomous Zone). Seattle's Democratic mayor, Jenny Durkan, proceeded to withdraw the police, in effect ceding that part of the city to lawless warlords, as she went on CNN to defend the takeover as simply "the *summer of love.*" She tweeted that CHOP "is not a lawless wasteland of anarchist insurrection—it is a peaceful expression of our community's collective grief and their desire to build a better world." In the chaos that ensued, two people were murdered, four more were shot, and multiple women were sexually assaulted.

When these rioters weren't looting stores, they were tearing down monuments to people they believed were racist. Of course, their definition of racist was impossibly broad, encompassing just about anyone who happened to be White and born before they were. In Portland, Oregon, several statues of great Americans came down. The same happened in Washington, D.C., where protestors attempted to bring down the famed statue of the Marquis de Lafayette, the French hero of the American Revolution, just a few blocks from the White House. In Rochester, New York, absurdly, vandals even tore down a statute of Frederick Douglass, the great Black abolitionist.

Amid the chaos, the *New York Post* wrote an article about the violence unfolding in the streets, titling it "Call them the 1619 riots." In a tweet that has since been deleted, Nikole Hannah-Jones, the primary author of the 1619 Project, wrote, "It would be an honor. Thank you."[7]

Tragically, these riots are what happen when ridiculous doctrines such as Critical Race Theory, once an obscure set of radical ideas taught mainly on college campuses, are spread by the corporate press and social media companies. How else would an idea as loopy as "defund the police," a slogan shouted by rioters during the summer of 2020, become a serious policy position that would eventually be supported by my Democratic colleagues in the Senate?

Throughout 2020, prominent Democrats catered to an increasingly radical left-wing base, and the results were predictable. Crime rates skyrocketed. So did murder rates and carjacking rates. But the Democrats were not concerned. They cared only about saying the right slogans, pushing the right policies, and hating the right people—anything that would keep the rioters and looters on their side.

During the early stages of rioting in June, Kamala Harris expressed support not for law enforcement, but for the protestors who were, at the time, chanting "ACAB" (all cops are bastards) in the street. On June 1, she tweeted a link to the Minnesota Freedom Fund, a group that was posting bail to get violent rioters out of jail so they could go out and continue to wreak havoc. Around the same time, thirteen members of Vice President Joe Biden's campaign staff also donated funds to get the violent rioters out of jail. One referred to our system of cash bail as a "modern day debtors' prison," expressing the same views as many of the left-wing district attorneys who had recently come to power.[8] Several other prominent Democrats supported similar charities, as did Hollywood celebrities such as Steve Carell, Don Cheadle, Chrissy Teigen, and Seth Rogen.

Many prominent Democrats also supported the calls to "defund the police." During an interview with the *View* in June, Kamala Harris refused to disavow calls to abolish or defund police forces. Instead, she attempted to give this radical idea a more palatable spin, saying that "a big part of this conversation really is about reimagining how we do public safety in America" and that "we have confused the idea that to achieve safety, you put more cops on the street" when we should be spending more money on social services and job training.

I suspect that Harris, herself a former district attorney in the horribly crime-ridden city of San Francisco, knew fully well that the words coming out of her mouth were outright lies. She didn't care. She knew that this was the nonsense she needed to spew in order to get elected, so that's exactly what she did. All around the country, Democrats hoping for a few more years in office did the same thing.

And the Soros money was flowing in to support them. After the success of 2016, the Hungarian billionaire continued pouring money into local races. In the 2018 midterm elections, several more prosecutors were elevated to public office with massive donations from Soros-backed groups. One of them was a lawyer named Rachael Rollins, who had campaigned for Suffolk County DA in Massachusetts on the usual platform of racial "equity" and cash bail reform. During the debates, she repeatedly invoked racism rather than discussing the potential negative consequences of some of her policies, saying at one point that she "really [didn't] have much time for more White men telling me what communities of color need, because they don't know."[9]

Thanks to the massive cash infusion, Rollins won easily, and she spent the majority of her tenure enacting the same left-wing agenda that had already failed in Minneapolis, Philadelphia, and the rest of the cities that had been targeted by the Soros machine. Time and time again, she made it clear that she came into the job of DA as a crusader. In 2021, she declared, with remarkable candor, "If you want to change the criminal legal system, become a prosecutor, because they have the power to determine charges, what crimes to decline to prosecute or divert, [and] how to fashion bail hearings."

She didn't care about keeping criminals off the street. She cared about having the power to say "I *won't* prosecute these crimes." With

Rollins, this power was not hypothetical. In March 2019, she wrote a lengthy memo to her office that would come to be known simply as the "Rachael Rollins Policy Memo," a list of fifteen crimes whose prosecution "should *always* be declined" or "dismissed without conditions.... The presumption is that charges that fall into this category should *always* be declined."

You might think that this had been some kind of reasonable criminal justice reform. Perhaps, you might think, Rollins was attempting to stop overzealous prosecution of crimes such as low-level marijuana possession. Perhaps she was looking out for young teenagers who might get caught with a couple of joints. Reasonable people can disagree about what to do in those circumstances.

Luckily, we don't have to guess about what crimes Rollins would no longer prosecute. She wrote them down in her memo, which is still available online as of this writing. These crimes, which would come to be known as the "Rollins Fifteen" are:

1. Trespassing
2. Shoplifting, including offenses that are essentially shoplifting, but charged as larceny
3. Larceny under $250
4. Disorderly conduct
5. Disturbing the peace
6. Receiving stolen property
7. Minor driving offenses, including operating with a suspended or revoked license
8. Breaking and entering, where it is into a vacant property or is for the purpose of sleeping or seeking refuge from the cold and there is no actual damage to property
9. Wanton or malicious destruction of property
10. Threats (excluding domestic violence)
11. Minors in possession of alcohol
12. Drug possession

13. Drug possession with intent to distribute
14. Resisting arrest where the only charge is resisting arrest
15. Resisting arrest if the other charges include only charges that fall under the list of charges for which prosecution is declined

So, in Boston during Rachael Rollins's time as district attorney, it was effectively legal for a criminal to break into someone's house and steal $249. It was also functionally legal for that person to take something from the house they had just broken into and destroy it on the front lawn, given that number nine on the Rollins Fifteen prevents someone from being charged with wanton or malicious destruction of property.

Rollins was not an outlier. She wasn't a crazy example of someone who wanted to carry out a radical agenda but would advance no further than her current station. Rather, she was doing exactly what she had been put in place by George Soros and his allies to do: disrupt our justice system from the ground up.

And it wouldn't stop there.

The Federal Level

There's a saying that all politics is local. The same is true for justice.

For the most part, criminals are punished in district courts at the level of the city or county. They are arrested by local police, charged by local officials, and sent to serve their sentences in local prisons. If you disrupt that process, the whole criminal justice system falls apart. George Soros and his band of cronies in liberal political action groups knew this, which is why they had such success tearing down our major cities during the summer of 2020. They attacked our system at its very roots, knowing that a small amount of damage there would have major implications all across the United States.

But for the most part, the worst violence was contained to a few left-leaning cities. The antics of the terror group Antifa, the black-clad psychopaths who burned down buildings and attacked counter-protestors with bike locks and baseball bats, were not often seen outside of Portland, Oregon, where brave journalists such as Andy Ngo worked hard to expose them at great personal risk to themselves. In August 2020, I introduced a bill that would have officially designated Antifa as a terrorist organization, which made perfect sense to me (and the millions of Americans who had already been terrorized by them by that point in the "summer of love"). But my colleagues on the left, several of whom had openly praised the work of Black Lives Matter and ignored the many lives that had already been lost due to leftist violence, didn't even let it get out of committee.

Still, the consequences for Americans all over the country had been severe. Already, we had seen the most severe increase in violent crime in decades. Ironically, the people who are suffering most are African Americans—the very people that Antifa, Black Lives Matter, and other violent rioters claim that they were trying to protect. By the end of 2020, 8,600 Black people had been killed by homicide, up from 7,484 the year before. In July, a four-year-old boy named LeGend Taliferro had been killed by gunfire in Kansas City.

When President Trump and Attorney General Bill Barr heard this story, they decided that something more had to be done—not on the ground by local police or prosecutors, too many of whom had already demonstrated an unwillingness to be tough on the terrorists who were running wild in the streets, but at the federal level. Clearly, a strong response from the federal government was needed. That summer, they sent federal agents to local task forces in several high-crime cities across the United States, naming the effort "Operation Legend" after the four-year-old boy who'd been murdered in Kansas City. The results were astounding.

According to Attorney General Barr's account of the operation, the surge resulted in "over 6,000 arrests across nine cities, including approximately 467 for homicide. Of the total arrested, approximately 1,500 were charged with federal offenses. More than 2,600 firearms were seized, as well as more than 32 kilos of heroin, 17 kilos of fentanyl, 300 kilos of methamphetamine, and 135 kilos of cocaine."[10] When you consider these numbers in light of the Soros prosecutors, who insist on leaving drugs out on the street because arresting people who carry those drugs *might* have negative effects on mass incarceration or racial "equity," it is difficult not to be infuriated. If it were up to someone like Marilyn Mosby, for example, who has declared that the war on drugs is "over," all that heroin, cocaine, and meth would have remained on the streets of Detroit, Cleveland, St. Louis, Memphis, Albuquerque, Milwaukee, Indianapolis, and Kansas City, circulating from drug dealers to drug users in a deadly game that would almost certainly have ended in many more dead bodies.

Without a strong intervention at the federal level, many more lives would have been lost. In fact, Operation Legend is a perfect example of how law enforcement by the federal government can somewhat counterbalance bad political decisions at the level of the state, county, or community. It also happens in courtrooms. When a district attorney refuses to prosecute a crime, for instance, a United States Attorney—someone nominated by the president of the United States and confirmed by the Senate—can take up the crime and charge the criminal under federal law. It is a fail-safe measure that is integral to the functioning of our justice system.

And so of course, at the end of 2021, Joe Biden nominated Rachael Rollins, the district attorney in Boston who had directed her office not to prosecute fifteen serious crimes, to become the United States Attorney for Massachusetts. This meant that the federal prosecutors, who might have prosecuted at least some of the serious crimes that Rachael Rollins wouldn't, would now become just as radical as the county DAs that George Soros had targeted with his national campaign in 2016. During Rollins's confirmation hearing, I vigorously opposed her, reading out loud each of the fifteen crimes she declined to prosecute.

I begged my colleagues on the Judiciary Committee to say enough is enough, to finally say no to the rampant lawlessness of the Soros DAs.

When Trump was president, we of course confirmed the vast majority of his nominees, but there were some whose qualifications and records made them unsuitable for the positions for which they were nominated. When that happened, Republicans on the Judiciary Committee raised our substantive concerns, and the Trump White House would withdraw the nominees. That's what "advise and consent" is supposed to be all about.

But not for Democrats. On the Judiciary Committee, Senate Democrats have rubber-stamped every single Biden nominee, no matter how radical. With Rachael Rollins, they did the same. And, when her nomination went to the floor, *every single Senate Democrat* voted to confirm her. So now, an unrepentant Soros DA—who refuses to enforce criminal laws she disagrees with—is the chief federal law enforcement officer for the Commonwealth of Massachusetts.

In February 2022, Joe Biden stood before a joint session of Congress and delivered his first State of the Union address. Near the middle of his speech, he addressed the calls that had been coming from his party for the better part of the last two years to "defund the police." After acknowledging the spike in crime that had occurred in major cities over the past two years, Biden said, "We should all agree, the answer is not to defund the police. It is to fund the police. Fund them. Fund them. Fund them with resources and training."

Nearly every lawmaker in the chamber, myself included, stood up and applauded. The message was the right one, even if it demonstrated stunning hypocrisy on the part of the Biden administration. Because though he may have suggested support for the police before the nation, Biden also nominated two of the leading advocates of abolishing the police (Vanita Gupta and Kristen Clarke, detailed in Chapter Eight) to senior positions in the Justice Department, and every single Democrat voted to confirm them. So when Biden nominates these radicals, and every single Democrat votes to confirm them, the Democrats cannot pretend they somehow oppose defunding the police.

For years, Democrats have been demonizing law enforcement, spreading outright lies about police brutality and disseminating massive misinformation about the killings of young Black men by officers. They have advocated—and passed—radical agendas slashing funding for police departments, in cities like Minneapolis and New York City and Austin, Texas. They have elevated radicals like Gupta and Clarke and Rollins to major positions of power within the Justice Department, ensuring that many more people would be put in danger. They were able to do so because they know that the corporate media will cover for them, repeating their propaganda and ignoring the lives lost because of their radical policies.

But it speaks volumes about just how scared Democrats are that the voters have figured it out anyway, that they rightly blame the skyrocketing crime rates nationally on Biden's radical soft-on-crime policies. That's why Biden laughably claimed that he doesn't support defunding the police, and why Democrats sheepishly stood and applauded. They want to hide the truth.

But nobody who's paying attention believed them.

CHAPTER SIX

JANUARY 6

B y the night of the 2020 presidential election, the United States of America was more bitterly divided than it had been in decades. Watching with friends in Houston, I saw clearly that no matter what happened, this would not be an ordinary election. Due to the massive volume of mail-in ballots, there would likely be significant delays in getting results. It was possible that we might see a repeat of the 2000 election, when the American people had to wait weeks to find out who would become their next president. And like that election, there would almost certainly be grave concerns about the validity of the results. No matter which side won, the other side would very likely raise allegations of foul play, fraud, or electoral misconduct.

This wasn't surprising. Throughout 2020, the American people had been watching primary elections play out all over the country, and the results had not been encouraging. During the primaries in Georgia, for instance, voters waited on long lines for hours. Many people gave up on waiting, deciding not to vote at all. Those who persisted often got inside to find that the voting equipment wasn't working. At one point, the mayor of Atlanta tweeted that not a single voting machine was operational. In Wisconsin, which held its primary elections in April 2020, the story was largely the same. Voters waited in long lines in their cars, finding that there weren't enough poll workers to effectively run an election. Rather than having 180 polling locations, there were only five. Speaking to the *Guardian*, an election official said they were "over our heads in chaos right now. The level of public confusion will be so rampant that the access to voting will be so limited."[1]

The answer to this chaos, at least for Democrats, was universal mail-in voting. To them, there was simply no other choice. However, as we learned from the 2005 Carter-Baker Commission, there are few better ways to ensure fraud—or the perception of fraud—than the widespread use of mail-in ballots. According to the report, they are "the largest source of potential voter fraud."[2] This played out in several states across the country.

After waiting more than four hours in line, one woman in Georgia told the *Guardian* why she had come to vote in person despite the hardship involved in doing so.

"I requested [a mail-in ballot]," she said. "I received it, but I don't trust anybody. I don't trust them to count it."[3]

Thanks to a confluence of factors, the country found itself in the same position that Catherine Engelbrecht, the founder of True the Vote, was in during the 2009 elections. They looked around their hometowns and saw massive dysfunction in our election systems. They saw broken machines, long lines, and people leaving rather than waiting several hours to vote. They heard stories about widespread corruption during the primaries, most of which involved the mail-in ballots that Democrats were actively pushing as the only safe way to vote.

Clearly, we were heading for trouble.

Still, when I went to sleep on election night, it appeared that the outcome would be undeniable. President Trump seemed to be leading in every major battleground state, and it appeared as if he would win by a healthy enough margin to dispel any doubts about the validity of the election. For a moment, I thought things might go smoothly after all.

But that's not what happened. I awoke on the morning of November 4 to find that the race was much closer than it had first appeared. Media reports indicated that sometime in the very early hours of the morning, while America slept, Vice President Biden had taken the lead in several key districts—a lead that seemed, in the opinion of at least some analysts, to be unnatural. I wasn't sure what the facts were at the time; instead, I wanted to reserve judgment until all the votes were in.

This, as it turned out, was easier said than done. For the next few days, while the corporate press was busy loudly declaring Joe Biden the winner, several close states kept counting the votes. And allegations of voter fraud arose across the country. These claims, of course, were amplified greatly by President Trump, who had long been warning about the danger posed by universal mail-in ballots. Within days, the White House had compiled a series of allegations of fraud that seemed very much worth looking into. Clearly, they believed that there had been significant foul play during this election, as did many Americans. They weren't going to give up without a fight.

In the two months after the election, more than sixty lawsuits were filed by President Trump's legal team or his allies, all of them alleging fraud or electoral misconduct. There were cases in Pennsylvania, Georgia, Arizona, Wisconsin, Nevada, and Michigan, all of which had gone heavily—and somewhat unbelievably, given the pre-election polling—for Joe Biden. Unfortunately, many of the lawyers bringing these cases were inexperienced and ill-prepared for the fight ahead. Two months earlier, in September, I had gone to the White House and urged them to bring in a substantially stronger legal team—warning that there was likely to be massive litigation on and after election day—but Trump's staff, with the wave of a hand, dismissed my concerns and assured me that they had everything taken care of.

For the next month, these election challenges failed in court. Sometimes, they failed due to shoddy lawyering; other times, they failed on procedural grounds unrelated to the merits of the claims. And every time one of these lawsuits failed, the corporate press took it as proof that voter fraud did not, in fact, exist; they maintained that President Trump was simply filing lawsuits in a desperate attempt to hold on to power rather than attempting to remedy a serious problem with the integrity of our elections.

I knew that the case could soon end up before the Supreme Court, and the factual record being built in the trial courts would be pivotal to the outcome. That job wasn't getting accomplished. So I called President Trump, and told him that he needed to assemble a far better legal team, and he needed to do so immediately. There were some talented lawyers working on the cases (like my friends Cleta Mitchell and Adam Laxalt), but many of the lawyers bringing cases lacked the experience required to prevail. I told President Trump that he needed a team of world-class litigators, the kind you hire in multi-billion-dollar bet-the-company lawsuits. Trump knew that, two decades earlier, I had been part of the legal team in *Bush v. Gore*, the pivotal Supreme Court case that arose in the aftermath of the 2000 election. I told him about the historic legal team that came together during those thirty-six unforgettable days in Tallahassee, Florida. Extraordinary lawyers, like Ted Olson, Mike Carvin, Fred Bartlit, Phil Beck, and also a little-known constitutional litigator named John Roberts, who would soon go on to have a career in government. And all of them led by the incomparable James Baker. Never had such talented and experienced litigators been assembled on the same team, I told President Trump, and I had the great privilege of being a young lawyer carrying their bags, assisting them, and learning from them.

I then told him that if he wanted to have any hope of winning the cases he was about to bring before the Supreme Court, he would need to assemble a comparable legal team.

President Trump expressed a willingness to bring new lawyers on board, and I offered to try to help him do so. What followed was an experience unlike any I'd had before. I called multiple top-tier litigators—the kinds of people who could bring these cases, carefully build the factual record in the trial court, and then prevail before the Supreme Court.

To a person, every one of them said no. One of them replied, "Let me get this straight: the client will demand that I make frivolous claims in court, he'll publicly blame me when those claims fail, and then...at the end of the day, he won't pay my bill!" Although I tried, there was nothing I could say to convince him otherwise.

In an odd coincidence, most of the conversations happened while I was having a picnic in a park in Houston with Heidi and the girls; it was surreal, while sitting on a blanket eating a ham and cheese sandwich, I talked to lawyer after lawyer, all of whom declined to take the case. It was astonishing. The president of the United States was having a hard time hiring a lawyer.

So, frustratingly, the same legal team remained in place bringing the cases. Some of the claims being tossed around, in court and swirling on the Internet, were bizarre and unfounded. For example, the idea that Hugo Chavez, the dead Communist leader of Venezuela, had somehow hacked into voting machines in America to rig the election, was just nutty. It reminded me of the Russia collusion stories we had been hearing from the left from the past four years. There was simply no evidence for them.

But there were also cases that had real substance and merit. One of them was a case challenging the election results in Pennsylvania, a state President Trump had lost by a narrow margin. In Pennsylvania, the state constitution explicitly prohibits mail-in voting except in a few narrow, specified circumstances (such as illness or physical disability). In the wake of the COVID-19 pandemic, however, with the citizens of Pennsylvania mostly confined to their homes thanks to the stay-at-home orders of Governor Tom Wolf, a Democrat, the state legislature had enacted a new law providing, essentially, for universal mail-in voting. At the time, the state legislature had a Republican majority—although clearly, at least some of them were Republicans who were willing to be bullied and intimidated by Democrats and by the corporate media, who had insisted all along that mail-in voting was the only way Pennsylvanians could vote.

Previously, the Pennsylvania Supreme Court had repeatedly struck down efforts by the state legislature to expand mail-in voting. They did so in 1862 and again in 1924, following the plain text of the Pennsylvania Constitution. I believed Pennsylvania courts should continue to follow its state constitution, and so did many other people in Pennsylvania.

One of them was Congressman Mike Kelly, a Republican who represents northwest Pennsylvania, deep in the Rust Belt alongside Lake Erie. Kelly played football at Notre Dame (until a knee injury sidelined him), and he owned several automotive dealerships; his district's blue-collar electorate typifies the working-class voters who elected Donald Trump. And those voters were furious with what was happening. Congressman Kelly had brought his challenge to the illegal universal mail-in ballots results because of the overwhelming concerns he had heard from his constituents.

Eventually, his challenge went all the way to the Pennsylvania Supreme Court. But the Court, a 5–2 majority of whom were partisan Democrats, issued a decision that I found both lawless and politically charged. The state constitution explicitly forbade what the legislature had done, but the supreme court justices refused to enforce that constitution, thereby abdicating their duty to the people of their state. Instead, they dismissed the case based on the doctrine of *laches*, which means that the plaintiffs waited too long to file the lawsuit.

While the case was pending, I put out a lengthy statement calling on the United States Supreme Court to hear the case. In it, I argued:

> This appeal raises serious legal issues, and I believe the Court should hear the case on an expedited basis.... This appeal argues that Pennsylvania cannot change the rules in the middle of the game. If Pennsylvania wants to change how voting occurs, the state must follow the law to do so.
>
> The illegality was compounded by a partisan Democrat Supreme Court in Pennsylvania, which has issued multiple

decisions that reflect their political and ideological biases. Just over a month ago, Justice Alito, along with Justice Thomas and Justice Gorsuch, wrote—correctly, I believe—concerning the Pennsylvania court's previous decision to count ballots received after Election Day, that "there is a strong likelihood that the State Supreme Court decision violates the Federal Constitution."

In the current appeal, the Pennsylvania Supreme Court dismissed the claim based on a legal doctrine called "laches," which essentially means the plaintiffs waited too long to bring the challenge. But, the plaintiffs reasonably argue that the Pennsylvania Supreme Court has not applied that doctrine consistently and so they cannot selectively enforce it now.

Even more persuasively, the plaintiffs point out that the Pennsylvania Supreme Court has also held that plaintiffs don't have standing to challenge an election law until after the election, meaning that the court effectively put them in a Catch-22: before the election, they lacked standing; after the election, they've delayed too long. The result of the court's gamesmanship is that a facially unconstitutional election law can never be judicially challenged.

Shortly after my statement went out, I got a call from a lawyer on the litigation team with a request. If the U.S. Supreme Court did grant a writ of certiorari—meaning if it agreed to hear the appeal—would I be willing to argue it?

I thought carefully about this request, recalling the nine cases that I had previously argued before the Supreme Court. No two of these cases were alike. In part, that's because Supreme Court cases are typically extremely complicated by nature. When a case makes it all the way to the highest court in the land, that often means the case is of national importance and the law is unsettled. And, in a case as politically charged as this one, you could anticipate that the justices would be sharply divided. There is no doubt this case would be incredibly difficult, but after seriously considering it, I said yes, if the justices granted certiorari, I was willing to argue the case.

I knew that, in this case, there were two major challenges. First, it would not be easy to articulate the precise question of federal law at issue. As a typical matter, the United States Supreme Court does not (and cannot) decide questions of state law. The Pennsylvania Supreme Court was clearly wrong as a matter of Pennsylvania law, but that doesn't necessarily mean that the U.S. Supreme Court can step in and overrule the decision. The Pennsylvania Supreme Court, usually, is the final arbiter of state law. I did believe there was a cognizable federal interest in the Pennsylvania case, and the Pennsylvania court's refusal to follow state law in a presidential election potentially raised both federal constitutional issues and federal statutory issues. Still, articulating the precise federal questions would have been challenging.

Second, there was the question of remedy. If the Supreme Court agreed that the state legislature had indeed violated Pennsylvania law, then what should the solution be? Obviously, the solution could not be that the Court would simply invalidate all the votes in Pennsylvania. The Court, rightly, would not want to disenfranchise millions of people, so finding a potential remedy would require some form of trying to identify illegally cast votes and somehow separating them from votes that were legally cast. That would not be easy.

If the Supreme Court had taken the case, I fully imagine that the oral argument would have focused front and center on those two challenges. And my preparation for that argument would have entailed brainstorming with leading Supreme Court advocates and constitutional scholars to try to develop a careful strategy for navigating both of those minefields. But first, the Court had to take the case (as I had urged it to do). I believed the Supreme Court had a responsibility to tackle these hard and important questions and to help provide much-needed resolution and confidence to the tens of millions of Americans who, even a month after the election, still had profound doubts about the integrity of our election system.

Unfortunately, on November 16, the Court declined to take the case. This, I believe, was a mistake. The American people had grave doubts about the outcome of the 2020 election, and rather than listening to these doubts and hearing the evidence, the Supreme Court had decided to shut down the argument before it could even begin. When the news came, many Americans were outraged. It was clear that the challenges were not going to stop coming.

A few days later, my home state of Texas, along with six other states, filed an original jurisdiction lawsuit in the Supreme Court against four other states. The suit was novel and creative; it alleged that the states being sued had violated state and federal law and improperly administered their elections, thereby unfairly altering the results of the presidential election, to the detriment of voters in Texas. Unfortunately, this case was on even on shakier legal ground than the Pennsylvania case. It was really stretching the bounds of Supreme Court precedent. But the American people were demanding answers.

That night, while the case was pending, I was having dinner with a friend at my favorite steakhouse near my Senate office. A few minutes into the meal, President Trump called me on my cell phone, as he often did during times of crisis. He said he was deeply dismayed that the Supreme Court had declined to take the Pennsylvania case. I agreed, saying it was a serious mistake and very disappointing. He asked if I was surprised.

"No, Mr. President," I said. "I wasn't surprised. There's no doubt that was the easier decision, the more risk-averse decision, for the Court to decline to take the case. I think it's very unfortunate. I think it's a mistake that the Court didn't take the case. But I wasn't surprised that that's what they decided to do."

President Trump was furious, and deeply frustrated. Then he asked a question that I wasn't anticipating: "If the Supreme Court takes this Texas case, would you be willing to argue it?"

I paused for a long moment. Clearly, this case would be an even more challenging endeavor than the Pennsylvania case. The facts of the

Texas case had been hastily assembled, and the overall lawsuit was incredibly far reaching. Preparing for oral argument would be one of the most difficult endeavors of my legal career, to put it mildly. Still, I believed it was too important—the stakes were too high—to shirk from the task.

Taking a deep breath, I replied, "Yes, I will. In my judgment, the chances that the Court will decide to take the Texas lawsuit are extremely low. It's overwhelmingly likely that the Court will decline to hear it. But if the Court does choose to take it—if four justices decide that the case merits oral argument—then I believe the parties deserve effective advocacy. I am willing to argue it."

The next morning, just as I had predicted to President Trump, the Supreme Court declined to take the case.

As the days and weeks went on, the same story played out over and over again. Case after case alleging fraud was rejected. Sometimes, these cases were rejected on the merits of their particular claims, but many others were rejected on procedural grounds that had nothing to do with whether voter fraud had occurred. Rather, they were rejected because of the manner or timing in which the lawsuits were brought. In countless reports, the corporate media conflated these two types of outcomes, claiming that *all* of the cases were invalid based on the handful that were rejected based on actual substance.

And so, the United States justice system—which should have been the primary venue for President Trump and his campaign to make their case to the American people—was not functioning properly.

Something else needed to be done.

Objections

As it became more and more clear that the litigation over the contested election results was not going to yield a definitive outcome, and that the United States Supreme Court was not going to step in and resolve the matter, I struggled with what the best approach in Congress would be. Under federal law, specifically a statute called the Electoral Count Act, the process of counting electoral votes is arcane and convoluted.

As discussed in a previous chapter, the United States Constitution gives Congress the power to count electoral votes and officially certify the results of a presidential election. Under the Electoral Count Act, members of Congress may raise objections to the results from any state, but there are rules for doing so. For the objection to trigger a vote, it cannot be made by a House member alone. Instead, the objection must be made by both a House member and a senator. When an objection is raised by a House member *and* joined by a senator, the joint session of Congress is suspended and both chambers divide to debate the issue for a maximum of two hours and then vote on whether to sustain the objection. Typically, certification has been seen as a largely ceremonial power, and objections have been relatively rare throughout our history.

But they have happened. Indeed, Democrats have objected repeatedly in modern times. In Chapter Three, for instance, I discussed the various objections that were raised by Democrats after President Trump was elected in 2016. Evidently, the Democrats believed that a few unfounded rumors of Russian collusion presented circumstances that were sufficiently dire to stop the process of democracy in its tracks indefinitely. The same was true of the Democrats who objected to George W. Bush's win during the long, hard-fought election of 2000. But in both of these instances, the objections had been raised by members of the House alone. No senator had joined them.

However, in both 1969 and 2005, a Democratic senator *had joined* with a Democratic House member in objecting to presidential electors, and had therefore twice triggered debate and a mandatory vote on the objections. Ironically, in 2005, one of the Democratic objectors was Congressman Benny Thompson—whom Nancy Pelosi would shamelessly name as chairman of the kangaroo court known as the January 6 "select" committee. In none of these previous instances of Democratic objections did the corporate media insist that Congress exercising its constitutional authority was somehow a "threat to democracy."

In the Senate, in 2020, Majority Leader Mitch McConnell was fervently urging all Republican senators to decline to join the objections of any members of the House. During the month of December, I was on multiple conference calls during which Republican leaders attempted, rather forcefully at times, to make the case against objecting.

As I was contemplating the best course of action, my colleague Josh Hawley, a Republican from Missouri, announced that he would object to certifying the electors from Pennsylvania. The objection of Senator Hawley, a good man and a friend (and also a former Supreme Court law clerk), was met like a bombshell in the Senate. Suddenly, every senator and every member of the House was going to be forced to vote on the objection, and go on record about whether or not to sustain it.

I was deeply conflicted. I knew that if I declined to object, or voted "no" on another senator's objection, that would be heard and understood by tens of millions of Americans as my saying that I did not believe voter fraud was real, significant, or a problem. That was, emphatically, not the case. I've spent two decades fighting against voter fraud, and I know full well that it has been a persistent challenge in elections since the dawn of our country.

However, I also knew that if I objected or voted in favor of an objection, it might be taken as my saying that we should simply throw out the results of the election because the candidate I had supported didn't win. That, of course, was an altogether unprincipled and indefensible position.

There are times when my training as a constitutional and Supreme Court lawyer is helpful in trying to decide how best to carry out my responsibilities as a senator. This was one of those times. As I analyzed the best course of action, I began to examine history. My experience as a lawyer had taught me to always consider precedent—what other people in similar positions have done when presented with similar circumstances. As a legislator, there can be wisdom in this approach.

As I examined history, the precedent that seemed most applicable was the election of 1876. That year was the closely contested presidential election between Republican Rutherford B. Hayes and Democrat Samuel

Tilden. During that election, as with the 2020 election, there were serious allegations of fraud in three states: South Carolina, Florida, and Louisiana. When faced with these allegations in 1877, Congress did not simply throw up its hands and say, "Well, there's nothing we can do! There are real questions here about the validity of this election, but we are powerless. Therefore, we must accept the results at face value." Had today's Republican leadership been around in the late nineteenth century, they might very well have taken that approach.

But instead, they did something very different. They appointed an election commission, which consisted of five House members, five senators, and five Supreme Court justices. The election commission examined the results in painstaking detail, looked carefully at the evidence of election fraud, and made a determination as to what the evidence demonstrated. In the end, Rutherford B. Hayes won by a slim margin, becoming the nineteenth president of the United States.

As I struggled to ascertain the most principled path for Congress to take, the precedent of 1876 seemed to provide the best answer. I discussed my thoughts with my senior advisors, and initially, I was prepared to go it alone in suggesting that Congress do something similar. But as my team discussed the matter, we all agreed that it would be far stronger if I could possibly assemble a larger coalition of senators to agree collectively upon this course of action.

The Coalition

On New Year's Eve of 2020, I was in Houston attending my birthday party. It was a festive event. I had turned fifty just a few days earlier, and my wife, Heidi, had organized the black-tie affair long before we knew what kind of fireworks would follow election night. Even with the chaos unfolding around the country, many of our closest friends attended the party, and we had a wonderful time.

During the party, many friends expressed deep dismay about where things stood with the election. Almost to a person, they believed fraud had affected the outcome of the election, and they did not believe the evidence of fraud had been fairly considered by the courts. The ubiquity of these concerns only strengthened my resolve to find a way for the full body of evidence to be assessed on the merits.

Early the next morning, on New Year's Day, I sleepily boarded a plane back to Washington. There was a vote that afternoon, and my colleagues and I would all be together for the first time since Senator Hawley's announcement. As I sat in the aisle seat midway back on my Southwest Airlines flight, multiple passengers expressed the same sentiments to me, saying we had to do something to get to the bottom of the voter fraud. I pulled out my laptop, and on the flight to D.C. I typed out a two-page statement that explained the course of action I had been mulling over.

When I arrived on the Senate floor, one of the first of my colleagues I saw was John Kennedy. An incredibly talented trial lawyer from Louisiana, Senator Kennedy is a brilliant man and a good friend. He speaks with a homespun sense of humor that is unique in the Senate. He is, by far, the funniest of my colleagues (although Lindsey Graham disputes that!), and he's also a ruthlessly effective cross-examiner during hearings.

I pulled John aside. We had both been thinking hard about how to handle the vote on the electors that was set to occur on January 6. I told him that I found both options before us—either certifying the Electoral College results and allowing Joe Biden to take office without any scrutiny, or objecting to the results and demanding that President Trump, our preferred candidate, be installed, no questions asked—were deeply problematic. Speaking with John, I'm sure I may have put the situation in slightly more vulgar terms. But he agreed that both of these options were really lousy. This was my opening.

"What if we created a third option?" I asked.

John looked at me, obviously intrigued.

"What if, when we are presented with either door number one or number two on January 6, we instead choose door number three?"

He asked what I meant.

I suggested that we could object to certifying electors only in states where there were significant claims of fraud. We would not object based on conspiracy theories or the many baseless claims that were floating around the Internet. Then, instead of attempting to throw out the results and simply install our preferred candidate, we would call specifically for the appointment of an election commission modeled after the commission of 1877. Thus, no matter what the results ended up being, we could be sure that the American people could have confidence that the right man was in office.

In the end, John expressed openness to this approach and said he would consider it. Encouraged, I went to my office and began making phone calls.

Over the next twenty-four hours or so, I called about fifteen more of my colleagues, spending anywhere from thirty to sixty minutes apiece on the phone with each of them. I walked through the issues, answering questions and laying out my idea in detail. It was well past one in the morning on January 2 when I made my last call, and I was up before dawn to make more calls. By that afternoon, a total of eleven senators had come together to sign the two-page statement I had written the day before on Southwest Airlines. The senators who joined me were Ron Johnson from Wisconsin, James Lankford from Oklahoma, Steve Daines from Montana, John Kennedy from Louisiana, Marsha Blackburn from Tennessee, Mike Braun from Indiana, Cynthia Lummis from Wyoming, Roger Marshall from Kansas, Bill Hagerty from Tennessee, and Tommy Tuberville from Alabama. Our joint statement, in full, read as follows:

> America is a Republic whose leaders are chosen in democratic elections. Those elections, in turn, must comply with the Constitution and with federal and state law.
>
> When the voters fairly decide an election, pursuant to the rule of law, the losing candidate should acknowledge and respect the legitimacy of that election. And, if the voters

choose to elect a new office-holder, our Nation should have a peaceful transfer of power.

The election of 2020, like the election of 2016, was hard fought and, in many swing states, narrowly decided. The 2020 election, however, featured unprecedented allegations of voter fraud, violations and lax enforcement of election law, and other voting irregularities.

Voter fraud has posed a persistent challenge in our elections, although its breadth and scope are disputed. By any measure, the allegations of fraud and irregularities in the 2020 election exceed any in our lifetimes.

And those allegations are not believed just by one individual candidate. Instead, they are widespread. Reuters/Ipsos polling, tragically, shows that 39% of Americans believe "the election was rigged." That belief is held by Republicans (67%), Democrats (17%), and Independents (31%).

Some Members of Congress disagree with that assessment, as do many members of the media.

But, whether or not our elected officials or journalists believe it, that deep distrust of our democratic processes will not magically disappear. It should concern us all. And it poses an ongoing threat to the legitimacy of any subsequent administrations.

Ideally, the courts would have heard evidence and resolved these claims of serious election fraud. Twice, the Supreme Court had the opportunity to do so; twice, the Court declined.

On January 6, it is incumbent on Congress to vote on whether to certify the 2020 election results. That vote is the lone constitutional power remaining to consider and force resolution of the multiple allegations of serious voter fraud.

At that quadrennial joint session, there is long precedent of Democratic Members of Congress raising objections to presidential election results, as they did in 1969, 2001, 2005, and 2017. And, in both 1969 and 2005, a Democratic Senator joined with a Democratic House Member in forcing votes in both houses on whether to accept the presidential electors being challenged.

The most direct precedent on this question arose in 1877, following serious allegations of fraud and illegal conduct in the Hayes-Tilden presidential race. Specifically, the elections in three states—Florida, Louisiana, and South Carolina—were alleged to have been conducted illegally.

In 1877, Congress did not ignore those allegations, nor did the media simply dismiss those raising them as radicals trying to undermine democracy. Instead, Congress appointed an Electoral Commission—consisting of five Senators, five House Members, and five Supreme Court Justices—to consider and resolve the disputed returns.

We should follow that precedent. To wit, Congress should immediately appoint an Electoral Commission, with full investigatory and fact-finding authority, to conduct an emergency 10-day audit of the election returns in the disputed states. Once completed, individual states would evaluate the Commission's findings and could convene a special legislative session to certify a change in their vote, if needed.

Accordingly, we intend to vote on January 6 to reject the electors from disputed states as not "regularly given" and "lawfully certified" (the statutory requisite), unless and until that emergency 10-day audit is completed.

We are not naïve. We fully expect most if not all Democrats, and perhaps more than a few Republicans, to vote otherwise. But support of election integrity should not be a partisan issue. A fair and credible audit—conducted expeditiously and completed well before January 20—would dramatically improve Americans' faith in our electoral process and would significantly enhance the legitimacy of whoever becomes our next President. We owe that to the People.

These are matters worthy of the Congress, and entrusted to us to defend. We do not take this action lightly. We are acting not to thwart the democratic process, but rather to protect it. And every one of us should act together to ensure that the election was lawfully conducted under the Constitution and to do everything we can to restore faith in our Democracy.

If we'd had more time, I have no doubt that even more senators would have come on board. But in the few hours we had, I was able to speak with only a limited number of senators. On the morning of January 2, I boarded a plane and flew to Georgia to campaign for my colleagues David Perdue and Kelly Loeffler, both of whom were in hotly contested run-off elections scheduled for January 5. Their elections would decide control of the Senate, and I could see on the ground just how frustrated and angry our voters were. (Unfortunately, that volcanic frustration resulted in far too many Republicans staying home on January 5, and Georgia ended up replacing two Republican senators with two Democrats—which made Chuck Schumer the next majority leader and resulted in the disastrous and radical legislation he's been able to ram through over the past two years.)

Right before our joint statement went out, I made two more phone calls. One was to Mark Meadows, President Trump's chief of staff. Mark had been a friend for some time, and I knew he was working hard to come up with a good approach for the White House to take in finding legitimate claims of voter fraud. My second call was to Majority Leader Mitch McConnell. Both calls were brief. Prior to those calls, neither had known my plans. Obviously, Mark was much happier to hear the news than Leader McConnell was. But they both appreciated the heads-up.

On January 5, later in the evening before we were set to carry out our plan, I got another call from President Trump. He had heard what the eleven of us were planning to do, and he was elated. But he wanted more. Over a call that lasted about thirty minutes, President Trump urged me and my colleagues to object to *all seven* of the contested states, not just one or two. I told him that although I understood his frustration, it was really important that we keep our coalition of eleven senators together. It maximized our chance of prevailing. I'd held multiple conference calls with those senators trying to keep everyone on the same page, and I knew that if we did prevail and managed to actually set up an electoral commission, there would be strength in numbers. Finally, I told President Trump that several members of our group were deeply uncomfortable with objecting to all seven of the contested states.

I told him the plan the coalition had agreed to. I would object to Arizona, and then I would support Senator Hawley's objection to Pennsylvania. The eleven of us would force the debate, and we would try with all our might to win on the merits.

A few hours later, on the morning of January 6, I sat in my office preparing for the upcoming debate. I had heard that one of my closest friends disagreed strongly with my proposed course of action, so I called him and spent nearly an hour on the phone explaining my reasoning. He told me that he still could not support my decision, which I said I respected. Like Heidi and me, my friend and his wife have two young daughters (who are our goddaughters), and our families had vacationed together every single year for over a decade. Our girls had grown up together, and we both agreed on the phone that nothing would get in the way of those lifelong friendships.

A few minutes later I walked over to the Capitol, and the proceedings began. We sat on the floor of the House of Representatives, and the state electors were presented in alphabetical order. The first contested state was Arizona. When a representative from Arizona stood up and objected to the results, Vice President Mike Pence asked if there was any senator who would join the objection.

I stood up and said that I would. Applause broke out throughout the chamber.

As a result, pursuant to statute, the joint session of the Congress was dissolved, and each house retired to its own chamber to debate the question for two hours. Because I was the one who had raised the objection, I stood to speak. Over the course of the five minutes allotted, I laid out the case for why I believed it was vital for the Senate to take this course. To Democrats who were worried about the proposal, I put things in simple terms.

"If you're right," I said, "and there is no voter fraud, then you should support the course of action I'm suggesting. If the evidence isn't there, the electoral commission presumably would conclude that."

But at that time, some 39 percent of Americans *did not* agree with the Democrats in the Senate chamber. Many of them were my constituents. It was my duty to stand up and speak for them. So, I did. But for Democrats, it didn't matter. Most of them were going to vote the party line no matter what. Unfortunately, we would never find out how the vote might have gone had the debate concluded under those circumstances.

Toward the end of our two-hour session, as Senator James Lankford from Oklahoma was speaking, there was a commotion from outside the chamber. Suddenly, Capitol Police officers rushed in and hastily escorted the vice president off the dais. Shortly thereafter, we paused the proceedings. In the fog of the confusion, it was difficult to tell what exactly was happening. We were informed that a riot had broken out and that rioters were attempting to violently breach the Capitol building.

At first, Capitol Police instructed us to remain on the Senate floor. And so we did. Then, a few minutes later, they instructed us to evacuate rapidly. While most of us were able to comply with these orders easily, some of my older colleagues who don't move too well had trouble getting quickly out of the chamber. As we scrambled chaotically out of the Senate chamber, moving together to an undisclosed location on the grounds of the Capitol, there was a great deal of speculation about what was happening outside.

Rumors abounded. "Shots fired," we were told. People had been killed, others said. None of us really knew what was happening.

Political Theater

In the secure location, tempers were high. Many senators were scared. Others were angry. Amid the chaos, more than one senator expressed rage at those of us who had objected to the certification of the election, blaming us explicitly for the violence that was occurring. As we evacuated the floor, Mitt Romney turned to me and the other objectors and said with a snarl, "This is what you've gotten us!" And the Democrats were even angrier.

Ironically, many of these Democratic senators were the very same people who had found absolutely nothing objectionable about the hundreds of violent riots that had convulsed our country during the summer of 2020. Many of them had cheered on these riots as they were occurring (or, in the case of Kamala Harris, had raised money to bail the rioters out of jail).

On the televisions in the room, CNN was playing nonstop footage of the protest unfolding outside the Capitol, cutting frequently to their left-wing panelists. Jake Tapper led the way, calling those of us who had objected to the results the "sedition caucus" for standing up for election integrity and calling for Congress to appoint a commission to consider the facts and evidence. For several hours, we received reports that rioters had breached the Capitol and that law enforcement did not have control.

While we waited for the Capitol to be secured, I assembled our coalition in a back room (really, a supply closet with stacked chairs) to discuss what we should do next. Several members of the group argued that in the face of the riot, we should suspend our objections and vote to certify the election. I understood the sentiment. But I vehemently disagreed with it. I urged my colleagues that the course of action we were advocating was the right and principled one. I said, "I'll be damned if I allow a handful of violent rioters to change our willingness to fulfill our constitutional responsibility." When they stormed the Capitol that day and assaulted police officers, these rioters wanted to stop the government from working; I wasn't going to let them.

Several hours later, when we finally returned to the Senate chamber to finish our work, the first order of business was the vote on my objection. As predicted, every Democrat voted no. But several senators out of the eleven who'd agreed with me going into that day also voted no.

Had the Capitol riot not occurred, I'm certain we would have held all eleven, and I think we would have had a real shot of getting twenty or more senators overall to support the course of action we were urging. But that is not what transpired.

In total, eight senators voted for either my objection or Senator Hawley's subsequent objection. But eight was not enough. The objections were rejected, and there would be no commission empowered to look into the results of the election. Instead, Joe Biden would take office in a few days, and no one would ever find out whether there had been serious fraud that tipped the election in one direction or the other. The tens of millions of Americans who had real concerns about voter fraud would not be listened to that day. Their public officials had failed them.

● ● ●

For the next few weeks, Washington and the country saw a level of political theater rarely experienced in public life. Almost immediately after the events of January 6, Nancy Pelosi and Chuck Schumer ordered the construction of massive metal fences surrounding the Capitol grounds, atop which razor wire sat in thick, menacing coils. The Capitol looked like Baghdad. Thousands of members of the National Guard were summoned to Washington, D.C. In full camouflage gear, they stood along the fence and by the gates holding machine guns. The guns, however, were all unloaded. They held M16s without any magazines or any bullets. Very soon, when it became clear that these guardsmen were being used as political props, red state governors called them home. For the next several months, the Capitol was guarded by soldiers from nearby blue states: New York, New Jersey, Rhode Island, and others.

Regularly, I would stop on my way into work and talk to these guardsmen. To a person, they were deeply frustrated that they were being used as actors in a bad political drama. This drama included some of the most highly charged rhetoric I had ever heard in American politics—words like "sedition" and "insurrection" and "treason" were now spoken daily on cable news. The reason Pelosi and Schumer wanted the image of thousands of guardsmen with scary guns, of course, was to convey that every Republican in America—especially those who voted for Donald Trump or expressed doubts about the election—was a dangerous terrorist and a threat to our nation. It was cynical. It was partisan. And it was a lie.

All of this extreme rhetoric has done enormous damage to our nation. With tempers raging and emotions hot, too many families have been torn apart and countless friendships have been destroyed. Sadly, those include some of my own friendships. The dear friend with whom I spent an hour on the phone just minutes before the January 6 debate—who pledged with me that our families and our girls in particular wouldn't pay the price for our political disagreement on this issue—publicly denounced me the next day. And our lifelong friendship, which I deeply, deeply treasured—and for which I grieve to this day—was discarded as yet another casualty of these angry, divided times.

In the end, my view of what happened on January 6 can be summed up neatly. Anyone who committed acts of violence should be prosecuted. If you assaulted a police officer, you should go to jail—for a very long time. That is true whether you're left-wing, right-wing, or have no wings whatsoever. Violent criminals should be prosecuted, regardless of whether they belong to Black Lives Matter or Antifa, or they committed acts of violence on January 6. And finding and prosecuting the actual terrorist who planted pipe bombs at both the RNC and DNC on January 6 should be a critical priority for the Department of Justice. Had those pipe bombs actually detonated, dozens of bystanders could have been murdered.

Conversely, anyone who engaged in peaceful protests on that day (or any other day) had the constitutional right to do so. Tens of thousands of peaceful protestors gathered on January 6 to speak up for their nation and to defend President Trump. Democrats and the media cravenly attempted to paint these peaceful protestors as violent criminals.

The day after January 6, I was at BWI airport flying back to Texas. A group of people who had participated in the January 6 protests were there as well. Most of them were little old ladies. They were crying. They came up to me and hugged me.

"We were standing on the Mall waving American flags and singing 'God Bless America,'" they said. "Now the media is calling us terrorists."

Demonizing patriotic Americans for expressing their political views was cynical and wrong. And on the part of Democrats in the media, it was entirely deliberate.

In the days and months that followed, I repeatedly laid out the distinction between ordinary protestors like those little old ladies and the small number of people who had committed violent acts. Some months later at a hearing where the chief of the Capital Police was testifying, I made off-the-cuff remarks praising the brave men and women of law enforcement, as I have done thousands of times previously. In so doing, I made reference to the violent assaults on those police officers as a "terrorist attack." Because it was not a broader discussion of what should happen following January 6, I failed to include what I had previously said repeatedly, which was that peaceful protestors were of course exercising their constitutional rights. Within hours, a huge number of people heard my comments and misunderstood them without context, believing that I was referring to anyone protesting on January 6 as a "terrorist." That was not at all what I said, and it's not remotely what I believe. On that day, more than 140 police officers reported being physically assaulted in the riot, many suffering serious injuries. The *only* people I was describing as "terrorists" were those who violently assaulted police officers.

However, after a year of being demonized and vilified by Democrats and the corporate media, many people were understandably raw and sensitive to the misuse of political rhetoric. I understand why people reacted with horror when they thought they heard me refer to anyone who'd attended the January 6 protests as "terrorists." Obviously, I wasn't talking about the tens of thousands of peaceful protestors on the National Mall that day, much less about the tens of millions of Americans who voted for and passionately support President Trump. It would've been utterly absurd—truly crazy—for me to be talking about them, given that at that very moment, *I was the one literally standing and leading the objection* to the certification of the elections and exercising both my First Amendment rights and my responsibilities as a United States senator.

Any time you hear someone describing what occurred on January 6 as an "insurrection," you know they are engaging in misleading political rhetoric. It was not an insurrection. An insurrection is an armed rebellion organized to overthrow the government. We *have* had insurrections throughout our history, most notably the Civil War. There is a good argument to be made as well that the Antifa "autonomous zone" that was violently established in Seattle during the summer of 2020 was likewise an attempt (successful, for twenty-four days) to overthrow the government and install a new one. But what happened on January 6 does *not* remotely meet the definition.

Revenge

Of course, to Joe Biden and his vengeful Justice Department, legal definitions don't matter very much. To them, January 6 was the perfect opportunity to attack their political enemies—a group that now included President Trump and just about anyone who dared support him during or after the election of 2020—using the machinery of the federal government. Now that the corporate press was unabashedly on their side, they could use the Justice Department as a weapon without so much as a peep from the media.

Shortly after he came to office, Joe Biden ordered the Justice Department to marshal the full forces of the federal government against the protestors who came to Washington that day. There was no legitimate law enforcement purpose for him to do this. By any measure, a handful of violent protestors does not pose even a fraction of the threat to American democracy posed by, say, radical Islamic terrorists in the days before 9/11 and every day since. But this Department of Justice, much like the Democrats forcing National Guardsmen to hold unloaded machine guns outside the Capitol throughout the spring of 2021, was eager to play its appointed part in the political theater of today's radical Democrats.

As of today, the Biden Justice Department has arrested more than 775 people, charging just one with seditious conspiracy. According to the *New York Times*, more than 280 people have been charged with "obstructing Congress's duty to certify the election results."[4] In fact, according to that same article in the *Times*, the White House's complaint was that Attorney General Garland hasn't gone far *enough* in his prosecution of January 6 protestors.

"As recently as last year," according to the *Times* article, "Mr. Biden confided to his inner circle that he believed former president Donald J. Trump was a threat to democracy and should be prosecuted, according to two people familiar with his comments...he has said privately that he wanted Mr. Garland to act less like a ponderous judge and more like a prosecutor who is willing to take decisive action over the events of January 6."[5]

Less than two years into his presidency, Joe Biden seems to have found himself in the position of a late-term Richard Nixon. He is eager to attack his enemies—so eager, in fact, that he's willing to say it out loud in the White House—but those around him won't fully carry out his wishes, at least so far.

Of course, that doesn't mean that the Justice Department hasn't already carried out gross miscarriages of justice on Biden's behalf.

As of this writing, far too many defendants from January 6 have been held in prison an exceedingly long time, many reportedly in solitary confinement. And the precise details remain deliberately hidden. When pressed in oversight about how many have been charged with crimes of violence, how many have been denied bail, and how many have been placed in solitary confinement, the Biden Justice Department has repeatedly refused to answer.

In June 2021, I joined a letter written by Senator Ron Johnson that compared the treatment of political prisoners from January 6 to the treatment of violent rioters and looters arrested—or, more importantly, *not* arrested—during the summer of 2020.

The letter concluded with a series of important questions for the Biden Justice Department about the treatment of January 6 protestors compared to the treatment of violent rioters who burned down buildings in the summer of 2020. Among the questions we asked, concerning both sets of defendants, were: "How many of these individuals are or were placed in solitary confinement?" "What was the average amount of consecutive days such individuals were in solitary confinement?" And "How many of these individuals have been released on bail?"

Four months later, in October 2021, DOJ responded...by answering none of the questions we asked. Instead, they spewed the following pablum:

> The Department has dedicated investigative and prosecutorial resources commensurate with the significance of these events. The Department's investigation and prosecution of cases related to this matter are ongoing, and longstanding policy and practice across Administrations has been not to disclose non-public information related to pending matters. We would therefore direct you to the public information that is available about the charged cases.

At a Judiciary Committee hearing in January 2022, I asked the Department of Justice about their non-answers:

> **CRUZ:** "How many people have been charged with crimes of violence in connection with the events on January 6?"

DOJ: "Senator, I'm not sure exactly how many have been charged with crimes of violence. I know that there are many—"

CRUZ: "How many have been charged with nonviolent crimes?"

DOJ: "I don't have the numbers of people charged...."

CRUZ: "Okay. How many people are currently incarcerated concerning the events of January 6?"

DOJ: "I don't know the number of people incarcerated...."

CRUZ: "How many people have been placed in solitary confinement concerning the events of January 6?"

DOJ: "I don't have any information about that, Senator."

CRUZ: "Back in June of 2021,...I and [three] other senators sent a letter to the Department of Justice asking these questions, asking about the differential prosecutions. Let me ask you. During 2020 Black Lives Matter and Antifa riots, all across the country, there were over 700 police officers injured by Black Lives Matter and Antifa riots. How many people have been charged with crimes of violence concerning those riots all across the country?"

DOJ: "I don't have information on how many—I would say, you know, hundreds of people have been charged...."

At this point, I unloaded on them:

You would say, but you don't know. You know, when we asked you why the Biden Department of Justice has such wildly disparate standards, going after January 6, targeting some people who committed crimes of violence, and anyone who commits a crime of violence should be prosecuted, but also targeting a lot of nonviolent individuals.

We asked you why is it that you won't target the rioters and terrorists who firebombed cities across this country. The answer we got from the Department of Justice was shameful. On October 22, you came back and said, "The department has dedicated investigative and prosecutorial resources commensurate with the significance of these events." By significance, I guess it means the political benefit to the Biden White House.

And I will tell you there are a great many Americans who are understandably deeply concerned about the politicization of the Department of Justice under President Joe Biden. It has been 218 days since we sent you that letter. DOJ refused to answer the letter. Today, when Senator Lee and I asked you about it, your answer to every damn question is "I don't know. I don't know. I don't know." You're under oath. You may believe at the Department of Justice that you are unaccountable to the American people, but that is not the case. And the wildly disparate standards are unacceptable.

Who Is Ray Epps?

In the days after the protests at the United States Capitol, several videos of the event emerged. Some of these were disturbing, such as the ones that showed police officers being beaten with flagpoles or violently slammed in door frames, while others were downright silly. It was hard not to laugh, for instance, when you saw the shirtless "QAnon Shaman" doing his bizarre "spirit calls" with a fuzzy horned hat on his head. But there was one video that drew my attention more than the rest, and I wasn't alone.

The clip, obviously captured on someone's smartphone camera, showed a middle-aged man in a tan shirt and vest speaking with the crowds outside the Capitol. He wore a red "Trump" hat that seemed to have been pulled off the rack just a few hours earlier.

In the video, the man—whose name, we would later learn, was Ray Epps—seemed intent on speaking to everyone who happened to be around him, almost as if he wanted to make them do something.

"I don't even like to say it because I'll be arrested," he said, speaking into a camera phone held aloft by another protestor. "I'll say it. We need to go *into* the Capitol!"

In another video, Epps can once again be seen arguing with people out on the streets. This time, when he suggests "going into the Capitol," those around him react vehemently, as if the argument had been going on for a while. They reject the idea of going into the Capitol and begin chanting the word "Fed" in Epps's face, obviously suggesting that he was an undercover FBI agent.

Given what we had learned about the politicization of the FBI over the past few years, I didn't think it was implausible that they might have sent federal agents to the Capitol in an attempt to make sure things went as badly as possible. After all, they had already spied on President Trump's campaign and attempted to manufacture false evidence that he was in cahoots with Russia; riling up a few protestors to make him look bad was certainly not beyond the pale.

But Crossfire Hurricane wasn't the only precedent for FBI malfeasance. Far from it, in fact. In October 2020, shortly after the state-enforced lockdowns due to COVID-19 were being lifted, four men were charged with a conspiracy to abduct Gretchen Whitmer, the Democratic governor of Michigan. The men (along with two other men who pleaded guilty) were members of an extremist group called the Wolverine Watchmen, a mostly online group of young men who spoke frequently about guns and explosives. They were motivated to kidnap Governor Whitmer, according to prosecutors, because her COVID-19 policies had been particularly harsh. In the news, Americans heard stories about how these dangerous White men planned to take the governor from her lake house in the night and then set off explosives on a bridge to cause a diversion. It would have been scary stuff, if it was true.

But it wasn't. At least not entirely. As more details about the plot emerged, it became quite clear that these men did not come up with the kidnapping scheme on their own. They were, it seemed, actively enticed into doing so by as many as twelve informants of the FBI.

In March 2022, one of these informants—an army veteran named Dan—came forward at trial to tell his story. He said that he had been brought in by the FBI "when the group talked about killing police," and undertook covert work for the Bureau. Eventually, he said, that work led to a plot to kidnap Gretchen Whitmer.[6] Remember, of course, that this "plot" was undertaken when Donald Trump was still president. Every day, he was expressing anger at various governors who were keeping their states locked down, and the dramatic arrests in the months before the 2020 election underscored the media narrative that his followers were White supremacist maniacs bent on violence.

That narrative ran into a substantial impediment, however, in April 2022, when a federal jury declined to convict any of the four men of any of the charges. Two of the defendants were acquitted, and two received a mistrial from a hung jury. Given that the principal defense offered at trial was entrapment by the FBI, the natural inference is that the jury believed that the FBI—and not the defendants—was the impetus for the criminal plot.

To anyone familiar with the history of the FBI, this should not be shocking. As we've seen, the Bureau has a long and sordid history of being directed to carry out "black bag jobs" and other dirty tricks. And, where the FBI is deployed for a political agenda, they pose enormous potential for abuse.

The Whitmer case illustrates an important distinction. Law enforcement frequently uses undercover officers to penetrate criminal organizations and to gather evidence against them. And, in so doing, they often—and quite rightly—engage in deception. An undercover cop going into a drug cartel or into the mafia is not going to tell the criminal bosses, "I'm a cop." But what they cannot do is themselves *cause* the criminal activity. They cannot *entrap* otherwise law-abiding citizens in illegal conduct. That means, among other things, it cannot be law enforcement that suggests, urges, or encourages criminality—an undercover cop can't go to a bunch of teenagers hanging out on a street corner and suggest, "Hey, wouldn't it be a good idea if we robbed the liquor store?"

And if they do—if it was law enforcement that was the impetus for the law-breaking—then the defendants will be acquitted because the cops engaged in entrapment (as with the Whitmer prosecution).

Which brings us back to Ray Epps. On January 11, 2022, I had the opportunity to question a senior FBI official about the Bureau's involvement in the January 6 attack on the Capitol. Unsurprisingly, they were not forthcoming with information. Speaking to Jill Sanborn, the executive assistant director of the FBI's national security branch, I asked a point-blank question: "How many FBI agents or confidential informants actively participated in the events of January 6?"

"Sir," she said. "I'm sure you can appreciate that I can't go into the specifics of sources and methods."

That much was unsurprising. Having undercover agents there was not problematic; entrapping people in illegal conduct would be, however, a big problem. Which led to the following exchange:

> **CRUZ:** "Did any FBI agents or confidential informants actively participate in the events of January 6? Yes or no."
> **FBI:** "Sir, I can't—I can't answer that."
> **CRUZ:** "Did any FBI agents or confidential informants commit crimes of violence on January 6?"
> **FBI:** "I can't answer that, sir."
> **CRUZ:** "Did any FBI agents or FBI informants actively encourage and incite crimes of violence on January 6?"
> **FBI:** "Sir, I can't answer that."

After that back-and-forth, I turned to Ray Epps. Earlier that week, I had directed my staff to print out large photographs of the footage that showed Epps wandering around the crowd outside the Capitol. I put them up behind me, and pointed out that the crowd had begun chanting "Fed, Fed, Fed" at him.

I asked Jill Sanborn if Epps was indeed "a Fed."

"Sir, I cannot answer that question."

I continued showing Sanborn—and the American people—how Epps had whispered in the ears of someone who ... *just seconds later* ... went on to tear down barricades in front of the Capitol building. I also showed her the post that the FBI had put up showing a picture of Epps under the headline "OFFERS CASH REWARD FOR INFORMA-TION LEADING TO ARREST," then another one showing that his photograph soon disappeared.

Next, I asked, "Did Mr. Epps urge them to tear down the barricades?"

Her response, predictably, "I cannot answer that."

Soon after, the outcry for public accountability grew. The American people began to realize that it was quite possible—likely, even—that the FBI had placed undercover agents and informants at the Capitol who didn't just observe or investigate, but who actively initiated and encouraged others to engage in illegal conduct. To what extent did the FBI actively incite the riot? They still refuse to answer. The FBI surely knew that violently entering the Capitol—which was exactly what Epps was directing all those people to do—was a criminal offense, giving them the narrative they had so longed for since the early days of the Trump presidency.

To this day, we have not gotten a straight answer from DOJ or the FBI. But that does not mean that I will not keep fighting in the Senate to expose what really went on that day.

CHAPTER SEVEN

TARGETS

When I'm at home in Texas, I try to spend as much time as possible speaking with and listening to my constituents. I have had hundreds of town halls all over the state, and have hosted countless roundtables to hear the concerns of Texans in every region. I have about two dozen staff working across the state—from East Texas to West Texas, from the Panhandle to the Rio Grande Valley—who are devoted to listening to the concerns of Texans and helping them deal with problems with the federal government. That includes helping tens of thousands of veterans resolve problems with the VA, helping seniors with Social Security, helping Texans deal with immigration problems, and helping people whose passports have expired and need to get expedited passports from the State Department. My job is to fight for all 29 million Texans, regardless of whether they're Democrats or Republicans.

Some time ago, the conservative intellectual Dinesh D'Souza moved to Houston to join his new wife, Debbie, an immigrant from Venezuela who happened to be a Houstonian. I didn't know Dinesh well at the time, but I had long been an admirer of his work. I believe that his relatively brief biography of Ronald Reagan, subtitled *How an Ordinary Man*

Became an Extraordinary Leader, is one of the finest books ever written on our fortieth president. Unlike other historians who have taken on Reagan as a subject, Dinesh seemed to understand in a fundamental way what made the man tick, writing with an appreciation not just of President Reagan, but also of the conservative Americans who elected him twice. I had seen several of his documentary films as well, and I had come to believe that he was one of the most vital thinkers in the conservative movement.

As it so happens, my father, who is a pastor, had officiated the wedding between Dinesh and Debbie, and he told me it was a wonderful ceremony. He, too, admires them both.

During their first few months in Houston, my wife and I invited Dinesh and Debbie over to our house for dinner. If nothing else, I thought it would be good to spend a little time with one of my newest constituents. And for a while, that's exactly what the four of us did. We spoke about our families, our work, and the state of American politics in general. During dinner, I was impressed by the speed at which Dinesh's mind seemed to work. While he could be caustic and combative during his debates and public appearances, I found that here in my living room he was kind, affable, and self-deprecating. He was, in short, living the American dream: a kid who had grown up in Mumbai, India, then clawed his way up the ladder of success using nothing but his quick wit and work ethic. He attended Dartmouth College and ended up a policy advisor to President Ronald Reagan shortly thereafter. Having made my own way as the son of an immigrant (and having gone through the travails of being a conservative in the Ivy League), I felt an instant kinship with him.

Toward the end of dinner, Dinesh began speaking about something that had clearly been bothering him for a long time. For the past few years, he said, he had been paying for a minor campaign finance violation that had completely upended his life. The story was familiar to me. But hearing about the fallout—eight months in a community center, years of forced community service, and a lifetime ban from voting in any elections—I thought again about the details of Dinesh's crime. I was astounded by how minor it had been, especially in relation to the drastic punishment he eventually received for it.

The facts were simple. During the 2012 Senate primary in New York State, a woman named Wendy Long had run against Senator Kirsten Gillibrand, a Democrat who was sure to win the race. Long had attended Dartmouth with Dinesh, and the two had grown close in the years since, fighting for the same causes and running in the same social circles. (I'm friends with Wendy too.) Just about everyone watching the race knew that Long, who was running a campaign of ideas against the Gillibrand Democratic machine, did not have any hope of winning. She was going to lose in a landslide, and everyone—from the press and the voters to Dinesh and even Long herself—knew it.

That is when Dinesh made the foolish mistake that would haunt him for years to come. In what he would later call "an act of misguided friendship," he asked three friends to donate $5,000 each—then the maximum contribution for an individual—to Long's campaign, and then he reimbursed them each for the money by check. He did this after he had already given $5,000 under his own name, meaning that his total contributions to the Long campaign totaled $20,000, four times the legal limit. Clearly, Dinesh had not done this to influence the outcome of the election. Nor had he done it so that Long would have a materially better chance of winning the race.

Presumably, he did it so that his friend would not be embarrassed in public, or so that she could keep waging her battle of ideas for a little bit longer. It was a crime, to be sure, but one that typically would be punished with a fine and a light slap on the wrist. Indeed, had Dinesh not been a public figure and an enemy of the Obama administration, this is almost certainly what would have happened.

Unfortunately, the case against Dinesh was brought in 2013 by Preet Bharara, the left-wing U.S. Attorney in New York City who clearly harbored a grudge against him. Like Dinesh, Bharara was the son of Indian immigrants who had worked his way up from the bottom.

Bharara was so nakedly political that he became the inspiration for Paul Giamatti's character, the corrupt and wildly ambitious U.S. Attorney Chuck Rhoades, in the Showtime drama *Billions*. In later commentary, Dinesh would suggest that Bharara had prosecuted him, "a fellow Indian," in order to curry favor with his bosses in the Obama administration. Reviewing the facts of the case, I found that easy to believe.

Dinesh's trial came shortly after he released the film *2016: Obama's America*, a sweeping indictment not only of President Obama's policies, but indeed of his entire worldview. In making the film, Dinesh had gone to Kenya to interview several members of Obama's family, including his brother, who had unkind things to say about the president. Shortly after the film was released in around two thousand theaters, President Obama began denouncing Dinesh on his website, BarackObama.com, and venting about the film in private.

It wasn't long after that Preet Bharara brought the government's case against Dinesh for his campaign finance violation—which, as Dinesh was willing to admit, was a crime. He was completely willing to receive the same punishment as anyone else. But anyone else who committed a similar violation—one in which there was no conspiracy or quid pro quo—would have received only a nominal fine. Given that Dinesh had never committed this crime before and was almost certain never to do so again, it is unlikely that the crime should have even gone to trial.

There is no doubt that the prosecution brought this case because Dinesh was a public figure—one who, as everyone knew, was a passionate and effective critic of the Obama administration. The person who took him down, Bharara must have reasoned, would be favored by the White House. So, Bharara brought the full force of the government to bear on D'Souza, going so far as to argue in front of a judge that he should serve time in prison for his crime. When Dinesh's lawyers asked for the FBI's files on him—which, they argued, could have proven collusion between Bharara and, say, Eric Holder at the DOJ—the judge refused. In these files, later obtained by a congressional oversight committee, Dinesh was explicitly "red-flagged" as a conservative and a prominent critic of the Obama administration.

In the end, Dinesh was sentenced to five years' probation and eight months at a community confinement center. This meant that for eight months, Dinesh was allowed to spend all day at his house, then forced to go to a center with other convicted felons to sleep in a bunk bed in the middle of a large room. There was no real reason for his confinement, and everyone who watched the proceedings knew it.

As a result of this ordeal, Dinesh was now a convicted felon. This meant that he could not vote. He could not legally own a firearm. He also needed to report to mandatory community service one day a week, meaning that for one day, he was not able to write his books, make his films, or advance the conservative movement with his ideas. For his enemies, whom he routinely shreds in debates and online altercations, I'm sure this was a good arrangement. But for the rest of us, not so much.

After telling me about what he had been through, Dinesh asked me, very politely, whether I would be willing to ask President Trump to consider granting him a pardon for his crime.

I hadn't expected that. So I thought about it for a moment.

The crime itself was minor, and the sentence Dinesh had been given was, on its face, needlessly harsh. If Dinesh had not been such a vocal supporter of conservative causes—and, more importantly, such a vociferous critic of President Obama—he would not have been punished as he was. But he *was* an effective critic of Democrats, and he had made himself a thorn in the side of the Obama administration. Therefore, as soon as his critics saw a chance to strike, they did.

In this sense, Dinesh was in good company. He was one of many prominent critics of the Obama administration who had been targeted for their political beliefs. Unlike Richard Nixon, however, President Obama and his cronies got quite good at precision attacks, always making sure they had plausible legal basis for their political hit jobs.

At the dinner table, after mulling it over for a moment, I told Dinesh that I would be happy to raise the issue with President Trump.

I knew that the president had shown similar understanding when it came to other people who had been attacked for their conservative beliefs. Just months earlier, for instance, he had recently pardoned I. Lewis "Scooter" Libby, a former aide to Vice President Dick Cheney who had likewise been caught in the political crosshairs by over-zealous prosecutors looking to settle scores. I made a mental note to reference the Libby pardon during my conversation with President Trump, when it occurred.

As Dinesh was leaving, I told him not to get his hopes up. The pardon power, although (rightly) delegated to the head of the executive branch to use as he or she sees fit, is one that presidents—even those who seem to take glee in breaking with tradition, as President Trump certainly did—use sparingly. While I certainly believed that Dinesh had learned his lesson, served a severe punishment for a one-time foolish indiscretion that hurt no one, I could not be sure that President Trump, or the people around him, would agree. I said that the next time I spoke with President Trump, which I typically did every week or two, I would raise the issue and argue Dinesh's case in as convincing a manner as possible.

In the following days, I ran through the facts of Dinesh's case again, thinking of the various other people who had been victimized by our justice system for their beliefs. The first, of course, was Scooter Libby, a man who served his country for decades only to get caught up in one of the most notorious—and dumbest—instances of political persecution in the history of our justice system. Unlike Dinesh, Libby did not make a foolish youthful mistake. He didn't do anything to deserve what ultimately happened to him.

Instead, he committed the crime of supporting a Republican president, and that was enough to ruin his career—at least for a while. Today, Libby's story stands as a paradigmatic instance of a group of rogue prosecutors who went looking for a crime, found nothing, and then started charging anyone they could find with anything they could dream up.

The Fall of Scooter Libby

When the presidential election of 2000 was finally decided—after weeks and weeks of "stolen election" claims from Al Gore and the Democrats—President George W. Bush had to begin staffing the government. Although I had served as a domestic policy advisor on the Bush campaign and had helped to coordinate our legal strategy for arguing in front of the Supreme Court, I wasn't hired to come into the White House with President Bush. Instead, I worked for six months at the Department of Justice as an associate deputy attorney general, then spent the rest of my time in the administration as the head of policy at the Federal Trade Commission.

Not working in the White House was a crushing disappointment. In time, I grew to recognize the mistakes I had made that had cost me the chance. It was my own fault; when I joined the Bush campaign, I was a twenty-eight-year-old, cocky kid. I was deeply passionate about conservative ideas, and I stepped on more than a few toes in fighting to advance those ideas. And, up to that point, I had enjoyed a lot of early success, and desperately needed to learn some humility (involuntarily, if necessary). In hindsight, I'm genuinely grateful for my failure to get the job I had hoped for in the Bush White House; I needed to get my teeth kicked in (figuratively) to fundamentally change my attitude. And I'm convinced I never would have been elected to the Senate had I actually gotten the White House job I yearned for. As I learned a decade later, sitting down with thousands of grassroots activists, answering questions face-to-face from Republican women, being cross-examined at Tea Party forums—all of those are powerful tools for determining authenticity and for detecting, rejecting, and punishing arrogance.

In the weeks between his victory and inauguration, President Bush and his transition team worked to staff the White House with good, principled conservatives who would implement the agenda we had campaigned on. Many of my friends went on to work in the Bush White House, and when filling out the ranks of his senior staff, President Bush preferred to work with people he knew he could trust.

Often, this meant hiring people who had been in Republican politics for a long time, meaning they had probably worked for Bush's father, President George H. W. Bush, during his four-year term in the White House. This is best exemplified by his choice of Dick Cheney, a long-time friend of the family and a ruthlessly effective conservative, for the job of vice president.

During his time in President George H. W. Bush's cabinet (and previously, when he was just thirty-four years old, serving as President Ford's chief of staff), Cheney had built up a strong circle of acquaintances and advisors, many of whom had also spent long careers in government. Along with these men, Cheney learned how the levers of power worked in Washington as he developed his worldview. Among his close aides were Paul Wolfowitz and Elliott Abrams, two foreign policy experts who would go on to define the neoconservative movement. But there was perhaps no one closer to Dick Cheney than I. Lewis Libby, known around the White House by his nickname "Scooter."

From the first days of President George W. Bush's time in office, Scooter Libby worked hand in hand with Vice President Dick Cheney on foreign and domestic affairs. Soon, he became one of the president's most trusted aides. Unlike some presidents who preferred to be involved in the gritty details of every decision, President Bush preferred to lead from the top, delegating a great deal of power to his vice president and the team that surrounded him. It was a task Scooter and his colleagues had been preparing for all their lives.

Throughout the eight years of the Clinton presidency, these men had antagonized the administration in power, writing memos that criticized Clinton's foreign policy and called for renewed investment in America's military. In 1997, they founded the Project for the New American Century to further their goals, a move that made them plenty of enemies in the Clinton administration. When the tables turned and the Republicans again took the White House in the year 2000, that hatred remained, this time spurred on by the belief that the Republicans had somehow "stolen" the election.

The trouble for Scooter Libby began, in some sense, with President George W. Bush's 2003 State of the Union address. During that speech, given just weeks before the invasion of Iraq, President Bush alluded to a report from British intelligence that claimed that Saddam Hussein, then the president of Iraq, had attempted to purchase five hundred tons of yellowcake uranium from Niger. At the time, the world was on the brink of chaos, much like it is today. Anyone listening would have understood "yellowcake uranium" to be code for "weapons of mass destruction." If the report was accurate, then it meant that Saddam Hussein, a brutal dictator, was on the verge of acquiring and potentially using nuclear weapons against his enemies.

The report would later turn out to be based on false information. But it was in all likelihood not a deliberate lie. In the weeks before the State of the Union, President Bush and his team had, in fact, received what seemed to be concrete evidence that Saddam Hussein was attempting to buy uranium to make nuclear bombs. Leaders in Congress had been briefed on the same intelligence, and most (all, really) believed it was accurate at the time.

But to President Bush's critics, that didn't make a difference. One of them, a former ambassador to Gabon and São Tomé and Príncipe named Joseph Wilson, wrote an op-ed in the *New York Times* that accused President Bush of lying. "Based on my experience with the administration in the months leading up to the war," he wrote, "I have little choice but to conclude that some of the intelligence related to Iraq's nuclear weapons program was twisted to exaggerate the Iraqi threat."[1]

Months earlier, the CIA had sent Wilson to Africa to investigate an earlier report from Italian intelligence services that also claimed Saddam Hussein was trying to purchase uranium from Africa, and he'd determined that the rumor was based on bad intelligence. Wilson never filed a written report of his findings. He had also undertaken the mission without the knowledge of George Tenet, then the director of the CIA. One week after Wilson published his op-ed in the *New York Times*, columnist Robert Novak wrote a story about his mission to Niger to investigate the rumors about nuclear weapons. Toward the bottom of that story, there was a passing disclosure that would lead, quite strangely, to the end of Scooter Libby's political career.

"Wilson never worked for the CIA," Novak wrote, "but his wife, Valerie Plame, is an agency operative on weapons of mass destruction. Two senior administration officials told me that Wilson's wife suggested sending him to Niger to investigate the Italian report. The CIA says its counter-proliferation officials selected Wilson and asked his wife to contact him."

At first glance, this was a minor detail in the story. But its implications would be severe. At the time, Plame's relationship to the CIA was not public knowledge; it wasn't something a newspaper columnist could have easily found on his own. Someone at the highest levels of government, possibly the Bush White House, must have leaked Plame's name and employment status to Novak.

For the next several years, a manhunt ensued to find out who leaked the name. The investigation soon became the talk of the town, though it caused a mere ripple compared to the Mueller investigation that would come years later. On December 31, 2003, Deputy Attorney General James Comey—a man whose thirst for praise and attention was just beginning to grow—appointed his old friend Patrick Fitzgerald as a special counsel to lead the investigation. Fitzgerald and Comey had been colleagues at the United States Attorney's office in New York City, where they developed a close personal friendship. At the time he was appointed, Fitzgerald was godfather to one of Comey's children.

For the next few years, Fitzgerald and his team of prosecutors pursued their enemies in the Bush White House with zeal. Because the mandate of the special counsel was broad and apt to change as the lead prosecutor saw fit, the investigation broadened considerably during that time. Rather than investigate a single leak, Fitzgerald and Comey used their powers to take out their anger over the Iraq war and other policies that they did not agree with. It is no surprise that they focused the majority of their ire on anyone who had ever been close to Vice President

Dick Cheney, one of the chief architects of the invasion of Iraq. (Although I personally disagree with the decision to invade Iraq, I don't believe that those who made that decision did so out of malice or that they deserved the political persecution that followed.)

Almost immediately, Patrick Fitzgerald found the leak. It had come from Richard Armitage, the deputy secretary of state in the Bush administration. Armitage admitted that he had told Bob Woodward, the famously dogged Watergate reporter who had become the assistant managing editor at the *Washington Post* in the years since, that Plame was an employee of the CIA. That, in turn, is how her name ended up in the Novak column, also published in the *Washington Post*.

That should have been the end of it. Patrick Fitzgerald and his team had set out to find the person who leaked Valerie Plame's name to the press, and that person had come forward before they even had a chance to order office supplies. Had I been put in charge of the investigation, I might have broken early for lunch and delivered my final report by the end of the first day.

But Fitzgerald didn't stop. Much like the Mueller team that would come together more than a decade later, Fitzgerald's office was filled with anti-Bush partisans who wanted to take someone down. It mattered little whether that person had actually committed a crime. Indeed, they had already declined to prosecute Richard Armitage because his disclosure, improper though it may have been, was not a crime. Under the Intelligence Identities Protection Act of 1982, disclosing the name of a covert CIA employee is a crime punishable by time in prison. But Valerie Plame, a mid-level employee at the CIA, hardly fit that description. There were likely hundreds of people who knew she worked for the CIA, and no CIA source or operation was placed in jeopardy when her identity was disclosed. Moreover, the barrel-chested Armitage, who was Colin Powell's deputy, was seen as a moderate and an Iraq war skeptic; he was not deemed a good target for a political witch hunt.

So, the investigation went from a hunt for leaks to a game: they would ask a series of incredibly detailed questions to anyone they came across, then prosecute the first person who got an answer wrong, probably through no fault of their own.

Eventually, the Fitzgerald team settled on Scooter Libby, Vice President Cheney's chief of staff. They knew that Libby was not the one who disclosed Valerie Plame's identity—that was Richard Armitage—and that it would not have been a crime even if he had. But if they could trip him up with questions, they might be able to charge him with perjury, or get him to flip on someone higher up on the White House chain of command.

That's exactly what happened (at least the first part). At some point during a lengthy line of questioning, Libby was asked about a phone call that took place in July 2003 between himself and Tim Russert, then the host of *Meet the Press* on NBC. Libby remembered that during this phone call, Russert had mentioned casually that Valerie Plame was married to Joseph Wilson, the diplomat who was haranguing the Bush administration over the Iraq war in public. Libby had mentioned this phone call, presumably, to prove that many people in the media already knew that Plame was an employee of the CIA. But when Tim Russert was questioned in November 2003, he testified that he did *not* recall mentioning Valerie Plame on a phone call with Scooter Libby.

This, amazingly, was the question on which Libby's conviction was based. Libby said that he'd heard Valerie Plame's name on a phone call four years ago, and the person he'd been on the phone with said he hadn't mentioned it. This did not prove that Libby had leaked Plame's name to the press, and it did not prove he was lying about the phone call. It proved, simply, that he was a human being who had trouble remembering the minute-by-minute details of phone conversations he had four years ago (or that the other person on the call disagreed about what was said). If you doubt that, think back to a random day in September 2018, roughly four years ago. Did you speak with anyone on the phone that day? What did you speak about? Can you recall every name mentioned and say with absolutely certainty—under penalty of perjury—that you did or did not, in fact, hear those names?

Probably not.

As anyone who's ever tried to remember something similar knows, the human memory is faulty. We are always forgetting things, editing things, and misremembering events. There is a wealth of clinical literature in psychology that proves this. In fact, Libby's lawyers attempted to have an expert in human memory come into court and testify. I have reviewed such testimony before, and it can be extremely convincing. But Fitzgerald and the special prosecutor's office managed to block that from happening.

Instead, they called a reporter from the *New York Times* named Judith Miller, who had spoken with Libby in the past for stories. In her notes, she had scribbled four words—"wife works in bureau?"— that Fitzgerald took as proof that Libby had discussed the identity of Valerie Plame with her. When she refused to testify, Fitzgerald took the heavy-handed step of sending the reporter to jail for eighty-five days, releasing her only when she agreed to answer questions on the stand. Thanks to this coerced testimony, Scooter Libby was ultimately found guilty of perjury and sentenced to thirty months in prison. He was also ordered to pay a fine of $250,000, and stripped of his license to practice law.

Many in the Bush White House were outraged, but none more so than Cheney. Libby had been targeted in a political prosecution, with Fitzgerald hoping he could coerce him (like he had with Miller) into revealing something politically or legally damaging about Cheney or Bush. Libby had steadfastly refused to participate in this political vendetta, and he paid a heavy price for his loyalty. Critically, the prosecution was not focused on investigating an actual crime (they determined at the outset that Libby was not the Plame leaker, and that, even if he had been, doing so was not a crime), and Libby was not in the role of Nixon's henchmen of covering up their boss's actual criminality. Rather, Fitzgerald was targeting people, trying to find anything he could get; he was looking for scalps, and willing to abuse the vast power of the Department of Justice to try to get them.

Cheney vigorously urged President Bush to pardon Scooter Libby, which would have been the right thing to do. Unfortunately, other voices in the White House were concerned with the political downside of a pardon; they were worried that it would be portrayed as a corrupt deal, much like Bill Clinton's infamous "midnight pardon" of Marc Rich, the former hedge fund manager who hid in Switzerland after being charged with tax fraud and participating in illegal oil deals. Not coincidentally, during his time in Switzerland, Rich had donated enormous amounts of money to the Clinton campaign through his ex-wife, effectively buying himself a presidential pardon on the black market.

Ultimately, the Bush White House cut the baby in half: President Bush commuted Libby's sentence, sparing him jail time, but declined to issue a pardon. So Libby remained a convicted felon, which among other things prohibited from earning his livelihood practicing law.

As the years went on, the evidence that Libby had been railroaded by the special prosecutor mounted. It reached new heights in 2015, when Judith Miller revealed in a book that she was led into giving a false confession by Patrick Fitzgerald. The four words in her notebook, she realized, could not have referenced an attempt by Libby to leak the fact that Valerie Plame was an employee of the CIA, because the CIA did not have bureaus; it had divisions, something Scooter Libby would surely have known.

For a few more months, this evidence hung in the air, waiting for someone to do something about it. President Obama certainly wasn't going to pardon Libby, no matter how much evidence was on his side. Then, in January 2017, President Trump took office and upended the traditional rules of Washington, D.C. This included the norms governing presidential pardons.

Typically, presidents issued the bulk of their pardons on their way out of office, almost as if they were ashamed of giving clemency to people who'd been convicted of crimes. Far too often, these pardons were given to people who were major donors to the president's campaign (like Marc Rich). But President Trump did not wait until his final days in office to begin issuing pardons. When he saw someone who'd been unfairly treated by our justice system, he moved to make things right. On April 13, 2018, he granted a full pardon to Scooter Libby, saying that he hoped the pardon would "help rectify a very sad portion of his life."

Unfortunately, not all victims of political persecution are lucky enough to receive pardons—or to live to see themselves exonerated. This brings me to another of the most prominent examples of prosecutorial misconduct in modern history: the case against Senator Ted Stevens.

A Case of Concealment

By the time the charges against Senator Ted Stevens emerged, he had been in the United States Senate for forty-five years, making him the longest-serving Republican in Congress. A talented lawyer who had served his country in World War II, Senator Stevens had a remarkable career. During his time at the Department of the Interior in the 1950s, he was even involved in the process of making his adopted home state of Alaska the forty-ninth state of the Union.

His "crime," first reported by the *Anchorage Daily News*, involved a renovation he'd done on his home in Girdwood, Alaska. According to the report, later taken up by the Department of Justice, Senator Stevens had failed to pay full price for the remodeling of the home, and then attempted to "conceal" this fact by not including the cost of the renovations on his mandatory Senate financial disclosure forms. As the evidence would later reveal, all of this was false. Senator Stevens and his wife had paid a fair price of $160,000 for the renovations, and they had attempted to do the whole thing in accordance with Senate rules.

Senator Stevens had also written a note to Bill Allen, who would later become the star witness for the Department of Justice, expressing his intention to do everything according to the rules of the Senate.

"Send me a bill," the note read. "We have to do this ethically."

The case went to trial in 2008, just as Senator Stevens was beginning his re-election campaign. If he won, it would be his eighth term in the

Senate. All along, he maintained his innocence, saying the whole thing had been a misunderstanding. But he was worried, as anyone would have been. The prosecutors argued that he had accepted the renovations—paid for, they said, by Bill Allen as an illegal campaign gift—and then attempted to hide them. While testifying on the stand, Bill Allen said that the note from Stevens about "doing this ethically" was just an attempt by the senator to "cover his tracks" when he realized he might get caught. This testimony was at the heart of the DOJ's case against Senator Stevens.

And it worked.

In the end, the jury found Senator Stevens guilty of seven counts of failing to report hundreds of thousands of dollars in improper gifts.

Amid the fallout from this scandal, Senator Stevens lost his re-election bid to Anchorage mayor Mark Begich. Interestingly, Begich was the only Democrat that year who managed to flip a Senate seat in a state that Barack Obama lost, a pretty good indication that had it not been for the trumped-up charges against his opponent, he would not have stood a chance in the election. To this day, Senator Stevens remains the longest-serving United States Senator ever to lose a re-election bid.

Just two years later, while on his way to a fishing trip in a small plane, the plane crashed and Senator Stevens died. He was eighty-six years old.

Tragically, Senator Stevens never lived to see himself exonerated. He did not live to see the flurry of headlines that came in March 2012 when a special investigator looking into his conviction found that "federal prosecutors knowingly concealed exculpatory evidence and allowed false testimony to be presented at trial in their overzealous pursuit of criminal charges," according to a summary in *Politico*. He didn't live to see the multiple books that have been published about the blatantly illegal conduct of DOJ prosecutors, all in pursuit of convicting him and getting him out of office (and keeping Democrats in control of the Senate).

Reading some of these books, as well as various newspaper accounts of the trial, it is clear just how much damage even a single rogue prosecutor—especially one who has the full backing of the United States government—can do to an innocent person.

We now know that in order to nail Stevens, a Republican who was just then up for re-election, prosecutors at the Department of Justice refused to turn over notes from the renovation foreman at Stevens's home that would have supported the senator's contention that he did indeed ask for a bill so they could "do things ethically." They also failed to disclose that Bill Allen, the government's star witness, had a sexual relationship with a fifteen-year-old girl that he asked the girl to lie about under oath. During the trial, Allen and his family were granted immunity in exchange for testifying against Senator Stevens. These facts only scratch the surface of how corrupt the prosecutors in the case were.

In the weeks after the report about the Stevens prosecution was released, Attorney General Eric Holder said that the DOJ had imposed "sweeping new training courses on thousands of federal prosecutors to remind them of their legal obligations." Apparently, Holder was disgusted by how unfairly the prosecutors had treated Senator Stevens, and he was going to make some changes.

Given what was about to happen to Senator Bob Menendez, however, the changes did not last long.

Keeping Menendez in Line

After Barack Obama's second inauguration, the focus of his White House shifted to Iran. Shortly after President Obama was elected again, his advisor Ben Rhodes—a failed novelist who helped design some of his boss's most extreme policies—said that he wanted the Iran nuclear deal to be the "Obamacare of the second term." Somehow, he meant this as a compliment.

In my Senate office, this came as deeply unwelcome news. At the time, I had ambassadors from major European allies coming to my office asking for my help pushing back against the deal, which had become the Obama administration's top foreign policy objective. They were getting enormous pressure from the White House to support the deal, and they wanted out. (Ironically, some of these allies have now become enthusiastic cheerleaders of the Iran deal, but they certainly were not at the time.)

The Ayatollah Khamenei is a theocratic zealot who routinely leads chants of "Death to America" and "Death to Israel." I believe he means it. Allowing his despotic regime to acquire nuclear weapons would pose an enormous national security threat to America, and an existential threat to our close friend Israel.

Israel tried to do everything it could to stop the Iran deal, right down to Prime Minister Benjamin Netanyahu's giving an impassioned speech against it in a joint session of Congress. I was there on the floor of the House chamber for that historic speech, which was positively Churchillian in its gravity and foresight. Numerous Democrats boycotted Netanyahu's speech.

There has long been considerable bipartisan support for Israel, and that bipartisan support is incredibly important. But the Obama administration wanted the Iran deal more than anything else. And so the administration gave Democrats in Congress a binary choice: either you could support Israel, or you could support Democrats in the White House.

You could not do both.

As a staunch supporter of Israel, and a hawk when it comes to keeping America safe, I knew which side I was on. The Iran deal, even if the Obama administration could come up with its perfect, platonic ideal, would inevitably lead to Iran developing nuclear weapons. I knew it, and so did everyone else. And clearly, the deal was far from perfect. Every Senate Republican agreed with me, as the Obama administration surely knew they would. The problem, of course, was that there were still some Democrats who occasionally had the courage to part ways with the Obama administration.

One of them was a senator from New Jersey named Bob Menendez. Bob is a fellow Cuban American, one of three in the Senate (the two of us and Marco Rubio). Unlike Marco's family, which came to Florida, and my father, who came to Texas, Bob's family came to New Jersey, and he became a Democrat. At the time, on questions of foreign policy, Bob was by far the most moderate of the Senate Democrats. When I joined him on the Senate Foreign Relations Committee (where he was the senior Democrat), I told him, tongue-in-cheek, "Bob, on foreign policy, you're by far the least crazy of your party." He laughed heartily.

At the beginning of 2015, Senator Menendez began seriously questioning the wisdom of coming to the negotiating table with the vicious theocratic regime in Iran, especially on a subject as serious as nuclear weapons. He often did so in public, much to the consternation of his Democratic colleagues, most of whom were so blindly obedient to the Obama White House that I'm surprised they didn't consult the West Wing before deciding what color ties to wear to work. Around the Capitol building, it was common knowledge that Senator Menendez was leaning against the Iran deal. The question was whether he would follow through on his opposition in public.

He did. On March 2, he gave an impassioned speech at the annual AIPAC conference in Washington. As the *Atlantic* reported,

> Menendez's speech marked a crescendo in a long and—at times—tense relationship with the Obama administration. As the White House seeks to negotiate a nuclear deal with Iran, Menendez has been the leading Democrat questioning the process. While President Obama has demanded cooperation from Congress, the Foreign Relations Committee's top Democrat sponsored legislation in December that aimed to bog Iran down with more economic sanctions. His intent was to put more pressure on the country to cooperate with the United States, but the White House claimed it undermined its months-long discussions.... Menendez has continued to carry the torch publicly against a "bad deal."[2]

Just one week later, CNN reported on a leak from the highest levels of the Department of Justice that DOJ was planning to bring "criminal corruption charges" against him.

"People briefed on the case say Attorney General Eric Holder has signed off on prosecutors' requests to proceed with charges," the CNN report read. "Investigators have focused in part on plane trips Menendez took with [Salomon] Melgen. In 2013, after word of the federal investigation became public, Menendez paid back Melgen $58,000 for the 2010 plane trips, calling his failure to properly disclose the flights an 'oversight.' Menendez said he has been friends with Melgen for more than twenty years and the two families have spent holidays and other special occasions together."[3]

Much like the Steele Dossier, the rest of the CNN report (based on the DOJ leak) included salacious and unverified details. There was a rumor, for instance, that Senator Menendez had "solicited prostitutes in the Dominican Republic," and that he had carried out affairs with three mistresses. To anyone reading, it was meant to portray Menendez as a corrupt politician who could not be trusted; at the very least, it was certain to undermine and take the focus off his criticism of the Iran nuclear deal.

This, of course, was the point.

While the actual indictment against Menendez did not become public until months later, planted rumors of it were enough to make him seem guilty during the final stages of the Iran deal. The fact that the Holder DOJ leaked the prosecution within a week of when Menendez announced his opposition to a "bad deal" with Iran was not lost on anyone. The Obama administration was, in effect, telling the rest of the Democrats to get in line, *or else.*

To his credit, Senator Menendez stood his ground.

On August 18, 2015, as the Iran deal was in its final stages of being written—or, rather, cobbled together and rewritten for the thousandth time—Senator Bob Menendez made the brave choice to formally oppose

President Obama on the floor of the Senate. At the time, only one other Democrat had summoned the courage to do so.

"I have looked into my own soul," he said, "and my devotion to principle may once again lead me to an unpopular course. But if Iran is to acquire a nuclear bomb, it will not have my name on it. It is for these reasons that I will vote to disapprove the agreement and, if called upon, would vote to override a veto."[4]

But the other Democrats had received the message. On September 10, 2015, Republicans tried to force a vote on a resolution of disapproval on the Iran deal, and the Democrats in almost straight party line filibustered that resolution. Just three Democrats voted with Menendez against the deal, two short of what was needed to overcome the Democrats' filibuster. (One of these was Chuck Schumer, who quietly and hypocritically cast a "no" vote after doing everything he could to shepherd the Iran deal through Congress and ensure it would go into effect.)

While the criminal case was pending, Senate Democrats stripped Menendez of his role as ranking member of the Foreign Relations Committee, elevating Maryland Democrat Ben Cardin to take his place.

Of course, Senator Menendez would eventually see the end of his troubles in 2018, when a federal judge dismissed all the charges against him. In response, Senator Menendez issued a statement.

"From the very beginning," he said, "I never wavered in my innocence and my belief that justice would prevail."

He did not say whether he believed the prosecution was politically motivated from the start. On the merits of the case, I have no idea whether Senator Menendez was in fact guilty or innocent. But he did not deserve to have his case taken up and used by the Obama Justice Department as a political weapon to neutralize his opposition to the Iran nuclear deal.

Luckily for Menendez, the case ended in 2018, but only after his first trial ended with a hung jury. Only then (long after the Iran deal), did DOJ prosecutors ask the judge to dismiss the charges, and only then was the case dismissed. At the very least, his "crime" was always about much more than his actual conduct.

Senator Menendez was fortunate that the prosecutors on his case were willing to give up the fight when it became clear they had little chance of convicting him. This is what prosecutors, who usually get one shot to make the best version of their argument before a judge or jury, are supposed to do. He did not need to have a president intervene in his case to remove the stain from his legacy, which is not something that can be said for all victims of selective prosecution.

Which brings me back to Dinesh D'Souza.

Justice Served

"Thank you for pardoning Scooter Libby," I told President Trump. "It was the right thing to do. It was always disappointing that President Bush failed to do so, and thank you for having the courage to correct that injustice."

I was riding in the back of the Beast with President Trump and John Kelly, the White House chief of staff. Once again, I was amazed by the size and strength of the president's limousine. The steel doors were eight inches thick, and the windows could withstand a bazooka or several minutes of continuous machine gun fire. We were on our way to attend the annual NRA convention, which was in Dallas. It was just a couple weeks after my dinner with Dinesh and Debbie.

President Trump was happy, and opening a conversation with praise was always the best way to begin a productive discussion.

"You know," I continued, "There is another person whose story is very similar to Scooter Libby's. And that's Dinesh D'Souza. Like Scooter, Dinesh was targeted in a political prosecution, and his sentence was grossly disproportionate. It was an abuse of power, directed at him because Dinesh is such an effective advocate, and I would encourage you to pardon Dinesh as well."

President Trump paused, though only for a moment. Then he nodded, smiled, and turned to John Kelly, who'd been half-listening for most of the ride.

"Okay. I'll do it. John, make it happen," he said.

And that was it. On one level, I was dismayed at how quickly the matter had been decided—with no consideration of pros or cons, no briefing from the Department of Justice—the entire conversation had taken less than two minutes. But President Trump could be decisive and bold, and that's one of the many things millions of Americans love about him. And, in this instance, I was glad that he was following good counsel (if I might immodestly observe).

After a moment, John Kelly—the four-star general who'd been charged with carrying out President Trump's order—turned to me with a confused look.

"Who's Dinesh D'Souza?" he asked.

Needless to say, this didn't surprise me. John was a decorated Marine and a tremendously efficient leader at making the trains run on time, but his background was not political. (That may be one reason his tenure as chief of staff was short-lived.) Of course he didn't know who Dinesh D'Souza was. Trump, I knew, did, because every day Trump watches hours of Fox News, where Dinesh was a fixture.

After the ride in the Beast, I called Dinesh, who was thrilled. I told him not to pop champagne yet, but he should be encouraged that things seemed to be moving forward. A short time later, I had dinner with Don McGahn, the White House counsel and a friend. The subject of the pardon came up again, and Don told me, almost as an afterthought, that according to the Constitution, the requirements for a presidential pardon were quite loose. Historically, when presidents have sought to pardon people, they've done so by printing out official documents with a gold seal and lots of lofty-sounding writing and elegant calligraphy. But the Constitution requires none of that. As long as you have a signed piece of paper that says "I, the president of the United States, hereby pardon you, person, for this crime," you have a pardon.

I filed the conversation away in my mind and went about my business. Dinesh did the same. Then, a few days later, I got another call from Don McGahn. He asked me for Dinesh's cell phone number, and I gave it to him.

The next day, I saw this tweet from President Trump's account:

"Will be giving a Full Pardon to Dinesh D'Souza today. He was treated very unfairly by our government!"

Again, I had a hard time believing that it had really been that easy. But with President Trump, some things were. When he believed something was right, he had the courage to do it, no questions asked.

Today, Dinesh D'Souza continues to fight valiantly in the arena of ideas. He can vote, and he can own a gun. His latest movie and book, *2000 Mules*, is a powerful exposé of voter fraud in 2020, exposing ballot harvesters caught on camera stuffing drop boxes with handfuls of ballots in the middle of the night. It's also the top-grossing political documentary since his prior film *2016: Obama's America*. Dinesh's new movie highlights, among other things, the great work that continues to be done by Catherine Englebrecht and True the Vote.

I am proud to have played a part in helping to clear his name.

CHAPTER EIGHT

AFFIRMATIVE ACTION

During the presidential campaign, Vice President Joe Biden promised repeatedly that he would keep politics out of the Department of Justice. He argued, although never convincingly, that President Trump had deeply politicized the DOJ, using it as a vehicle to settle his own political scores and attack his enemies. During one speech, he argued that President Trump had turned the Department of Justice into "his personal law firm," vowing never to do the same thing if he were allowed to take office.

This, of course, was an egregious misrepresentation of the truth. But Biden never let facts get in the way of his partisan rhetoric.

Nevertheless, Vice President Biden repeatedly assured crowds on the campaign trail—if a few dozen people sitting in white chalk circles in half-empty parking lots can be called a "crowd"—that the Department of Justice was hopelessly broken. He claimed that he, a lifelong politician who had finished near the bottom of his class in law school, was the one to fix it. He would do this, he claimed, by staying away from the DOJ altogether. The department, he promised repeatedly, would operate completely independently of him and his political cronies.

During an event in Charlotte, North Carolina, held shortly before the election, Biden was asked about his plans for the Justice Department, specifically the civil rights division. The question came from one of the many far-left activists that the Biden campaign was then attempting to win over. The vice president's answer, scattered and meandering though it was, covered all the talking points he'd been given.

"The Justice Department under my administration will be totally independent of me," he said. "I will not direct them when to prosecute, how to prosecute, what to prosecute, and I will not be injecting—I will not enter their decisions based upon the judgments they make about the cases they bring and what they don't bring."

Biden continued:

> Most of all, I would have an attorney general who understood his oath of office. Not a joke. An attorney general has an oath of office that could do and move on what the professionals in the department thought had to be pursued without my interfering and saying no, they're my friends; go after this person. Go after Hillary, or this kind of stuff...I get asked the following question: If in fact you get elected, would you prosecute Trump? Would you pursue prosecuting Trump? And the answer is I'm not going to pursue prosecuting anyone. I'm going to do what the Justice Department says should be done. And not politicize it.

That was a noble promise. Since taking office, however, President Biden has done precisely the opposite of what he promised to do. In fact, almost every word of the answer above has turned out to be a lie. Although he has shown a willingness to stay "independent" of certain aspects of his job—looking the other way, for example, while the United States military was embarrassed during its disastrous withdrawal from Afghanistan, or twiddling his thumbs while inflation climbed to record heights—he has been unusually present and engaged when it comes to the affairs of the Department of Justice.

Shortly after taking office, for instance, according to a report in the *New York Times*, he "confided to his inner circle that he believed former president Donald J. Trump was a threat to democracy and should be prosecuted."[1] Toward the end of that first year, he told reporters that he believed the Department of Justice should prosecute anyone who refuses to cooperate with the kangaroo-court demands of Congress's increasingly partisan January 6 select committee. Despite his press secretary Jen Psaki's attempts to walk these comments back during a briefing the next morning, the message from the Biden White House was clear. Now that the Democrats had seized power, their enemies were not safe from the claws of the federal government.

In other words, President Biden has picked up where President Obama, the man who taught him how to check names off his enemies list using the machinery of the federal government, left off. The only difference was that by the time Joe Biden took office, his list of enemies was much longer. It included not only people who attacked his administration directly, but also those who dared go against the new neo-Marxist, "woke" orthodoxy that he and his supporters are devoted to.

The Department of Justice began doing this work as soon as President Biden took office, moving on multiple initiatives long before any of his judicial nominees were even confirmed. Anything that might upset the new regime was summarily dismissed.

On February 3, for instance, months before any of President Biden's judicial nominees would even be confirmed, the Department of Justice formally dropped a case against Yale University examining the methods by which the school decided which students to admit to its undergraduate program. For years, Asian American students had been claiming—with mountains of evidence on their side—that major universities such as Harvard and Yale aggressively discriminated against them. In various lawsuits, Asian American groups claimed that by adhering to strict guidelines on affirmative action, these universities were deliberately putting Asian students at a disadvantage during the admission process.

Reviewing the evidence, it was difficult not to conclude that this was true. Even the most hardened Critical Race Theorists in the country could not dispute the fact of this discrimination. For years, Yale had openly and ostentatiously discriminated against Asian Americans. They had done so in much the same manner as other Ivy League colleges in the '50s had instituted quotas against Jews, and their reasoning was the same. Back then, the administrators of these schools knew that if the admissions were based on merit alone, they might end up with "too many Jews" in the schools. In today's context, schools worried that if they didn't discriminate against Asian American students in favor of victim groups that were more in vogue at the time, they would end up with "too many Asian Americans." Both were openly racist policies.

Over the course of two years, the Justice Department had worked hard to build its case, and the evidence they uncovered had been astounding. In a press release published on August 13, 2020, the Department of Justice described its findings:

> For the great majority of applicants, Asian Americans and Whites have only one-tenth to one-fourth of the likelihood of admissions as African American applicants with comparable academic credentials. Yale rejects scores of Asian American and White applicants each year based on their race, whom it otherwise would admit. Although the Supreme Court has held that colleges receiving federal funds may consider applicants' race in certain limited circumstances as one of a number of factors, the Department of Justice found Yale's use of race is anything but limited. Yale uses race at multiple steps of its admissions process resulting in a multiplied effect of race on an applicant's likelihood of admission, and Yale rarely balances its classes.

In response to the findings of its investigation, the Justice Department demanded that Yale agree not to use race in its upcoming admissions cycle. Had this demand been accepted, it would have been a major leap forward for fairness and equality—but not the left's demand for "equity"—in admissions.

Good Racism

In the minds of the Critical Race Theorists, the world is an unfair, racist place designed to oppress non-White people, and it is their solemn duty to alter the system until all racial groups are represented equally in all positions of power. Rather than seeking equality of opportunity, meaning that all people of all races would have an equal chance of succeeding, these people seek to bring about mandated equality of outcome.

"Equity" demands discrimination—discrimination against the "oppressors" and in favor of the "oppressed." And, for the left, that racial discrimination is a good thing.

As a student at Princeton, I was very active in the American Whig-Cliosophic Society, the nation's oldest political and debating society and the largest student group on campus. It had been formed by the merger of the American Whig Party, founded by James Madison when he was a student at Princeton, and the Cliosophic Party, founded by William Paterson (a signer of the Constitution and later a senator and governor of New Jersey and then U.S. Supreme Court justice). I was elected chairman of the Cliosophic Party, which had become the conservative party. I always found it ironic that although I agree with virtually every word James Madison (the "father of our Constitution") ever wrote, I could not lead the party he founded. By the time I got to Princeton, the Whigs had become the party of the left.

When I chaired the Clios, the Clio whip was a man named David Panton. David had come to Princeton from Jamaica, where he was born and raised. David is a remarkable man: brilliant, principled, funny, and immensely charming. He became my roommate, both in college and in law school, my debate partner, and my best friend. Together, he and I ran the student government at Princeton, and we also became the top college debate team in the country. David went on to win a Rhodes scholarship, earn a doctorate in business from Oxford, and then graduate with honors from Harvard Law School. Many people know that Barack Obama was the first Black president of the *Harvard Law Review*; far fewer know that the second Black president of the law review was David Panton, my roommate and later the best man at my wedding.

In the last debate David and I did together for the Clios, we proposed that Princeton should end racial affirmative action. We laid out a host of arguments against it: racial discrimination is morally wrong, it stigmatizes minorities, it fosters resentment, and it perpetuates false racial stereotypes. If Princeton was going to have any preferences, far better to give additional weight to economically disadvantaged students of any race—which would ensure a diverse student body, recognize real merit in overcoming adversity, and avoid the pernicious practice of discriminating based on skin color. For the liberal students in attendance, the fact that it was David and me arguing for this—a Black man and a Hispanic man, both conservatives—made their heads explode. Nevertheless, because Princeton (like most colleges) leaned overwhelmingly left, they assumed they would win the student vote that night.

At the end of the debate, the roughly 100 students in attendance cast their votes. And, that night at least (to the astonishment of the left), the Princeton students there voted by a large margin to end racial affirmative action.

At the time, the necessity of affirmative action policies to advance the interests of people of color was treated as gospel at universities like Princeton. Minority students who dared dissent were not treated kindly by the supposedly open and loving liberal students and professors on campus. It was during my four years at Princeton that I first learned a lesson that would come up again and again during my career in politics: liberals like their minorities quiet and submissive.

Of course, most institutions—including the United States government—were not willing to have open debates like the one we had at Whig-Clio. As a result, far too often the orthodoxy of racial affirmative action goes unchallenged in corporations, universities, and government agencies across the country. When there is opposition, it's usually quiet, voiced only in small venues behind closed doors.

The perniciousness of racial affirmative action was made all the more visible to me two years later when I entered my second year of law school. That year, I was selected to join the *Harvard Law Review*. Every year, the *Harvard Law Review* selected forty students out of a class of 560 to write student notes and edit articles written by legal scholars and law professors all over the country. In total, there were eighty editors—forty second-year students and forty third-year students.

At the time I was there, thirty-two of these slots were based on merit. Every year in late May, the law review conducted a grueling weeklong writing competition for students who wanted to become editors. Students would edit an article deliberately riddled with mistakes and would also write their own legal case comment. Based on a combination of this writing competition and first-year grades, thirty-two students were invited to become editors of the review. The other eight slots were expressly reserved for students of color, regardless of how they performed during their first year of school or on the writing competition. Although it was public that up to eight slots were reserved for affirmative action every year, it was not public which students were invited to join the law review based on something other than merit.

This put minorities such as myself and David in a difficult spot, never knowing ourselves (and nobody else knowing) whether we had actually earned our places on the law review.

During my first year on the law review, it happened that a number of editors selected were conservatives who opposed affirmative action. They decided to force a debate on whether the law review should end affirmative action. Unlike the debate I had participated in as a student at Princeton, this one could have immediate real-world consequences for future students at Harvard. Still, I wasn't particularly keen on the idea. I could count votes, and it was clear that, no matter what points we made during the debate, we would almost certainly lose. But my classmates wanted to proceed. And so, all eighty editors on the law review gathered one evening in a classroom to debate the issue.

For most of the debate, I stayed relatively quiet. The arguments for both sides proceeded along familiar lines, with opponents of affirmative action arguing that it was an impediment to true fairness and equality, and proponents arguing it was the only way that students of color would have any hope of attaining positions of power. Unfortunately, the second position was much more commonplace on campus in the early '90s.

But I knew how to pick my battles, so I remained quiet, sitting in the back of the classroom and listening to both sides tire themselves out.

Then, near the end of the debate, one supercilious liberal stood up and claimed that affirmative action was not only a net positive, but also necessary. He spoke with the assurance of all leftists on campus at the time—the ones who never had to have their ideas challenged because they aligned perfectly with the institutional ethos that surrounded us.

"We must keep affirmative action in place," he declared. "Without it, the law review would become be nothing but White men."

Again, I wasn't planning to speak. But this really pissed me off. I rose, hardly waiting for him to finish before pointing out how stupid—and how blatantly, nakedly racist—the young man's argument had been.

"If you want to understand just how noxious the assumptions behind affirmative action are," I said, "this one liberal has just told everyone here that he believes that in a system of merit, the only people who could possibly succeed are White men. What a nasty, bigoted lie."

Suddenly, every head in the room turned my way.

"I am a Hispanic man," I said, turning my attention directly to him. "If you want to pull out your damn transcript and lay it on the table, I'll put mine next to it. Then we can see who would prevail in a meritocracy."

The student did not take me up on the offer.

I also pointed out the most revealing aspect of his assumptions: "You claimed that only White men would prevail in a meritocracy. But the law review doesn't have affirmative action based on gender; it's only based on race. Your comment illustrates perfectly just how insidious affirmative action is. What you're saying to the dozens of women sitting in this room, who earned their spot on the law review, is that you don't think they deserve to be here either."

Interestingly, the issue of gender-based affirmative action had come up before in the offices of the *Harvard Law Review*, almost always suggested by well-meaning White liberal men who believed women and minorities were not capable of achieving things on their own. Almost every time the issue came up, it was invariably the female editors (themselves overwhelmingly left-leaning) who opposed extending affirmative action to gender. To a person, these women had attained remarkable success—acceptance to Harvard and earning a place on the law review—and they had done so based on merit. Everyone knew this. If the law review instituted gender-based affirmative action policies, however, going forward it would never be clear which women had gotten there based on merit and which ones were only there thanks to a quota system imposed by benevolent White liberal men.

In the end, the motion to end affirmative action died a quick death, as I knew it would. We hardly needed to count the ballots to know that racial affirmative action was not going anywhere anytime soon. Perhaps some of the people who were against it assumed that the practice would eventually die out. As the United States moved further toward Dr. Martin Luther King, Jr.'s dream of an equal and colorblind society, the need for such discriminatory rules would simply go away. Of course, these students needed only to take a short look around the campus of Harvard University to know that this wasn't happening anytime soon.

Over the next thirty years, the students who had been responsible for such ridiculous antics as the trial of Christopher Columbus on their college campuses graduated and started attaining positions of power, making the world more race-obsessed than it had ever been before.

Wherever these students went, they brought the misguided principles of Critical Race Theory with them, spreading the word that the United States was a racist, horrible place, and that the only way to fix this was by instituting rigid systems of affirmative action and other quota systems.

By the time Joe Biden became president of the United States, this dangerous ideology had spread far and wide. In universities, corporations, and the federal government, it was no longer merit that mattered. During the riots that occurred in the wake of George Floyd's killing in the summer of 2020, for instance, several major corporations vowed to implement quota systems for their boards. Major universities said they were more dedicated than ever to the cause of "antiracism." And when it came time for Joe Biden to staff the federal government, he leaned on the same affirmative action policies that his far-left supporters had been pushing for years.

In June 2021, the Biden administration released a list of political appointees, taking special care to note that more than 85 percent of them "identified as people of color, women or LGBTQ," according to a report in Axios the next morning.[2] And, of course, when it came to his first Supreme Court nominee, Biden announced that he would consider only African American women; the other 94 percent of Americans need not apply. During the campaign, Biden had promised to promote racial "equity"—the pursuit of equality of outcome for all races, genders, and sexual orientations—over all else. Apparently he believed that nominating people to positions of power based on those qualities (rather than, say, focusing on their abilities) was a step forward for the United States of America rather than backward.

When it came to political nominees, the Biden administration adopted the left-wing positions of its base, nominating people based on their skin color and sexuality rather than on their ability to do their jobs. As soon as he got elected, a kind of affirmative action on steroids began taking over the federal government.

Nowhere were the downsides of this approach more evident than in President Biden's appointees to judicial positions—appointments which, as a senior member of the Judiciary Committee, I was obliged to spend a great deal of time looking into.

Is Racial Discrimination Wrong? A Yes or No Question

In February 2022, I learned that another law school classmate of mine was up for a judicial appointment. Given the left-wing politics of Harvard Law School, this was not uncommon, especially during Democratic administrations. Often, when a former classmate is up for a nomination, I'll know them personally. Justice Ketanji Brown Jackson was on the law review with me, as was Trump's secretary of state Mike Pompeo. So too was Obama's court of appeals nominee David Barron.

This time, however, the name was Kenly Kiya Kato, and I didn't know her. During the research for Judge Kato's nomination hearing, I came upon a remarkable book review she had written as a student at Harvard that argued that all Asian Americans should be dedicated to the pursuit of racial equity. That pursuit required, she argued, policies that explicitly disadvantaged Asian Americans. Those Asian Americans who espoused "neoconservative" beliefs, she wrote, were simply "[internalizing] the dialogue of their oppressors, believing in the values of the status quo and condemning the activism of their group."[3] In English, this means that in the view of the author, Asian Americans who did not support discrimination against Asian Americans were insufficiently "woke" (although this was before that term was used) and were instead complicit in the racism of the evil White "oppressors."

When it came time for me to question her, I asked a simple question: "Do you believe racial discrimination is wrong?" She dodged the question: "Our Constitution prohibits discrimination on the basis of race....As a judge, I don't deal with issues of morality." I asked again. She dodged again. I asked a third time. Once again she refused to answer.

The reason was obvious: if she said "no," it would make clear to the American people just how radical her views were; but if she said "yes," that was in direct conflict with what she had written in law school.

So then I asked her directly what she had meant in her law school writing. She tried to deflect, saying she "didn't know" what she had meant and "didn't remember" what she had written. When I asked her if she had re-read the article—which was only eight pages long—in preparation for the hearing, she admitted she had, but she refused to discuss or defend any of the substance of what she had written.

After my questioning, Democratic senator Mazie Hirono tried to rehabilitate her testimony by arguing that, because Judge Kato's Japanese-descent parents had been detained as children in internment camps during World War II—a horrific and racist practice instituted by Democratic president Franklin Delano Roosevelt—she must "understand how terrible racial discrimination is." That should be true, but it doesn't explain why as an adult she was advocating explicit discrimination against Asian Americans.

Sadly, Judge Kato's views are not an outlier among the modern left. In 2021, Senator Hirono introduced a bill to punish "hate crimes" agaist Asian Americans. Like much of what the Democratic Party does on race, it was a bill designed as empty posturing. In this instance, their nakedly political argument went as follows: President Trump's referring to the Wuhan virus (which, in point of fact, originated in Wuhan, China) was by definition racist, and therefore any and all acts of violence that happened to be carried out against Asian Americans nationwide are the result of Trump's accurately identifying the origin of COVID-19. Ultimately, the bill was a messaging bill designed to have very little effect, and once Hirono's more egregiously political language was removed from the bill, it passed the Senate 94–1. Because I oppose all acts of violence, I voted for the bill.

When Hirono's bill was on the floor, I introduced a simple amendment that would have had a meaningful effect. It was just one paragraph, and it provided that no federal funds would go to any university that discriminates against Asian Americans in admissions or in granting scholarships. I forced a vote on my amendment, and every single Democrat voted against it. It failed by a single vote.

That's the unfortunate reality of today's Democratic Party: they support—actively, vocally, unequivocally—racial discrimination, when it favors their political objectives.

That fact was made clear again in 2021, when we voted on Biden's so-called "COVID relief" bill. I say "so-called," because only 9 percent of the bill went to healthcare spending for COVID-19. Instead, it was a liberal wish list paying off left-wing political interests across the country. I introduced amendments to prohibit federal stimulus payments from going to millions of illegal immigrants and also to prohibit those payments to criminals who were currently incarcerated. Astonishingly, yet again, every single Democrat voted no, and both amendments failed by a single vote.

But the single most offensive provision of that bill was, ironically, an agricultural lending provision. It was designed to forgive agricultural loans to "historically disadvantaged" races. Two aspects of the provision were particularly galling: first, it forgave loans at 120 percent of the loan amount (20 percent more than was owed), and second, it wasn't means tested, which meant people could qualify regardless of income. That meant an African American or Hispanic billionaire could have all his farm and ranch loans forgiven, but a poor White farmer was ineligible because he had the wrong skin color. I joked that, as a Hispanic, "I need to get me a farm, because you idiots are giving away free money." Along with several other senators, I introduced an amendment to strike this obviously unconstitutional provision, and…you know the rest: every single Democrat voted against it. It failed by one vote.

Extreme Nominees

Shortly after President Biden was inaugurated, his first slate of nominees came before the Senate Judiciary Committee. Looking at the list, it was clear that President Biden and the far-left ideologues who had put him in office were attempting to remake the federal judiciary in the name of racial and sexual equity. Nothing else—certainly not qualifications or experience—seemed to matter very much to them. Shortly before the hearings began, I wondered whether the administration would just attempt to nominate Ibram X. Kendi for attorney general and Robin DiAngelo to a federal judgeship.

The legal results, unfortunately, would be much the same.

One of the first nominees to come forward was Merrick Garland, the man who believed he had been unfairly denied a seat on the Supreme Court at the end of President Obama's first term. As payback for this perceived slight, President Biden had nominated Garland to serve as his attorney general, perhaps the most important legal position in the government. As a court of appeals judge, Garland had built a reputation of being relatively nonpartisan, so I had some hope that he might not be a terrible nominee. However, at his confirmation hearing, he refused to answer almost every single question of substance. He refused to commit to removing politics from the Department of Justice, and, sadly, he has since proven to be a profoundly partisan attorney general.

And that was reflected in the other DOJ nominees Biden put forward. One of the most radical was a former lawyer from the Department of Justice's civil rights division named Vanita Gupta. Biden nominated her to be associate attorney general, the number-three position in the DOJ. For years, Gupta had used her prior position at the DOJ to advance the extreme left's policy agenda, expressing outright hostility to anyone who dared to disagree with her. Just a few months earlier, she had spoken out against the Catholic charity Little Sisters of the Poor, which sought an exemption from the mandatory contraceptive coverage under Obamacare. As my other colleagues would soon point out, she had a long history of directing harsh and hateful insults at Republicans.

But I wasn't terribly concerned about bad tweets and foul language. This woman was up for one of the most senior posts at the Department of Justice, an agency that is supposed to be apolitical, and yet she seemed to be a thoroughly dedicated left-wing activist. During Gupta's hearing, I attempted to get her to answer several questions on her extreme left positions. Asked whether there were any circumstances under which a doctor could exercise his or her rights of conscience to refuse to perform an abortion, she declined to answer. Asked whether she believed that *District of Columbia v. Heller*, the landmark case that protected the right of individual citizens to keep and bear arms, was decided correctly, she declined again.

When she was before the Judiciary Committee, I asked if she agreed with the provisions in the Equality Act, a radical piece of legislation that among other things, explicitly repeals major parts of the Religious Freedom Restoration Act. It is a bill designed to take away the religious liberty of citizens. I knew that Gupta had been a vocal proponent of the misnamed Equality Act, and that she had lobbied for its passage—a fact that she did not initially disclose to the Judiciary Committee. But again she declined to answer.

Gupta was also profoundly hostile to school choice, an issue that I consider to be the most important civil rights issue in the nation. When she served in the Department of Justice during the Obama administration, she intervened in a case trying to kill a Louisiana school choice program even though many of the African American parents in Louisiana strongly supported and desperately needed that program. The federal court involved in that case even reprimanded the DOJ under her leadership for unethical and ineffective lawyering.

Asked whether she regretted this, she refused to provide a straightforward answer.

But it was Gupta's positions on defunding the police that were the most extreme. In 2020, in written testimony to the Senate, she had expressly encouraged Congress to "re-examine federal spending priorities and shrink the footprint of the police and criminal legal system in this country." She also encouraged reallocating federal resources, writing "some people call it defunding the police. Other people call it 'divest, invest,' but whatever you call it, if you care about mass incarceration, you have to care about skewed funding priorities."

These were not, as I would point out later during a floor speech on the issue, Gupta's college writings. They weren't scribblings on a Post-it note that she made somewhere. This was official testimony that was submitted to the United States Senate just a year before she came up for the job of associate attorney general.

With these writings in mind, I vigorously opposed Gupta's nomination to the Department of Justice. In a job that requires me to make difficult decisions every day, this was an uncommonly easy one. All of the other Republicans on the Judiciary Committee came to the same conclusion, resulting in a deadlocked vote.

A few days after that vote, I rose to lay out my objections on the floor of the Senate. Why, I asked in the middle of my speech, were Democrats so hell bent on making sure she got confirmed?

There were two reasons, I said. The first was headlines. Today's Democrats care so much about looking good in the press, they continue to press through partisan bills and partisan activists for adulation by an adoring media. The second was more complicated, and much more dangerous. Today's Democrats, I continued, are beholden to the far-left voices in their party, and nominations of people like Gupta fulfilled campaign promises they had made to the radical left.

Another such nominee was Kristen Clarke, who was also nominated to a senior position at the Department of Justice. Like Gupta, Clarke's record was one of an extreme radical. In 2020, she wrote an op-ed in *Newsweek* titled, "I Prosecuted Police Killings. Defund the Police—But Be Strategic." In that op-ed, Clarke wrote about the protests that erupted that summer and stated, "into that space has surged a unifying call from the Black Lives Matter movement: *defund the police.*"

Like Gupta, Clarke tried to run away from her record, and from her previous writings. At the prompting of Senate Democrats and chairman Dick Durbin, Clarke denied ever supporting the ridiculous "defund the police" movement that had worked its way into the brains of far-left ideologues like a virus in the summer of 2020. She instead attempted to push the responsibility onto whatever editor at *Newsweek* wrote the headline of her article, saying that she did not *really* mean we should defund the police.

So, when she came before the Senate Judiciary Committee, I met her halfway. I asked whether she still believed that "defund the police" was a "unifying call." That was not from the headline. She couldn't blame some poor editor at *Newsweek* for it. It was exactly what she wrote, right there in the text of the article.

She wouldn't answer the question. Instead, she repeated her talking points, saying that she did not (currently) support defunding the police.

That claim, I told her, is objectively ridiculous. In the op-ed she wrote, there is a lengthy section of about three paragraphs, each one beginning with the phrase "We must invest less in the police…" that lays out why and in what manner she believes we should "defund" the police. As a writer myself, I am willing to grant that some people get carried away with stylistic flair that might imbue certain phrases with meaning they did not intend. But when you begin three separate paragraphs in this identical way, you do not get to come in and say that you don't support defunding the police. Indeed, doing so was a bald-faced lie, as would be clear to anyone who actually read the article.

These two nominations were proof—as if we needed it—that the Democratic Party in the United States had changed in a fundamental way. The party has been fully radicalized. When it came to a vote, every single Democrat voted to confirm both Vanita Gupta and Kristen Clarke—two of the leading advocates in the country of defunding the police. When they're home on the stump, most Senate Democrats today claim they oppose defunding the police, but with the support of every single Democrat, both of these radical nominees were narrowly confirmed. This marked yet another sad step toward the politicization of the Department of Justice under President Joe Biden—one that would have immediate consequences.

CHAPTER NINE

INJUSTICE FOR ALL

I f you've ever wondered how much damage bad political appointees can do, the first two years of President Joe Biden's time in office presents an excellent example. Almost as soon as she was confirmed, Assistant Attorney General Kristen Clarke continued her left-wing partisan crusade. Only now, she had the immense power of the United States Justice Department behind her.

Like many zealots before her, Clarke sought first to consolidate power for herself and other left-wing crusaders who shared her agenda. During a press conference held on June 25, 2021, which began with a long speech from Attorney General Garland, Clarke attacked legislation that had been passed the previous year in the state of Georgia. The bill, which had been passed in response to enormous outcry over the irregularities of the 2020 election, was quite simple. Unlike most legislation that has come from Democrats in recent months, it was short and relatively easy to understand.

In clear statutory text, the bill laid out several steps that the state government would take to ensure that future elections did not descend into the kind of mass confusion that we saw in the aftermath of the 2020 race. It was a bill that Democrats should have welcomed. Most importantly, the bill limited the time that voters would have to request and cast their absentee ballots, also instituting strict identification requirements for doing so.

To most people, this was quite sensible. It also aligned squarely with the findings of the bipartisan Carter-Baker Commission.

To the Department of Justice under Joe Biden, however, an institution that had by this point become so saturated by left-wing politics and Critical Race Theory that its employees might as well have worn all-black Antifa outfits for uniforms, the legislation was deemed—to the surprise of no one—*racist*. According to the publicly stated position of President Biden's newest judicial appointees, voter ID laws adversely affected the African American community because Black people, unlike the rest of the adult population in the United States, don't know how to go to the DMV and get themselves a driver's license. Citing these provisions, President Joe Biden himself referred to the law as "Jim Crow 2.0."

There are no data to support the claim that voter ID laws hurt minorities. Overwhelming majorities of Americans support voter ID laws, including 69 percent of Blacks and 82 percent of nonwhite minorities.[1] And, although Democrats love to paint southern states as irredeemably racist, the data likewise do not back up that charge. Indeed, in 2018, 64.7 percent of Black Americans were registered to vote in Georgia, and 56.3 percent turned out to vote. Both of these are markedly higher than the national averages for Black voters (60.2 percent registration and 48 percent turnout). And many Democratic states do even worse than national averages (for example, in Connecticut in 2018, 49.6 percent of Black Americans were registered to vote, and just 39 percent voted; in California, 55.5 percent of Black Americans were registered to vote, and 48.8 percent voted).[2]

Nevertheless, claiming that voter ID requirements suppress Black votes is a lie that the Biden Department of Justice knows at least some of the American people will believe. The woke leadership of the Biden Justice Department knows that once they mention race, the chances that anyone will oppose them shrink dramatically. It is simply not worth the accusations of racism that will surely be hurled at anyone who expresses even mild opposition to their position.

Of course, it doesn't take very long to figure out the real reason that the Biden administration opposes the Georgia law. All you have to do is count the votes from previous elections. In the election of 2020, for instance, the official count shows that Joe Biden defeated President Trump by precisely 11,779 votes out of a total of just under five million ballots cast. We'll never know if this is a real number, of course, thanks to the unwillingness of Democrats to agree to a commission to examine the evidence of voter fraud, but assume for the sake of argument that the vote total is accurate.

Either way, these 11,779 votes represent a tiny margin of victory—one that we know the Biden team did not come by honestly.

About two years earlier, in November 2018, a local Democratic politician (and writer of romance novels) named Stacey Abrams ran for governor and lost. Rather than heading home and assessing what she had done wrong, Abrams insisted that the election was rigged against her, largely because of racism, as was and is the fashion for Democrats. She claimed that Brian Kemp, her opponent, had engaged in a campaign of "voter suppression" against communities of color, going so far as to file multiple lawsuits in an attempt to change the way elections in the state of Georgia are run. She said that the state's system of "ballot matching," whereby election officials made sure that the signatures on mail-in ballots match the signatures on voter registration forms, might have resulted in some Democratic ballots being thrown out.

In other words, elections in Georgia were *too* secure, and someone needed to do something about it.

So, for the next two years or so, that is exactly what Abrams did. Stopping in dozens of small towns in the state, saying that the election had been stolen from her the whole way, she set out to turn the state of Georgia—a longtime conservative stronghold—into a blue state. Curiously, no liberal media institutions accused her of being a conspiracy theorist or attempting to foment an insurrection when she made these claims, presumably because she was on the right team. In fact, they praised her effort, even publishing a fawning profile in the *New York Times Magazine* titled, "Why Stacey Abrams Is Still Saying She Won."[3]

A large part of Abrams's grand plan, which she had been pushing for about ten years already, involved loosening some of the restrictions that ensured free and fair elections in Georgia. She wanted more mail-in ballots, not fewer. And during the 2020 election, with the specter of COVID-19 hovering over the proceedings, she finally got her wish. More mail-in ballots—one of the surest ways to ensure more voter fraud, according to Jimmy Carter and James Baker—were flooded into Georgia than ever before. As a result, Americans were left with serious doubts about the outcome of this election—doubts that were summarily dismissed by the Democrats who benefited from Georgia's loose relationship with voting.

In response, the Georgia legislature passed a ninety-eight-page bill that addressed some of the most important concerns about election integrity. In addition to instituting identification requirements for absentee ballots, the bill also did away with "mobile voting centers," described by the *New York Times* as "an R.V. where you can vote."[4] It also set up an election hotline managed by the state attorney general, providing a direct line for citizens who see evidence of fraud, and it significantly limited the use of ballot drop boxes—in response to the multiple reports of fraudulent ballots being dropped in the dark of night.

To the Biden White House, however, the protections against fraud didn't matter. They had, after all, emerged victorious after one of the most fraud-ridden elections in the history of the United States. Any change to that system, they knew—especially one that had given them such a meager margin of victory—would not be good news. They knew that, by limiting fraud, the bill dramatically increased the chances that Republicans would be elected in the future. It had to go.

So, they sent out the Department of Justice, an institution that is supposed to be completely separate from electoral politics, to try to make sure there were no changes. Speaking about the law, Attorney General Garland said that the Department of Justice "would not hesitate to act" where it believed the "civil rights of Americans" had been violated. It was strikingly similar to when President Barack Obama, afraid of the attempts by concerned citizens to secure the 2012 presidential election, sent Attorney General Eric Holder down to Texas for a speech on "voting rights."

Earlier that same week, Attorney General Garland had said that the government would keep an eye out for new voting laws in states that had primarily Republican legislatures. He promised that the federal government would take action to stop these laws from being enacted.

In politics, this is what we call "saying the quiet part out loud."

Attorney General Garland knows that the Department of Justice is not supposed to take sides in political fights. He knows that the Department of Justice is likely to lose this legal fight in court. But that doesn't matter to Democrats. What matters is constantly appealing to an increasingly far-left base—one that wants to see all issues through the prism of race, and forces previously moderate Democrats to do the same thing. Often, they end up insulting the very people they purport to help.

During her speech on the issue, for instance, Assistant Attorney General Kristen Clarke said that African Americans in Georgia were much more likely to go to the wrong precinct to vote.

"It's well documented," she said, "that communities of color change residences more frequently than other populations. And because of this greater residential mobility, and polling site closures and consolidations, Black voters are more likely to end up at the wrong precinct on election day. SB 202 reduces the chances that those eligible voters will have their ballot counted."

Once again, it is striking that the Democratic Party's racism alarms—which seem to be ringing at all times—did not immediately go off when this statement was released. The process of changing one's voter registration is quite simple. According to the Biden administration, members of every other race in Georgia are able to see to it that their addresses are current, and that their voter forms are legal. But for some reason, the Biden administration claims that African Americans cannot do this. They know that this is a lie, but it allows the civil rights division—which was created to protect minorities from actual abuses—to step in with some semblance of legitimacy to advance the Biden administration's political goals. Once again, the Biden administration was hijacking the work of brave civil rights leaders in order to advance its own political ends.

Sadly, it would not be the last time.

Irreversible Damage

During the first two years of the Biden administration, the corporate press has, unsurprisingly, refused to write about the increasing politicization of the Justice Department. Even when the DOJ clearly acts in the interests of the party in power—even when it goes after personal enemies of Barack Obama, Joe Biden, and other high-level Democrats—the media seems perfectly willing to look the other way, buying whatever cover story the DOJ writes for itself.

For the most part, these excuses have involved some form of critical theory. Whenever the Biden DOJ wants to attack a Republican, as it did during the debates on election laws and abortion laws, it will come up with some perceived victim group that is allegedly being helped. In the case of voting rights, it was African Americans. In the case of the abortion laws, it was all women everywhere who faced unwanted pregnancies. This made it quite easy for the mainstream media to defend the clearly indefensible actions of the Department of Justice in both cases. All the corporate press had to do was run with the narrative that the Biden DOJ was, once again, protecting innocent victims from oppression.

The difference, of course, is that the word "oppression," much like "racism" and "injustice," has lost almost all meaning for Democrats. It is little more than a cover for the most extreme policies of the far left, devoid from actual substance. For example, on March 31, 2022, just a few hours short of April Fools' Day, the Biden Justice Department warned several Republican-led states that if they attempted to pass any legislation that infringed upon the so-called "right" of parents to submit their children to "gender-affirming care," they could be in violation of federal law. This, I submit, is what happens when you allow former students of disciplines such as Critical Race Theory and Critical Legal Studies—both of which involve performing radical and unhinged readings of legal texts—to mess around at the highest levels of federal law.

In the letter, once again penned by Kristen Clarke, the Biden DOJ warned that "a ban on gender-affirming procedures, therapy, or medication may be a form of discrimination against transgender persons, which is impermissible unless it is 'substantially related' to a sufficiently important governmental interest."[5] Here, I think, it is worth pausing to consider what the Biden DOJ means by "gender-affirming procedures." Like "antiracism" and "pro-choice," these words are so far removed from the horrific things they represent that just reading them probably does not conjure the right images in the mind.

In the world that the Biden Justice Department is trying to create, children are able to switch their genders at will. All a young boy needs to do is say that he feels like a girl today, for instance, or to reach for his sister's Barbie dolls, and the parents are well within their rights to send the child to a "gender conversion" specialist. Once the child reaches that specialist, a whole world of options is available. If the specialist, usually a firm believer in the "right" of all children to transition at will, deems it necessary for the child to take drugs to block puberty, or to begin therapy to better understand his or her gender identity, then that is what the child will do.

Many states, like Texas, believe that administering powerful drugs to young children to permanently halt their physical development is cruel and abusive. If an adult man wishes to live as a woman, or an adult woman wishes to live as a man—and if they want to undergo medical procedures to permanently alter their physiology—that is a choice they can make. Nobody is proposing restricting that. But children are different. An eight-year-old has no real idea about his or her sexuality or "gender identity." Young children sometimes think they're dinosaurs, but we wouldn't surgically alter them to add velociraptor claws. That would be absurd. Likewise, the voters of Texas can reasonably decide that young children should not be medically altered to permanently change or harm their physical development. The legislature can reasonably decide that young kids lack the maturity and emotional development to make such crucial decisions.

But not according to the Biden DOJ. If little Suzie wants powerful puberty blockers (or, more likely, if her woke parents want to force them on her), the Biden DOJ believes that there's nothing that can be done to stop permanent physical damage from being medically inflicted on this little girl.

That's not the law, and it's not common sense. It's radical politics.

The War on Texas

For years, the state of Texas has been a haven for Americans who want to keep the federal government at arm's length. When Davy Crockett fled Tennessee after losing his congressional election and came to the Lone Star State, he famously observed, "You all may go to hell. And I will go to Texas." Likewise, Sam Houston—another Tennessee transplant, who would later be the commanding general of the Texas army when we won our independence from Mexico, then president of the Republic of Texas when we were our own nation, and then a U.S. senator and then governor after we joined the Union—trenchantly observed, "Texas has yet to learn submission to any oppression, come from what source it may."

The state has a proud tradition of self-reliance, of writing our own destiny and ignoring the fashions of the time. Perhaps that is why, when hundreds of thousands of Americans left the major cities of this country after the various horrors that occurred during the

COVID-19 pandemic—prolonged lockdowns, riots, and skyrocketing crime rates—the largest percentage of them came down to the Lone Star State. In a sense, this mass migration was a direct repudiation of the policies of the radical left, which had taken over and shut down cities such as New York, Los Angeles, and Chicago.

In response, Democrats might well have taken a good, hard look in the mirror. They might have asked themselves why so many of their constituents were packing up, selling their homes, and running from Democrat-run cities as if Godzilla was about to crawl out of the ocean and attack.

But the Democrats didn't do this.

Instead, they took their usual course of blaming everyone else. The Biden Justice Department in particular, now staffed with political appointees who had either ignored or cheered on the rioting and looting that took place in major Democratic cities throughout the summer of 2020, was all too happy to take aim at places like Texas, where so many Americans had fled for a little more freedom and safety. If they couldn't stop people from moving to Texas, they seemed to reason, then they would just try to make Texas as bad as the places that Democrats controlled. This was a nearly impossible undertaking, of course. I'm sure anyone who's ever spent a few minutes in Dallas, Austin, or my hometown of Houston knows that. But if there was ever a team of people who were born for the job, it was the Department of Justice under President Joe Biden.

They began, as usual, by attacking the state's attempts to secure future elections. This is a fight, you'll remember, that had been going on in Texas for a long time, ever since a few volunteer poll watchers came together after the 2008 election to form True the Vote, an organization dedicated to finding and preventing voter fraud all over the country. In the aftermath of the 2020 election, which had been conducted under the dire circumstances brought on by COVID-19, the fight only intensified. Citizens all over Texas who had been concerned about fraud and election interference were now seeing dozens of stories a day indicating that something might be off about the results of the 2020 election. I was getting calls and emails nearly every hour asking what could be done about it.

Fortunately, a majority of state legislators were getting the same messages. This is why they acted quickly at the beginning of the year to pass Senate Bill 1, a sensible collection of reforms that would help ensure that the next election held in the state of Texas would be more secure and less contentious than the last one had been. In practice, it shared many elements with the bill passed by Georgia a few months earlier. The bill banned a practice known as "drive-through voting," which allowed volunteers to collect votes from people in their cars using portable voting devices. It also instituted strict requirements for mail-in ballots, requiring anyone who applied for one to provide either their driver's license number or the last four digits of their Social Security number, making it much harder for someone to commit fraud. Most importantly, it ensured that left-leaning officials would not send out millions of mail-in ballots—unrequested by the voters—in an attempt to undermine the security of our elections, as Democratic officials in Harris County had attempted to do in 2020.

Again, there was nothing in the bill that was inconsistent with the recommendations of the Carter-Baker Commission, which had explicitly warned against mail-in ballots and a lack of strong voter ID laws in the United States. Just a few years earlier, the legislation might have had bipartisan approval. People outside of Texas might not have found out that it even existed.

But the Biden Justice Department, which had by this point declared open war on anyone attempting actually to secure our elections, made sure that everyone knew it existed. On November 4, 2021, almost a year to the day after what might have been the most fraud-ridden election in the history of the United States, Attorney General Garland announced that the Justice Department had filed suit against the state of Texas over this commonsense election law. Their central allegation? That protecting the integrity of the election system and stopping voter fraud violates the Civil Rights Act of 1964.

To understand why the Biden DOJ is suing both Texas and Georgia for our election laws, you must understand the election system today's Democrats want to mandate. The very first bill filed in the Nancy Pelosi House was HR 1; the first bill filed in Chuck Schumer's Senate was S 1. Both are essentially the same bill: a federal takeover of our election laws that I and many others have dubbed the Corrupt Politicians Act. It would:

- Strike down every voter ID law in the country
- Strike down state prohibitions on ballot harvesting
- Strike down state restrictions on felons voting
- Mandate universal mail-in voting
- Automatically register millions of illegal aliens to vote

In the Senate, I've led the fight against this disastrous bill, on both the Judiciary Committee and the Rules Committee. I introduced amendments to preserve voter ID laws, to stop ballot harvesting, to stop felons from voting, to allow states to decide when (and if) to use mail-in voting, and to prevent illegal aliens from being registered to vote. Every single Democrat on the Rules Committee voted against each one of them.

The Corrupt Politicians Act reads as if Democrats read through the bipartisan recommendations of the Carter-Baker Commission on how to prevent voter fraud and then wrote legislation to do precisely the opposite. The only reasonable inference is that today's Democrats have cynically decided that voter fraud is good for them politically. That is, if more criminals are voting, if more dead people are voting, if more fraudulent voters are voting, if more illegal aliens are voting…they will be very likely to vote for Democrats.

Biden and the Democrats have repeatedly referred to the Texas and Georgia laws as "Jim Crow 2.0." As I explained at multiple hearings, while their rhetoric was misplaced as to those state laws, ironically it did accurately describe the bill that the Democrats were trying to ram through. The original Jim Crow laws were written by Democrats, and their objective was to prevent the voters from voting Democrats out of office. The Corrupt Politicians Act was likewise written by Democrats to disenfranchise the voters and make it impossible for the people to vote Democrats out of office. It was the opposite of democracy; it was partisan, incumbent protection.

After we beat this disastrous bill on the floor of the Senate, Schumer tried to force it through at three in the morning, after most senators had gone home to bed. In the dead of night, I stood up on the floor and objected, finally killing the bill.

Which is why the Biden DOJ is suing Texas and Georgia. Once again, the Biden administration's objection to the Texas bill had nothing to do with anyone's civil rights and everything to do with politics. The Biden administration knew that this bill—which, among other things, provided protections meant to ensure that millions of illegal aliens would not be allowed to vote—would result in fewer votes for Democrats. Just like President Obama before him, President Biden has a vested interest in making sure that voter fraud continues unabated in Texas and across the country. But there was a key difference. Where President Obama, ever mindful of his image, attempted to shut down election integrity groups in secret by using the well-hidden mechanisms of the Internal Revenue Service, President Biden was more than happy to do his dirty work in public. Whenever his Justice Department filed another suit attempting to prevent the securing of our elections, they had the audacity to hold a press conference about it.

They knew that by framing the whole thing as a matter of civil rights—and, therefore, as a matter of race—few would dare question them out of fear that they would soon be labeled a racist. As of this writing, the lawsuits have not yet been resolved in court. But I am confident that when they are, the American people will learn that both laws have been perfectly legal all along, just like the other reasonable election integrity laws that have been passed as a response to the 2020 elections.

In the meantime, the Biden administration will stay busy attacking Texas for political reasons, attempting to hit everything that sets the state apart from the deep-blue states that so many people don't want to live in anymore. In fact, they've already done so.

In September 2021, for instance, I attended a hearing of the Senate Judiciary Committee. The Supreme Court had just issued an emergency ruling declining to stop the Texas state law that effectively prohibits abortions after the unborn child has developed a heartbeat. During this hearing, which Democrats had titled "Texas's Unconstitutional Abortion Ban and the Role of the Shadow Docket," we were forced to endure hours of testimony by witnesses who described Texas as a legal hellscape where people were suffering unimaginably.

No doubt, abortion is a contentious issue that divides many Americans. It's been made all the more divisive by the Supreme Court's decision in 1973 in *Roe v. Wade* that effectively stripped democratically elected legislatures of deciding what the rules should be. At the time of this writing, the Supreme Court has not yet decided *Dobbs v. Jackson Women's Health Organization*, a case that presents a very real possibility of overturning *Roe*.

If *Roe* is overturned, it will not mean that abortion is immediately made illegal nationwide. Instead, it would mean that questions of abortion will be decided at the state level, by legislatures elected by the people—the same way they were decided for the first 185 years of our nation's history. That will mean that blue states like California and New York will almost surely continue to allow abortion on demand, and red states like Texas will adopt meaningful restrictions on abortion. I personally am strongly pro-life—I believe that every life is a precious gift from God that should be protected in law—but I recognize that not everyone agrees. I hope, over time, we will persuade those who disagree. But that's why the Constitution entrusts decisions like that to the elected legislatures of the fifty states, so that policies adopted in each state will reflect the values and mores of its citizens.

At some point in the hearing, my colleague Dick Durbin, the hyper-partisan Democrat from Illinois, railed on how horrible he believed the Texas law was. I couldn't resist asking him, if the laws in Texas were so bad, why were so many people fleeing blue states like Illinois and coming by the millions to Texas? He had no answer.

Clearly, as my colleague John Cornyn would point out, the real purpose of the hearing was to try to intimidate the Supreme Court, the one branch of our government that is supposed to be completely removed from partisan politics. A few days earlier, the Court had declined to block the Texas law from taking effect in an emergency ruling, with four liberal justices in dissent. In an unusual step, these four liberal justices had each issued separate signed dissents objecting to the Texas law, knowing full well that the Biden administration would back them.

On September 9, that's exactly what the Biden administration did. Claiming that the Texas law was "clearly unconstitutional," Attorney General Merrick Garland took direct aim at Texas, saying that "no state can deprive individuals of their constitutional rights through a legislative scheme specifically designed to prevent the vindication of those rights."

But that paled in comparison to the attack on the Supreme Court that occurred on May 2, 2022. Late that night, a draft of an opinion by Justice Samuel Alito, one of the strongest pro-life voices on the Court, was leaked to the reporters Josh Gerstein and Alexander Ward of *Politico*. This draft opinion, written to speak for a majority of the Court, would hold that "*Roe* and *Casey* must be overruled."[6] It was an astonishing disclosure, and one that would hopefully bring the nation one step closer to finally being able to provide meaningful protections for unborn children.

When I saw the leak, I was stunned. Truly speechless. As I said later in the Judiciary Committee, this leak represented the gravest possible breach of trust that every justice, law clerk, and employee of the Supreme Court owes that institution. It is impossible to overstate the gravity of the violation—the ethical violation, the potential legal violation, and the instantaneous damage to the independence and the integrity of the Court. By destroying confidentiality in its deliberations, this leak fundamentally undermines the ability of the Court to function. It may very well be a wound from which the Court never fully recovers.

After the leak, Justice Thomas described its potential enduring damage, memorably comparing it to the lingering harm of "infidelity" in a marriage:

> There's such a belief in the rule of law, belief in the Court, belief in what we're doing, that that was verboten. And look where we are, where now that trust or that belief is gone forever. And when you lose that trust, especially in the institution that I'm in, it changes the institution fundamentally. You begin to look over your shoulder. It's like kind of an infidelity, that you can explain it, but you can't undo it.

At the time of writing, we do not know who the leaker was. But, I am confident that we will. The universe of people with access to an opinion draft, along with details of the justices' votes at conference, is tiny. It consists, realistically, of the nine justices and thirty-six law clerks. I cannot believe it is remotely possible that a justice leaked the draft—it's too fundamental of a breach of trust at the Court. Instead, I believe it is overwhelmingly likely that the draft was leaked by a left-wing law clerk trying to put political pressure on the justices in the majority to change their votes. That means the likely pool of suspects is twelve: the four clerks who work for each of the three most liberal justices.

If the goal was to put political pressure on the justices, it worked. In the days that followed, there were protests all over the country. Abortion rights activists published the home addresses of Supreme Court justices. When White House press secretary Jen Psaki—serving her final days in that position before moving over to MSNBC to do effectively do the same job—was asked about doxing the justices and protestors screaming outside their homes, she refused to condemn these actions. Instead, she said that the Biden administration encouraged "peaceful protest."[7] It did not escape anyone's notice that the *last* time the left had encouraged "peaceful protests," multiple major cities burned for days at a time.

Moreover, these orchestrated left-wing protests outside the justices' homes are a federal criminal offense. Specifically, 18 U.S.C. § 1507 provides,

> *Whoever*, with the intent of interfering with, obstructing, or impeding the administration of justice, or with the intent of influencing any judge, juror, witness, or court officer, in the discharge of his duty, *pickets or parades* in or near a building housing a court of the United States, or *in or near a building or residence occupied or used by such judge*, juror, witness, or court officer, or with such intent uses any sound-truck or similar device or resorts to any other demonstration in or near any such building or residence, *shall be fined under this title or imprisoned not more than one year, or both.*

Notice the language of the criminal statute is mandatory: "*shall* be fined...or imprisoned." The purpose of the statute is similar to obstruction of justice; it is to prevent threats or intimidation of judges while decisions are pending—precisely what these angry mobs are trying to do. And protesting outside someone's home—where they sleep at night, where their children sleep—is by design threatening. I've publicly called on Attorney General Garland to prosecute these left-wing mobs. To date, he has refused to do so.

Importantly, this leak and the attempted intimidation of the Court didn't come out of nowhere. For years, Senate Democrats have been attempting to politicize and undermine the Court. Indeed, the Democrats have attempted to turn the Court into a mini-legislature, where five unelected judges decree the rules for the entire country regardless of what the voters decide.

In 2020, Senator Chuck Schumer went so far as to threaten, by name, two justices for the decisions they might make. Standing in front of the Supreme Court, he said, "I want to tell you Gorsuch, I want to tell you Kavanaugh, *you have released the whirlwind*, and *you will pay the price* if you go through with these awful decisions."

And criminal leftists heard the Democrats' call to violence. At 1:50 a.m. on June 8, 2022, police arrested Nicholas John Roske, a twenty-six-year-old man who had traveled from Simi Valley, California, to the home of Justice Kavanaugh. He came to murder the justice, and he was arrested carrying "a 'black tactical chest rig and tactical knife,' a pistol with two magazines and ammunition, pepper spray, zip ties, a hammer, a screwdriver, a nail punch, a crowbar, a pistol light and duct tape." The would-be murderer "told the police that he was upset about the recent school shooting in Uvalde, Texas, and about a leaked draft of a Supreme Court opinion suggesting that the justices were poised to overturn *Roe v. Wade*."[8]

In 2021, a year before the leak, leftist groups announced plans to protest in front of Justice Kavanaugh's home in a clear effort to intimidate him and threaten the safety of his family. Groups like Demand Justice have likewise launched shameful bullying tactics trying (successfully, it would turn out) to force Justice Stephen Breyer to retire and pave the way for a younger, more activist justice. They took out ads and even hired a mobile billboard truck to try to make this happen.

We are also seeing an ongoing, false, character assassination directed at Justice Clarence Thomas. In my view, Justice Thomas is one of the finest justices ever to serve on the Court, which is precisely why this deliberate effort to slander his character and to politicize the Court is so dangerous.

These efforts, of course, are massively funded by dark-money groups—the same dark-money groups that Democrats love to inveigh against—dedicated to putting leftists on courts and undermining our justice system. These groups, including Arabella Advisors, in turn fund Demand Justice, an organization led by Brian Fallon, a former press secretary to Chuck Schumer. On the night the opinion was leaked, Fallon tweeted that the SCOTUS leak was "good." Another leftist named Ian

Millhiser tweeted, "Seriously, shout out to whoever the hero was within the Supreme Court who said 'f**k it! Let's burn this place down.'"[9]

Sadly, the left no longer makes any attempt to hide its outright contempt for our justice system. The corruption that began with Richard Nixon and continued through Barack Obama is reaching a kind of culmination with the administration of Joe Biden and his band of angry left-wing activists. Today, they are leaking opinions on abortion and attacking parents who come to school board meetings to complain about transgender policy. They are waging war on states that pass laws that are offensive to their far-left base, and bringing good old-fashioned racism—which they cleverly call "antiracism"—back into American government.

I shudder to think of what they might do tomorrow. But as of this writing, the corruption shows no signs of slowing down. Having just seen the attempted murder of a Supreme Court justice, I fear the consequences of the politicization of our legal system will continue to get worse.

But, filled with hope, I know that only We the People can stop it. I believe that the 2022 elections will be historic and that Republicans will win substantial majorities in both the House and the Senate. In June 2022, Republican Mayra Flores won a special election in Texas's Thirty-Fourth Congressional District, which runs along the Gulf Coast from Corpus Christi all the way to Brownsville (the southern tip of Texas). I supported Mayra in the election, in a district that has the second-highest Hispanic population (84 percent) of any district in the United States. The victory marks the first time that Republicans have won a congressional seat in the Rio Grande Valley *since 1871*.

That election win foreshadows what I believe will happen in November: South Texas will likely turn red. For over a century, South Texas has consistently elected Democrats. And there is a real chance that, in 2022, South Texas will elect two or three Republican members of Congress—all Hispanic women whom I'm supporting vigorously—as part of a nationwide electoral tsunami. From Mexican Americans in

Texas to Colombian Americans in Florida to Puerto Ricans in New York, Hispanics of all backgrounds are abandoning the Democratic Party in droves. The Democrats are in big trouble with Hispanics, suburban moms, young people, and blue-collar workers who are fed up with their failed economic policies, elitism, and woke ideology.

And, if and when Republicans take over Congress, I hope and pray that it is just the first step to winning back the White House in 2024 and—critically—restoring integrity to the Department of Justice, the FBI, and our entire legal system.

If we value liberty, if we value the rule of law, it is incumbent on us to make that happen.

ACKNOWLEDGMENTS

Writing this book, my third, has been a joy. The topic is near and dear to my heart, and I have been blessed to work for and with multiple great lawyers and judges who revere the rule of law.

The corruption of the Department of Justice and the FBI is a terrible thing, deeply corrosive to our nation. But I want to acknowledge and thank the many extraordinary men and women who work at the DOJ and FBI who perform their jobs with integrity, and who are fighting back to prevent the law from being turned to political ends.

I am always immensely grateful to Heidi, Caroline, and Catherine. They put up with a lot, with Daddy getting on a plane every Monday morning, and with all the grief that comes with public life. There is far too much acrimony and bitter hatred in our political discourse, and my beloved wife and daughters have paid a real price for that. They have done so with grace, and I am deeply grateful to them for that.

I want to thank Sean McGowan, an incredibly talented writer who worked alongside me in writing this book. He did terrific work, performed invaluable historical research, and has a true gift in crafting an elegant turn of phrase.

I also want to thank my agent Keith Urbahn and his colleague Dylan Colligan, who as always provided sage counsel and wisdom. And my editor Paul Choix and the tremendous team at Regnery, who believed in this book and made the final product better.

Helpful edits were suggested by Steve Chartan, Sam Cooper, Nick Maddux, Chris Jaarda, and Nick Ganjei. Less helpful edits were suggested by Jeff Roe, Jason Johnson, and David Polyansky. I suppose I am grateful for both.

Any mistakes are mine.

NOTES

Preface

1. Luke Rosiak, "Loudon County Schools Tried to Conceal Sexual Assault against Daughter in Bathroom, Father Says," Daily Wire, https://www.dailywire.com/news/loudoun-county-schools-tried-to -conceal-sexual-assault-against-daughter-in-bathroom-father-says.
2. Sam Dorman, "Loudon Email Reveals Superintendent Notified School Board on Day of Alleged Sexual Assault," Fox News, October 22, 2021, https://www.foxnews.com/politics/loudoun-superintendent -email-sexual-assault-same-day.
3. "Full NSBA Letter to Biden Administration and Department of Justice Memo," Parents Defending Education, November 29, 2021, https://defendinged.org/press-releases/full-nsba-letter-to-biden -administration-and-department-of-justice-memo/.
4. Ibid.
5. "Bipartisan Judiciary Committee Senators Scold DOJ's Oversight Blockade," Chuck Grassley Senate website, June 17, 2021, https:// www.grassley.senate.gov/news/news-releases/bipartisan-judiciary -committee-senators-scold-dojs-oversight-blockade.
6. Justin Jouvenal, "In Case at Center of Political Firestorm, Judge Finds Teen Committed Sexual Assault in Virginia School Bathroom," *Washington Post*, October 25, 2021, https://www.washingtonpost .com/local/public-safety/in-case-at-center-of-political-firestorm-judge

-finds-teen-committed-sexual-assault-in-virginia-school-bathroom
/2021/10/25/42c037da-35cc-11ec-8be3-e14aaacfa8ac_story.html.

7. "Sen. Cruz Grills AG Garland: 'Apparently Ethics Are Not a Terribly High Priority in the Biden Justice Department,'" Ted Cruz Senate website, October 27, 2021, https://www.cruz.senate.gov/newsroom /press-releases/sen-cruz-grills-ag-garland-apparently-ethics-are-not -a-terribly-high-priority-in-the-biden-justice-department.

8. Hugh Hewitt, "Is This Terry McAuliffe's Last Hurrah?" *Washington Post*, October 11, 2021, https://www.washingtonpost.com/opinions /2021/10/11/why-glenn-youngkin-has-the-momentum-in-virginia/.

Introduction: The Way It's Supposed to Work

1. Ron Chernow, *Grant* (New York: Penguin Press, 2017), 708.

2. "Executive Order 6166—Organization of Executive Agencies," Office of the Federal Register, https://www.archives.gov/federal -register/codification/executive-order/06166.html.

3. Josh Gerstein, "Eric Holder: 'I'm Still the President's Wingman,'" *Politico*, April 4, 2013, https://www.politico.com/blogs/politico44 /2013/04/eric-holder-im-still-the-presidents-wingman-160861.

Chapter One: Enemies

1. Kenneth Thompson, *The Nixon Presidency: Twenty-Two Intimate Perspectives of Richard M. Nixon*, 81.

2. Nan Robertson, "Tricia Nixon Takes Vows in Garden at White House," *New York Times*, June 13, 1971, https://timesmachine .nytimes.com/timesmachine/1971/06/13/170503892.html ?pageNumber=1.

3. John A. Farrell, *Richard Nixon: The Life* (New York: Vintage Books, 2018), 416.

4. Douglas Brinkley and Luke Nichter, *The Nixon Tapes, 1971–1972* (New York: Houghton Mifflin Harcourt, 2014), 171.

5. Garrett M. Graff, *Watergate: A New History* (New York: Simon & Schuster, 2022), 44.

6. Tim Weiner, *Enemies: A History of the FBI* (New York: Random House, 2012), 277.

7. Ibid., 278.

8. Farrell, *Richard Nixon*, 422.

9. Patrick J. Buchanan, "Media Memorandum for the President," Nixon Library, May 21, 1970, https://www.nixonlibrary.gov/sites/default /files/virtuallibrary/documents/jan10/025.pdf.

10. Graff, *Watergate*, 49.

11. Ibid., 51.
12. Ibid., 24.
13. "I Really Need a Son of a Bitch," Miller Center, University of Virginia, https://millercenter.org/the-presidency/secret-white-house -tapes/son-of-a-bitch.
14. Ibid.
15. G. Gordon Liddy, *Will: The Autobiography of G. Gordon Liddy* (New York: St. Martin's Paperbacks, 1991), 104.
16. Dan Hall, "Criminal Mastermind: Watergate Scandal: How Ex-FBI Agent G. Gordon Liddy Carried Out the Break-In Which Led to Nixon's Scandal-Ridden Downfall," *The Sun*, March 31, 2021, https://www.the-sun.com/news/2613540/g-gordon-liddy-dead -watergate-scandal-nixon/.
17. Fred Emery, *Watergate* (New York: Simon & Schuster, 1995), 86.
18. Rick Perlstein, *Nixonland: The Rise of a President and the Fracturing of America* (New York: Simon & Schuster, 2008), 578.
19. "Transcript of News Conference by the President on Political and Other Matters," *New York Times*, August 30, 1972, https:// timesmachine.nytimes.com/timesmachine/1972/08/30/80801403 .html?pageNumber=20.

Chapter Two: The IRS Comes Knocking

1. NRATV, "CPAC Chicago: NRA News Interview with Catherine Engelbrecht— President of True the Vote," YouTube, June 14, 2012, https://www.youtube.com/watch?v=6ahohaYl5x0.
2. Bonnie Erbe, "Obama's ACORN Connection to Voter Fraud," U.S. News & World Report, October 10, 2008, https://www.usnews.com /opinion/blogs/erbe/2008/10/10/obamas-acorn-connection-to-voter -fraud.
3. Michael Falcone and Michael Moss, "Group's Tally of New Voters Was Vastly Overstated," *New York Times*, October 23, 2008, https:// www.nytimes.com/2008/10/24/us/politics/24acorn.html.
4. Brandon Darby, "Multiple Agencies Involved with IRS in Intimidation," Breitbart, May 13, 2013, https://www.breitbart.com /politics/2013/05/13/IRS-Scandal-Facts-Suggest-Other-Gov-Agencies -Involved/.
5. Burton W. Folsom Jr., "FDR and the IRS," Hillsdale College, https:// www.hillsdale.edu/educational-outreach/free-market-forum/2006 -archive/fdr-and-the-irs/.
6. Rick Perlstein, *Nixonland: The Rise of a President and the Fracturing of America* (New York: Simon & Schuster, 2010), 413.

7.   "A Conversation with Donald Alexander '48," *Harvard Law Today*, July 1, 2005, https://today.law.harvard.edu/conversation-donald -alexander-48/.

8.   Macon Phillips, "President Barack Obama's Inaugural Address," The White House, January 21, 2009, https://obamawhitehouse.archives .gov/blog/2009/01/21/president-Barack-obamas-inaugural-address.

9.   Ed Pilkington, "Obama Angers Midwest Voters with Guns and Religion Remark," *The Guardian*, https://www.theguardian.com /world/2008/apr/14/barackobama.uselections2008.

10.   "Presidential Approval Ratings—Barack Obama," Gallup, https:// news.gallup.com/poll/116479/barack-obama-presidential-job -approval.aspx.

11.   *Annual Report of the Commissioner of Internal Revenue for the Fiscal Year Ended June 30, 1938* (Washington, D.C.: Government Printing Office, 1938), available at the IRS website at: https://www.irs .gov/pub/irs-soi/38dbfullar.pdf.

Chapter Three: Crossfire Hurricane

1.   Paul Sperry, "Meet the Steele Dossier's 'Primary Subsource': Fabulist Russian from Democrat Think Tank Whose Boozy Past the FBI Ignored," RealClearInvestigations, July 24, 2020, https://www .realclearinvestigations.com/articles/2020/07/24/meet_steele_dossiers _primary_subsource_fabulist_russian_at_us_think_tank_whose _boozy_past_the_fbi_ignored_124601.html.

2.   "FBI Agent Peter Strzok's Texts with Lisa Page Disparage Trump throughout Campaign," CBS News, December 13, 2017, https:// www.cbsnews.com/news/peter-strzok-lisa-page-texts-trump-idiot/.

3.   Byron Tau et al., "Durham Probe Reveals Government Access to Unregulated Data Streams," *Wall Street Journal*, February 26, 2022, https://www.wsj.com/articles/durham-probe-reveals-government -access-to-unregulated-data-streams-11645871581.

4.   Sadie Gurman and Byron Tau, "Lawyer Michael Sussmann Indicted on Charges of Lying to FBI," *Wall Street Journal*, September 16, 2021, https://www.wsj.com/articles/lawyer-indicted-in-john-durhams -russia-investigation-11631825767?mod=article_inline.

5.   Charlie Savage, "Court Filing Started a Furor in Right-Wing Outlets, but Their Narrative Is off Track," *New York Times*, February 14, 2022, https://www.nytimes.com/2022/02/14/us/politics/durham -sussmann-trump-russia.html.

6.   Josh Gerstein and Kyle Cheney, "Judge Spares Clinton Camp in Sussmann Ruling," *Politico*, May 7, 2022, https://www.politico.com

/news/2022/05/07/judge-spares-clinton-camp-in-sussmann-ruling
-00030887.

7. Brooke Singman et al., "Hillary Clinton Approved Dissemination of
    Trump-Russian Bank Allegations to Media, Campaign Manager
    Testifies," Fox News, May 20, 2022, https://www.foxnews.com
    /politics/hillary-clinton-approved-trump-russian-bank-allegations
    -sussmann-trial.

Chapter Four: Critical Race Theory

1. Ibram X. Kendi, *How to Be an Antiracist* (New York: One World,
    2019), 163.
2. Ibram Rogers, "Living with the White Race," The Famuan,
    September 9, 2003, http://www.thefamuanonline.com/2003/09/09/
    living-with-the-white-race/.
3. U.S. Department of State, "Secretary Clinton Comments on the
    Passing of Robert Byrd," YouTube, June 28, 2010, https://www
    .youtube.com/watch?v=ryweuBVJMEA.
4. Alan Blinder, "Was That Ralph Northam in Blackface? An Inquiry
    Ends without Answers," *New York Times*, May 22, 2019, https://
    www.nytimes.com/2019/05/22/us/ralph-northam-blackface-photo
    .html.
5. Tom Kertscher, "Fact Check: Did Ketanji Brown Jackson Say Judges
    Should Consider CRT While on the Bench?" WRAL, March 25,
    2022, https://www.wral.com/fact-check-did-ketanji-brown-jackson
    -say-judges-should-consider-crt-while-on-the-bench/20205090/.
6. Rachel M. Cohen, "Why Teachers Are Afraid to Teach History,"
    New Republic, March 28, 2022, https://newrepublic.com/article
    /165598/teachers-afraid-teach-history.
7. "The World's Worst Writing," *The Guardian*, December 24, 1999,
    https://www.theguardian.com/books/1999/dec/24/news.
8. John Sedgwick, "Beirut on the Charles," *GQ*, February 1993, http://
    www.johnsedgwick.biz/pdf/GQ_BeirutOnTheCharlesFull.pdf.
9. "Bringing The 1619 Project into Classrooms: A Unique
    Collaboration," Penguin Random House, https://global
    .penguinrandomhouse.com/announcements/bringing-the-1619
    -project-into-classrooms-a-unique-collaboration/.
10. Christopher F. Rufo, "Failure Factory," *City Journal*, February 23,
    2021, https://www.city-journal.org/buffalo-public-schools-critical
    -race-theory-curriculum.
11. Ibid.
12. Tyler O'Neil, "Gavin Newsom's Wife Celebrates Angela Davis,
    Former Fugitive Communist Party Member, for Women's History

Month," Fox News, March 24, 2022, https://www.foxnews.com
/politics/gavin-newsom-wife-angela-davis-womens-history-month
-jennifer-siebel.

13. Christopher F. Rufo, "Bad Education," *City Journal*, February 11,
2021, https://www.city-journal.org/philadelphia-fifth-graders-forced
-to-celebrate-black-communism.

14. Ibid.

15. Rich Lowry, "How Southlake, Texas, Won Its Battle against Critical
Race Theory," *National Review*, June 3, 2021, https://www
.nationalreview.com/2021/06/how-southlake-texas-won-its-battle
-against-critical-race-theory/.

16. Ibid.

Chapter Five: Lawlessness

1. Jeffrey Toobin, "The Milwaukee Experiment," *New Yorker*, May 4,
2015, https://www.newyorker.com/magazine/2015/05/11/the
-milwaukee-experiment#:~:text=Chisholm%20stuck%20his
%20neck%20out,drawn%20attention%20around%20the
%20country.

2. David A. Love, "White Domestic Terrorists like Kyle Rittenhouse Are
Held to a Different Standard," Yahoo, November 24, 2020, https://
www.yahoo.com/video/white-domestic-terrorists-kyle-rittenhouse
-192659233.html?guccounter=1&guce_referrer=aHR0cHM6Ly93d
3cuZ29vZ2xlLmNvbS88&guce_referrer_sig=AQAAAAn7oJjiDc1YH
vVpn8wrLoi7viq4xKm0d4O2tkY6ej4HYgahq72wmy03gY0fI-
DCdLD1PvbWakNEQovicTnRtGu-AN3tNvIJtcUfD9s_lolSNXWoB
IxXe4TvhfVWnumke3o8bgyiDr6dHnILoq68J624pBx5xiHD4Gogr
Lsyp655.

3. Scott Bland, "George Soros' Quiet Overhaul of the U.S. Justice
System," *Politico*, August 30, 2016, https://www.politico.com/story
/2016/08/george-soros-criminal-justice-reform-227519.

4. Tim Prudente, "Marilyn Mosby Declares War on Drugs Over,
Formalizes Policy to Dismiss All Possession Charges in Baltimore,"
Baltimore Sun, March 26, 2021, https://www.baltimoresun.com
/news/crime/bs-md-ci-cr-mosby-stops-drug-prosecutions-20210326
-7ra6pn2a4zcexnj6hmfv4wj6li-story.html.

5. Heather Mac Donald, "The Myth of Systemic Police Racism," *Wall
Street Journal*, June 2, 2020, https://www.wsj.com/articles/the-myth
-of-systemic-police-racism-11591119883.

6. Heather Mac Donald, "I Cited Their Study, So They Disavowed It,"
Wall Street Journal, July 8, 2020, https://www.wsj.com/articles/i-cited
-their-study-so-they-disavowed-it-11594250254.

7. Conor Fitzgerald, "It would be an honour to name the thing that isn't happening after the thing I wrote," Twitter, June 20, 2020, 3:57 p.m., https://twitter.com/fitzfromdublin/status/1274431165437562880/photo/1.

8. Jason Lange and Trevor Hunnicutt, "Biden Staff Donate to Group That Pays Bail in Riot-Torn Minneapolis," Reuters, May 30, 2020, https://www.reuters.com/article/us-minneapolis-police-biden-bail/biden-staff-donate-to-group-that-pays-bail-in-riot-torn-minneapolis-idUSKBN2360SZ.

9. Charles Stimson and Zack Smith, "Meet Rachael Rollins, the Rogue Prosecutor Whose Policies Are Wreaking Havoc in Boston," Heritage Foundation, November 11, 2020, https://www.heritage.org/crime-and-justice/commentary/meet-rachael-rollins-the-rogue-prosecutor-whose-policies-are-wreaking.

10. Bill Barr, *One Damn Thing after Another* (New York: William Morrow, 2022), 353.

Chapter Six: January 6

1. Sam Levine, "'Over Our Heads in Chaos': Wisconsin on Edge of Election Fiasco amid Panic," *The Guardian*, April 3, 2020, https://www.theguardian.com/us-news/2020/apr/03/wisconsin-election-coronavirus-pandemic.

2. John R. Lott Jr., "Heed Jimmy Carter on the Danger of Mail-in Voting," *Wall Street Journal*, April 10, 2020, https://www.wsj.com/articles/heed-jimmy-carter-on-the-danger-of-mail-in-voting-11586557667.

3. Sam Levine, "Georgia Primary Blighted by Long Lines and Broken Voting Machines," *The Guardian*, June 9, 2020, https://www.theguardian.com/us-news/2020/jun/09/georgia-election-primary-long-lines-broken-voting-machines.

4. Katie Benner et al., "Garland Faces Growing Pressure as Jan. 6 Investigation Widens," *New York Times*, April 2, 2022, https://www.nytimes.com/2022/04/02/us/politics/merrick-garland-biden-trump.html.

5. Ibid.

6. "Army Veteran Who Became an FBI Informant Testifies about Plot to Abduct Michigan Gov. Gretchen Whitmer," CBS News, March 18, 2022, https://www.cbsnews.com/news/gretchen-whitmer-kidnapping-plot-trial-fb-informant-big-dan/.

Chapter Seven: Targets

1. Joseph C. Wilson, "What I Didn't Find in Africa," *New York Times*, July 6, 2003, https://www.nytimes.com/2003/07/06/opinion/what-i-didn-t-find-in-africa.html.
2. Lauren Fox, "At AIPAC, Sen. Menendez Goes Head-to-Head with the Obama Administration on Iran," *The Atlantic*, March 2, 2015, https://www.theatlantic.com/politics/archive/2015/03/at-aipac-sen-menendez-goes-head-to-head-with-the-obama-administration-on-iran/445692/.
3. Evan Perez and Shimon Prokupecz, "Sen. Bob Menendez: 'I Am Not Going Anywhere,'" CNN, March 9, 2015, https://www.cnn.com/2015/03/06/politics/robert-menendez-criminal-corruption-charges-planned/index.html.
4. Tal Kopan and Theodore Schleifer, "Bob Menendez Becomes Second Senate Democrat to Oppose Iran Deal," CNN, August 18, 2015, https://www.cnn.com/2015/08/18/politics/bob-menendez-corker-iran-nuclear-deal/index.html.

Chapter Eight: Affirmative Action

1. Katie Benner et al., "Garland Faces Growing Pressure as Jan. 6 Investigation Widens," *New York Times*, April 2, 2022, https://www.nytimes.com/2022/04/02/us/politics/merrick-garland-biden-trump.html.
2. Alayna Treene, "Exclusive: 85% Diversity on Biden People Team," Axios, January 24, 2021, https://www.axios.com/biden-personnel-team-opm-7df87473-3fd3-4ff7-9289-c89994e50879.html.
3. Nate Raymond, "Republicans Question Japanese-American Judicial Pick on Book Review," Reuters, February 1, 2022, https://www.reuters.com/legal/legalindustry/republicans-question-japanese-american-judicial-pick-book-review-2022-02-01/.

Chapter Nine: Injustice for All

1. Burgess Owens et al., "Op-Ed: Why We Black Leaders Support Voter ID Laws," The Center Square, April 18, 2021, https://www.thecentersquare.com/national/op-ed-why-we-black-leaders-support-voter-id-laws/article_1874e3b0-9f02-11eb-89a8-ff2ca4959a66.html.
2. "Voting and Registration in the Election of November 2018," U.S. Census Bureau, April 2019, https://www.census.gov/data/tables/time-series/demo/voting-and-registration/p20-583.html.
3. David Marchese, "Why Stacey Abrams Is Still Saying She Won," *New York Times*, April 28, 2019, https://www.nytimes.com

/interactive/2019/04/28/magazine/stacey-abrams-election-georgia .html.

4.   Nick Corasaniti and Reid J. Epstein, "What Georgia's Voting Law Really Does," *New York Times*, April 2, 2021, https:// www.nytimes.com/2021/04/02/us/politics/georgia-voting-law-annotated.html.

5.   Kristen Clarke, Letter to the State Attorneys General, March 31, 2022, available at Department of Justice website: https:// www.justice.gov/opa/press-release/file/1489066/download.

6.   Josh Gerstein and Alexander Ward, "Supreme Court Has Voted to Overturn Abortion Rights, Draft Opinion Shows," *Politico*, May 2, 2022, https://www.politico.com/news/2022/05/02/ supreme-court-abortion-draft-opinion-00029473.

7.   Jeff Mordock, "Psaki Refuses to Condemn Abortion Planned Protest at Churches, Justices' Homes," *Washington Times*, May 5, 2022, https:// www.washingtontimes.com/news/2022/may/5/ jen-psaki-refuses-condemn-abortion-planned-protest/.

8.   Maria Cramer and Jesus Jimenez, "Armed Man Traveled to Justice Kavanaugh's Home to Kill Him, Officials Say," *New York Times*, June 8, 2022, https://www.nytimes.com/2022/06/08/us/brett-kavanaugh-threat-arrest.html.

9.   Gabriel Hays, "Vox Journo Scorched for Cheering 'Hero' SCOTUS Leaker: 'Let's Burn This Place Down,'" Fox News, May 3, 2022, https:// www.foxnews.com/media/ vox-journo-scorched-cheering-hero-scotus-leaker-lets-burn-this-place-down.

INDEX